D1288915

The Book About Xu Bing's *Book From the Ground*

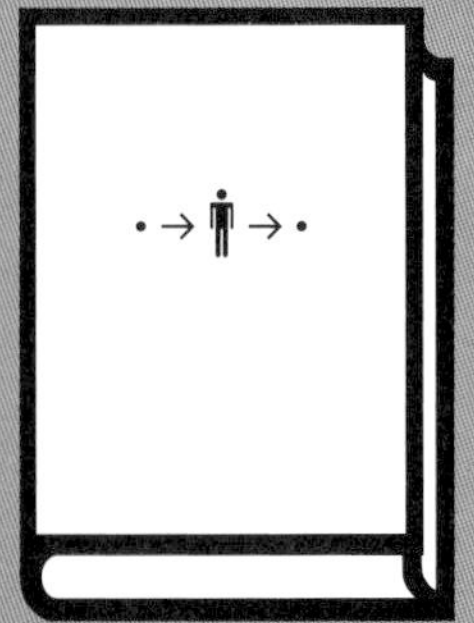

THE BOOK ABOU
BOOK FROM THE

Mathieu Borysevicz, editor

XU BING'S
GROUND

MASS MoCA
North Adams, Massachusetts

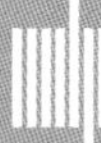

The MIT Press
Cambridge, Massachusetts

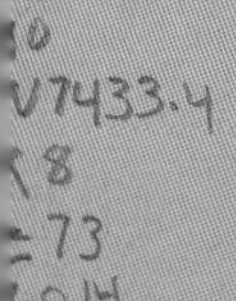

THE BOOK ABOUT XU BING'S *BOOK FROM THE GROUND*

Library of Congress Control Number: 2013950332
ISBN: 978-0-262-02742-7

Editor: Mathieu Borysevicz
Contributors: Mathieu Borysevicz, Xu Bing, Haytham Nawar, Kaimei Olsson Wang
Archivist: Xu Bing Studio
Illustrator: Xu Bing Studio (Wang Pei, Zhang Wenchao)
Translation: Kaimei Olsson Wang, Steven Huang, Jessie Xie, Sophie Huang, Faisal Sabbagh
Designer: Xie Wenyue
Photography: Dong Tianye, Gan Qi, Xu Bing, Xue Feng, Zhang Jia, Zhong Han
Copy Editors: Kaimei Olsson Wang, Marlaine Glicksman, Rachel Marsden, Jessie Xie, Sophie Huang, Mathieu Borysevicz

Printed and bound in China.

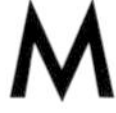

MASS MoCA
Massachusetts Museum of Contemporary Art
North Adams, Massachusetts 01247
massmoca.org

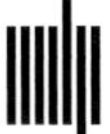

The MIT Press
Massachusetts Institute of Technology
Cambridge, Massachusetts 02142
http://mitpress.mit.edu

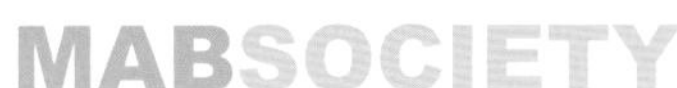

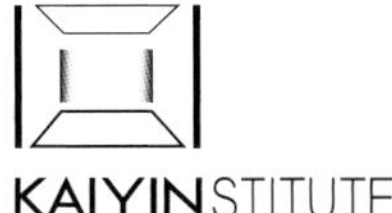

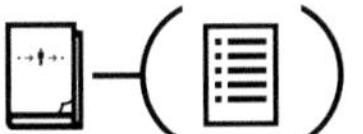

CONTENTS

P006-019:

BOOK FROM THE GROUND

2012

Pages from the original book, 148×220mm

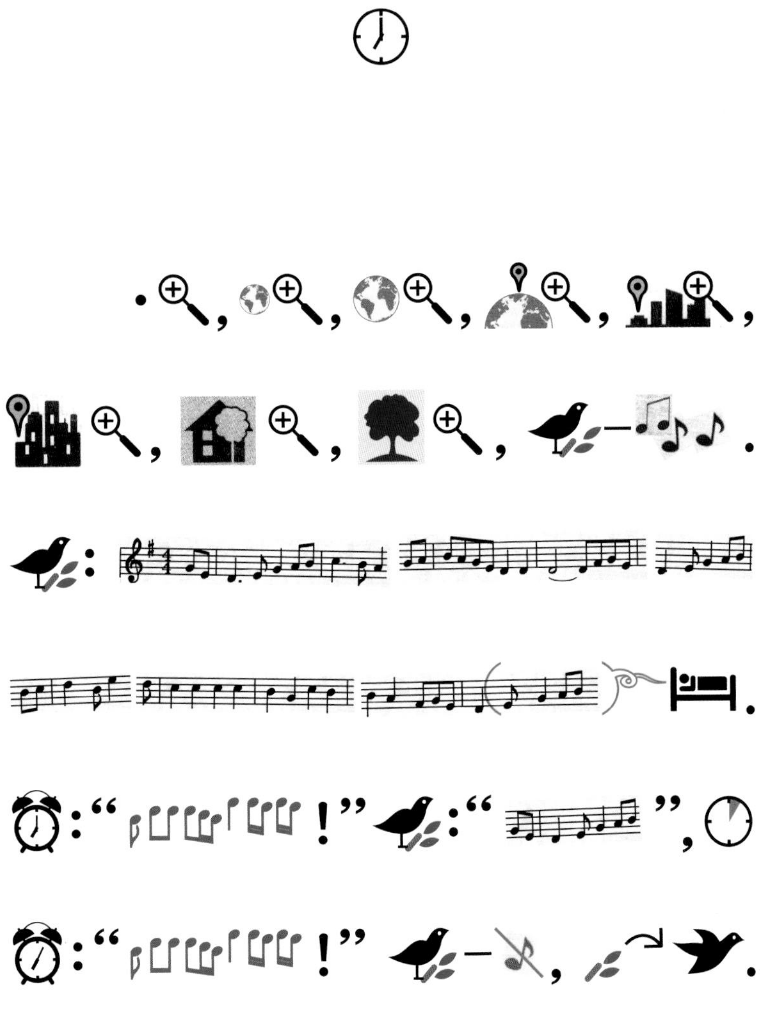

1

3

5

7

9

88F, 89F!

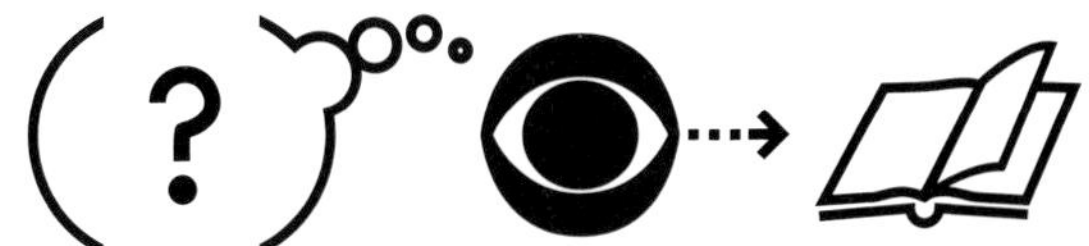

By Mathieu Borysevicz

(WHAT) ARE WE

Look back over the previous pages. Perhaps you skimmed or simply skipped over them searching for something more familiar, like this article here? Ahhh, standard English, something that you know so well, something that you have learned, absorbed, and practiced for most of your life — a system built of 26 squiggly lines that can communicate, illuminate, and educate. However, what if this system suddenly disintegratedddddy eituei;dhr thi szzznjsk hdkoh' io3xrb 4c08y4ioty biovtu3; 4'cnu13 Part 7- uv5opyu10-848n]0in1vi0 Part 7- m Part 7-0m-= ? You would be skimming again, frustrated by the unfamiliar, unbreakable code, much like wandering lost in a foreign city plastered with incomprehensible signs. Alas, such are the challenges of an increasingly consolidated planet wherein people of different languages rub elbows in increasingly smaller spaces.

The previous page shows an assemblage of pictograms that have been aligned into neat rows almost if they were mimicking words in a sentence, in a paragraph, in a book – almost like a written text. Could it be? The page begins with a dot: a point, a period, a simple punctuation mark that expands at the command of a

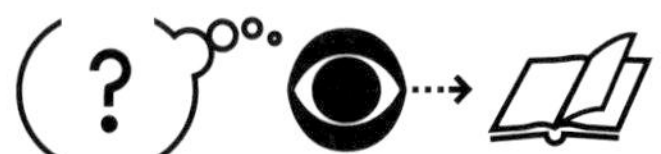

READING?

magnifying glass into our blue planet. Conditioned by a regular dose of Google Earth, we quickly fast-forward a few images into the icon of an anonymous city, which pushes further in on an anonymous house, outside which a bird on a branch is whistling a sonnet. It is the beginning of an epic, and like many classic fairy tales it begins "once upon a time, in a place far, far away..." However, here it is 7 a.m. sharp (the chapter title shows us), and this place is no further than your finger tips — the global village that we all inhabit with its attendant language of modern hieroglyphics.

This publication chronicles Xu Bing's *Book From the Ground*, a project that culminates in *From Point to Point*, a novel written entirely in a "language of icons." While the previous few pages were taken directly from *From Point to Point*, *Book From the Ground* is an extensive, ongoing project that explores visual communication through archival material, an animation film, a pop-up concept store, original artworks, and a computer program that translates Chinese and English into the intermediate language of pictograms. Through more than six years of research and development Xu Bing has stepped up to

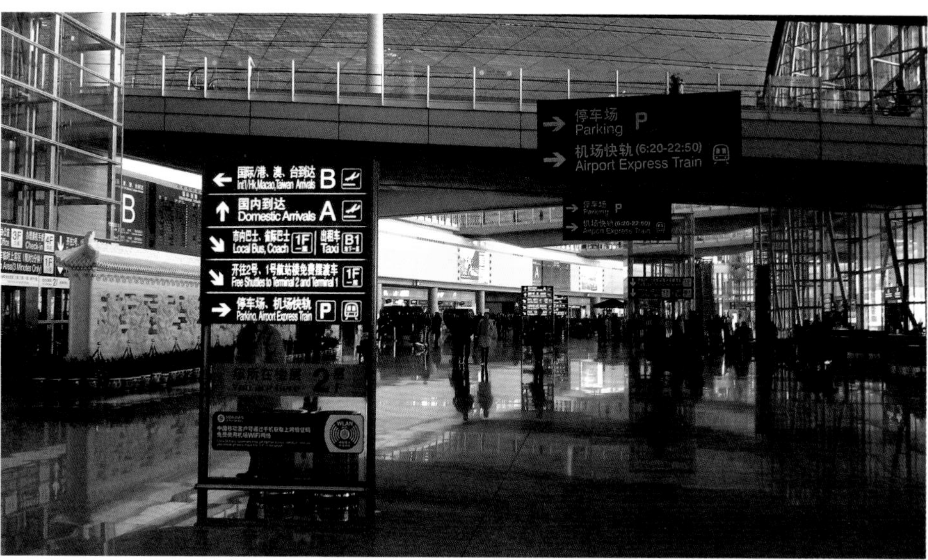

the challenge of producing a universally accessible language. However, this production involved no invention or fabrication. Xu simply indexed, organized, and employed an existent language that all of us are already guilty of using on a daily basis. He and his studio have culled and catalogued the lexicon of this utilitarian code from the millions of icons, logos, emoticons, and standardized illustrations that pervade our contemporary world. It is a language that Xu purports, "regardless of cultural background, one should be able to understand as long as one is thoroughly entangled in modern life."[1] *From Point to Point* is both a culmination of his great linguistic investigation in literary form as well as an assessment of this "language's" ability to compose a full-length narrative full of allusions, emotions, and evocations.

BOOK

From Point to Point's story follows a day in the life of Mr. Black — a young, white-collar, modern-day urbanite — over the course of 24 hours. Mr. Black's day is a lot like many of ours: filled with trials, tribulations, mundanity, and the pursuit of dreams. The story unwinds like a Twenty-first Century *Ulysses*, tracing the odyssey of this technophilic metrosexual through his corporate branded life in search of true love (or the simulacrum thereof).

The original *Ulysses* was divided into 18 episodes and foregrounded the stream of consciousness of Mr. Bloom, Joyce's main character, against any pretense of a clear narrative. Xu Bing presents a third-person view of Mr. Black, *From Point to Point*'s protagonist, and structures the book into 24 chapters, each representing an hour of the day.

While the differences between Mr. Bloom and Mr. Black are too far to measure, what we do gain by comparing *Ulysses* and *From Point to Point* is their landmark advancement of form, technique, and language. Upon its release in 1922, *Ulysses* confounded its readers, sending an uproar through literary circles. The New York Times book review of the day warned, "Only a few intuitive, sensitive visionaries may understand and comprehend it, but the average intelligent reader will glean little or nothing from it." In the same article, *Ulysses* was also pronounced "the most important contribution that has been made to fictional literature in the twentieth century."[2] *From Point to Point*'s

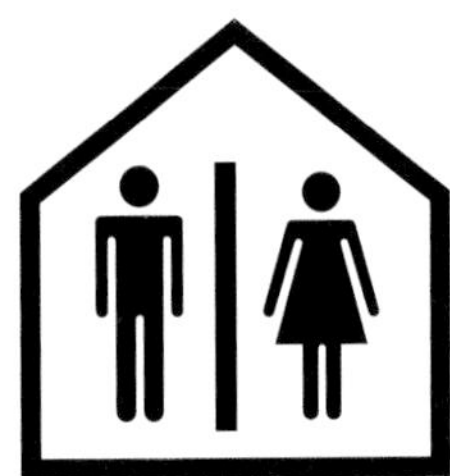

literary contributions may pale in comparison to that of *Ulysses*, but similar reactions may apply: Without patience and inspection it may appear inaccessible to the average reader, at the same time, it single-handedly liberates language from any pre-existing, traditional form.

AIRPORT

The inspiration for *Book From the Ground* began in the airport — that symbolic temple of supermodernity, the architectural embodiment of speed, movement, and human ingenuity. However, it was not the airports immediacy of transport that caught the interest of Xu Bing, but its ability to communicate instantaneously, through language barriers, in the form of signs, symbols, icons, and pictographs. Here, in this microcosm of the modern city — complete with its own shopping malls, banks, restaurants, post office, and living quarters — wanders a community of modern nomads, Xu Bing among them, looking for the bathroom.

The bathroom — yes, a place where both *Ulysses* and *From Point to Point*'s stories humbly begin. In the airport, the bathroom is attended by the ubiquitous symbol of man and woman — stark gladiators with oversized circular heads slightly separated from their Popsicle-looking bodies and identifiable as separate sexes only through what one may argue is a culturally specific dress code — a woman clad in a triangular skirt and a man, ostensibly naked.

It is curious here to pause and think of the elementary semiotic quandary of signification. While we see symbols for both a man and a woman, we also immediately read this as "toilet." This disconnect between the signifier and signified is only natural, or as Saussure maintains, arbitrary or unmotivated.[3] Certainly *cat* does not embody the essence of cat-ness, nor does any word, for that matter, have much to do with its signification. Similarly these symbols of a man and a woman do not indicate the bathroom's program or function but instead *who* uses *which* room. Its method of signification is certainly more refined than the "conceptual grid" of traditional language that has been imposed upon the world.

Xu Bing is not so keen about the disconnect of this communication tool as much as its potential utility. He

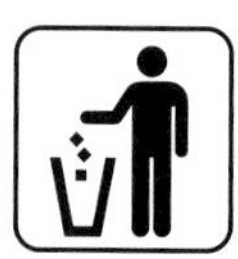
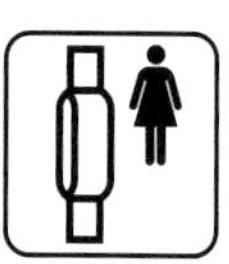

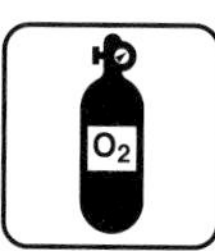

quickly realizes that an image of a cat would certainly signify more effectively than *cat*. No matter how imprecise these signs may be, we live in a system of social norms, and this twenty-first century Adam and Eve have been instrumental in guiding each and every one of us off the long plane ride directly to the right repository to unload our aching, weary bladders.

Xu belongs to a growing class of jet-set elite who spend much time flying cross-continentally from one cultural engagement to the next. For him, a native Chinese speaker who in the late 1980s migrated to the United States and has since visited every corner of the planet a number of times, the language barrier is a daily reality. It is only natural that the airport has provided his source of inspiration. The international airport is not only a linguistically confounded zone, it is a profoundly neutral nonspace dependent upon circulation, consumption, and forming shared identities. As anthropologist Marc Augé argues, "A person entering the space of nonspace is relieved from his usual determinants. He becomes no more than what he does or experiences in the role of passenger."[4] In fact, the entire experience of being in the airport is a transitory one, dependant not only upon leaving but also upon effective communication that will facilitate this exit. From checking in to exiting the destination city's airport, one is guided by a procession of demarcations, directions, and instructions composed mainly of pictograms.

Xu's revelation began while flipping through the safety cards commonly found in the back pocket of airplane seats. These colorful, laminated pamphlets instruct one, ever so didactically, what to do in the event of a crisis. Less concerned with crisis aversion than the slight aesthetic variations from airline to airline, as well as the ability of these cards to convey complicated ideas devoid of traditional text, Xu began to collect them. Starting in 1990 he amassed hundreds of cards. Over the years he observed that the amount of written language has increasingly subsided as ideograms began to dominate as the prime source of communication for these manuals.

His ongoing airport experiences made him increasingly aware of the plethora of symbols, pictograms, and logos that we, as participants of the global village, use, comprehend, and communicate to each other on a daily basis. The advent of personal computers,

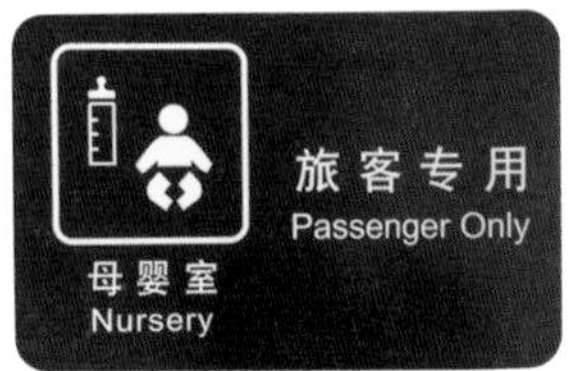

social media, and instant messaging has compounded this situation with their introduction of commands and emoticons that even further economizes communication. Extracting images from magazines, newspapers, instruction manuals, and computing devices, Xu and his studio began to develop an archive of pictograms. This ever expanding archive was then cataloged, digitized, and eventually transcribed into a software program that could translate English and Chinese text into this mediate language of icons. Beginning with simple translation exercises, Xu went on to test this language's ability to form narratives and, more importantly, abstract ideas and situations. Back in the airplane bathroom, an amorphous plastic vestibule punctuated by small pictographs, Xu muses on the intricacies of this icon language:

> There are many signs above the toilet stool inside the airplane. This one symbolizing changing the baby's diaper — this is good. I thought about using it for the part of the book to describe a girl who says she likes babies. But maybe it's not entirely proper. The one I saw at Terminal 3, about taking care of children, is more useful. [5]

Just as there is more than one word that denotes *baby* — *infant, child, tot, newborn, sweetie*, etc., there is also more than one icon per concept, each having its own contextual appropriateness. In discussion with writer Mian Mian later in this catalogue (page 134), Xu examines in detail what the ultimate freedom and limitations of this language are. Like any language system, many of its limitations are both formed and overcome from usage, convention, and license. Xu's *Book From the Ground* is an emerging system — a developing language that is alive and growing. What sets it apart from other systems is its open-source and ready-to-go user-friendliness. He has found a language "that is based on shared visual experience and commonly recognizable elements. The core study is about visual communication. The limitation of this book lies in your life experience, not in your educational level or your geographic location."[6] It is a language that one can grasp easily and immediately and, therefore it has infinite potential to remedy the age-old quandary of establishing a common, universal language.

UNIVERSAL LANGUAGE

Beginning as far back as the Tower of Babel itself,

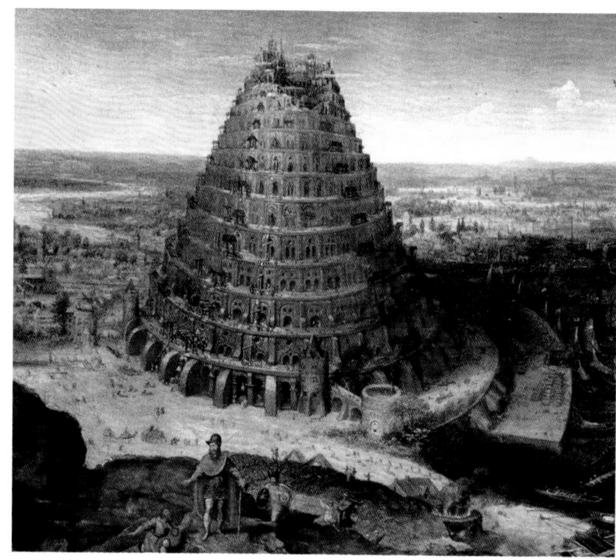

Lucas van Valckenborch
The Tower of Babel
1594
painting on canvas

mankind has strived to consolidate its diverse languages into a common one. In this biblical account of a post-great-flood world, a united people erect a giant tower hoping to penetrate the heavens. God, alarmed that these people are capable of extraordinary things, resolves to divide them by confounding their spoken dialects. The tower is called Babel because "there the Lord confused the language of the whole world."[7] Since then, many attempts have been made at re-unifying the languages of the Earth. Arabic, Chinese, and Latin have united distinct dialects and cultures with their standardized text but never realized global union. Xu Bing, later in this catalogue, discusses Jean Douet, a French thinker, who in the seventeenth century noted the potential for Chinese, or a script based on image recognition rather than an abstract system, to solve the problem of universal language. Similarly, philospher Gottfried Leibniz's *characteristica universalis* was, in his words, "an alphabet of human thought", which proposed that "all ideas are compounded from a very small number of simple ideas which can be represented by a unique 'real' character."[8] Liebniz's universal symbolic language consisted of visual diagrams that were intended to function as a medium for scientific exchange across languages and cultures.

Book From the Ground was historically anticipated, maybe even predetermined; yet this symbolic phenomenon was not a scientific innovation but rather a product of recognition. Xu's work is indexical — a great readymade — a found language and universal system that we are all complicit in exploiting. The alphabet of characters employed in the *Book From the Ground* project are neither created nor manipulated: They are culled from the kaleidoscope of signage that comprises our modern landscape — Xu's role was only to bring these images to our attention and to play on their potential.

BACKGROUND

The history of art is a history of images. From the cave paintings in Alsace Lorraine to Xu's *Book From the Ground* images have been fundamental to communicating complicated concepts to broad audiences. Whether it was renaissance-era murals conveying biblical stories to an illiterate mass-going peasantry or Leni Riefenstah's heroic film montages paving the way for Nazi fascism, images have both superseded and supplemented the printed word to educate, propagate, and shape ideology. Conversely,

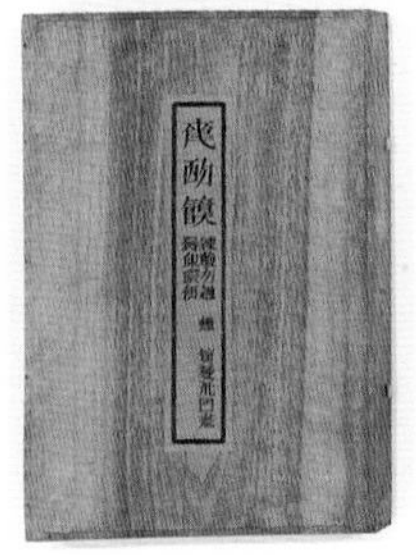
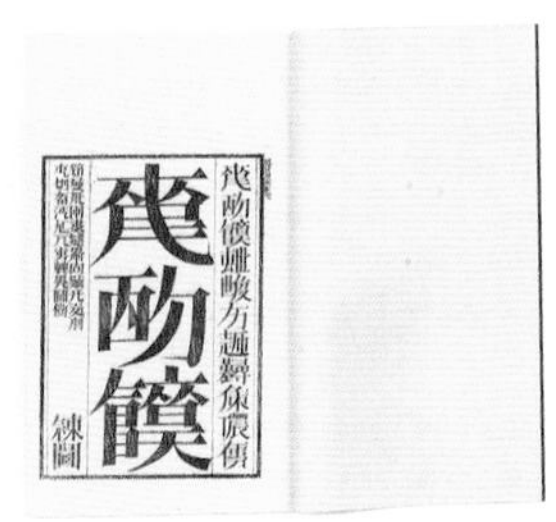
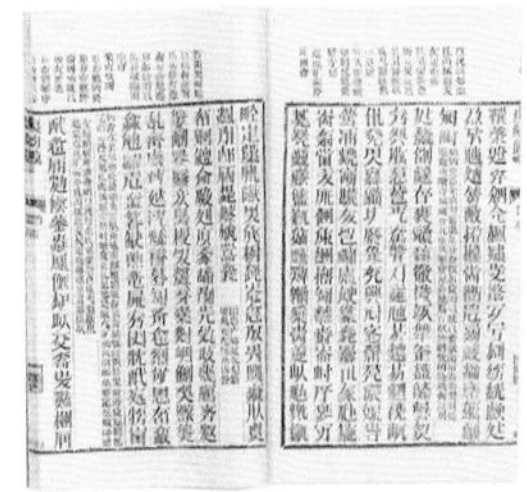
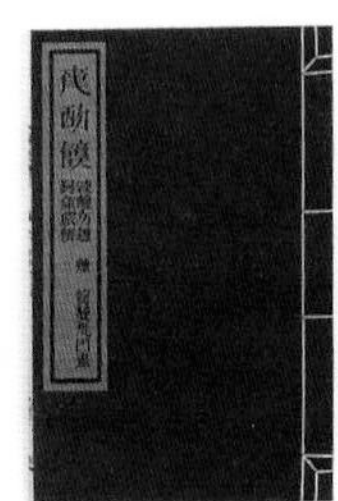
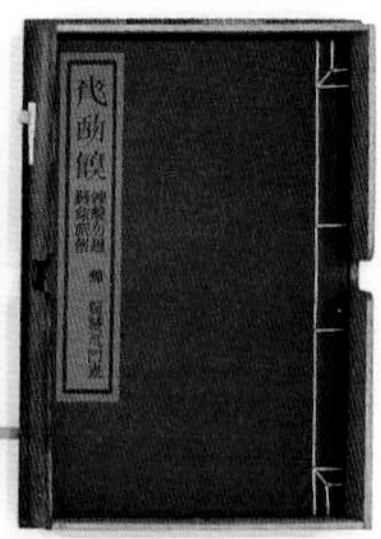

Xu Bing
Book From the Sky
1987-1991

there is a long tradition of language-based art in both the East and West. Calligraphy, still widely practiced in Asia, dates back some four thousand years, when ancient Chinese characters were written on the shells of turtles. Text collaged onto the canvases of Pablo Picasso, Georges Braque, and Kurt Schwitters were considered milestones for early twentieth century modernism. Today contemporary masters like Joseph Kosuth, Lawrence Weiner, and Jenny Holzer use text exclusively as their medium of choice.

Xu Bing's infatuation with language also began quite early on. When Xu was halfway through first grade, the People's Republic had a nationwide switch in writing systems, from traditional characters to a more simplified version that would, in Chairman Mao's mind, make literacy more accessible to the masses and help to unite the disparate outer reaches of the country. This sudden and great change left a deep impression on Xu. Language was not a God-given doctrine, as he previously imagined, but instead something that could be used for political leverage and manipulated at whim. In fact, the entire environment of Xu's youth was laden with examples of language's fallibility and efficacy. A strict routine of practicing calligraphy as a youngster not only laid a solid foundation in structure and composition for him, but also helped set him apart intellectually from those who didn't have this training — a tenuous class division during tense times. The Cultural Revolution's 大字报 *dazibao*, or big character posters — hand painted signs that openly criticized individuals and helped to seal the fate of many, Xu's father included — affirmed for Xu the maxim The Pen is Mightier Than the Sword, and set the precedent for language in his future work. His earliest artworks were actually produced while employed as a graphic designer for a propaganda magazine during the time he spent being re-educated in China's countryside. However, it was not until the end of the 1980s, with a decade of tumultuous change behind him, that Xu created his iconic *Book From the Sky*, (1987-1991) an artwork that set the foundation for all his later work, especially *Book From the Ground*.

In the eighties, with the Cultural Revolution giving way to economic reform, China had entered into a new phase of critical introspection ruled by contradictory social forces and extreme change. Xu's monumental *Book From the Ground* was in effect a rebuttal to the discourse of a culture besieged by modernization

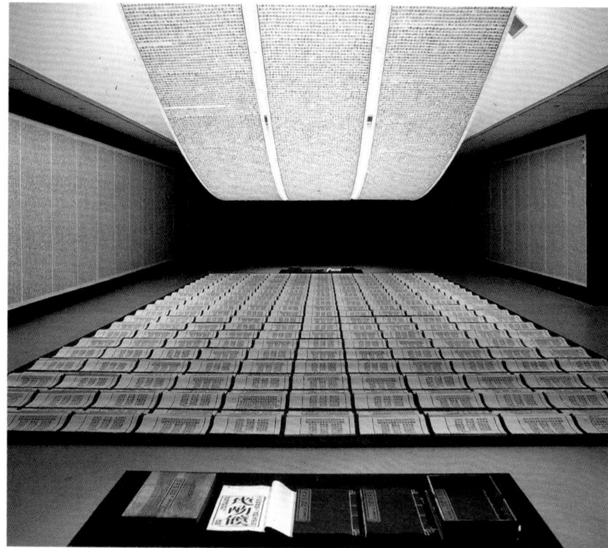

Xu Bing
Book From the Sky
1987-1991
Installation

and encroaching Westernism on one side and the stark reality of politics and tradition on the other. The "book" was composed out of four thousand characters (an amount considered standard for adult literacy in China) that were hand-carved into woodblocks and printed, as moveable type, on rice-paper scrolls. When exhibited the scrolls were strung up like billowing banners and graced the expanse of the space. Yet upon closer examination of these flowing texts, one could see that each and every one of these characters was garbled, nonsensical. In fact none of them were real but instead were invented by the artist. While these characters resembled the Chinese language, it was a deconstructed, bastardized version. Xu's assault of language was both a side effect of his early experiences as well as a response to the state's inability to face the growing unrest of its people. This incomprehensible book was a direct response to China's continual masking and manipulating of the truth through its state owned media.

Xu, in describing China's language simplification campaign of the nineteen-sixties, oddly enough expresses the severity of his own *Book From the Sky*: "To change the written word is to strike at the very foundation of a culture: To reconstruct language cuts to the heart of one's being and should be called a 'culture' revolution. The term is absolutely fitting."[9] In *Book From the Sky*'s confounding language Xu states, "A symbolic system fundamental to the integrity and perpetuation of a national culture is endlessly reproduced but vitiated of any functional value and thus made curiously unproductive."[10]

More than 20 years later the artist recalls that while "*Book From the Sky* was a book that nobody could read, *Book From the Ground* is a book that virtually everyone can read."[11] The cultural-political critique of *Book From the Sky* has been reshaped by *Book From the Ground* into an almost utopian proposition. These two products are clearly of different times. In the late eighties, the nation-state was still principally responsible for forming identity and cultural subjectivity in China. Xu, recognizing the growing irrelevance and frailty of this situation, felt that it was necessary to challenge it. Now fully midstream in the twentieth-first century, when the nation-state has subsided to transnational economic and cultural flows, Xu openly embraces our condition of globalization, technophilia and image saturation.

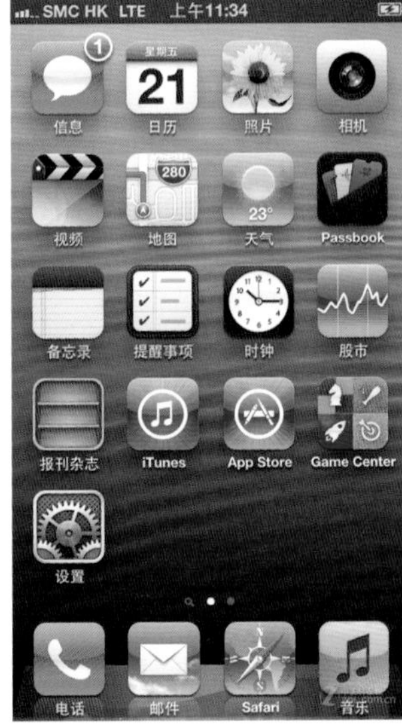

An iPhone Screen

At the time of writing, Apple's iPhone 5, chock-full of this so-called language of icons, was released with a record five million sales worldwide on the first day alone. China has 252,000,000 smartphone users[12] and close to 250,000,000 weibo (Chinese Twitter) users.[13] This infatuation with techno-consumption and instant communication are examples among many that indicate a shift in global ideological orientation. Today, we find our salvation not in the broken bastion of linguistic and cultural difference but in shared identities and connectivity.

In comparing his own two great artistic books Xu notes:

> These two books appear totally different but share some commonality, i.e. whatever language you speak, however you were educated, both are equally possible or impossible for everyone in this world to "read." Through *Book From the Sky* I expressed my shame on the then current state of Chinese language, while with *Book From the Ground* I try to pursue the dream that all humans can communicate freely without difficulty. I understand it's kind of too big to realize, but what matters is that I tried.[14]

1. Xu Bing. "Regarding *Book From the Ground*." Chinese Contemporary Art – Yishu Dangdai. April 2012.
2. Collins, Dr. Joseph. "James Joyce's Amazing Chronicle." New York Times. 28 May 1922.
3. Joseph, John E. *Saussure*. USA: Oxford University Press, p. 584. 2012
4. Augé, Marc. *Non-places: Introduction to an Anthropology of Supermodernity*, Translated by John Howe. New York: Verso, p. 103. 1995
5. Xu Bing. *Airport Notes*. previously unpublished
6. Xu Bing. Regarding *Book From the Ground*. Chinese Contemporary Art – Yishu Dangdai. April, 2012.
7. Babel sounds like the Hebrew for "confused." Genesis 11:9, *The Holy Bible: New International Version*. London: Hodder and Stoughton, p.10. 1981
8. Geiger, Richard and Rudzka-Ostyn, Brygida. *Conceptualizations and Mental Processing in Language*. Germany. De Gruyter. 1993
9. Xu Bing. "To Frighten Heaven and Earth and Make the Spirits Cry" Takatoshi Shinoda. *The Library of Babel*, Tokyo: NTT Publishing Co., Ltd., pp. 64-72. 1998
10. Yang, Alice. "Xu Bing: Rewriting Culture." *Why Asia? Contemporary Asian and Asian American Artists*, New York: New York University Press, pp. 24-29. 1998
11. Xu Bing Regarding *Book From the Ground* Chinese Contemporary Art, Yishu Dangdai, April issue, 2012.
12. *Monitoring Report of Smartphone Market in China*. Research Institute of Mobile and Internet Data, conducted by iMedia, 29th, May, 2012. http://www.iimedia.cn/29575.html
13. New Media Blue Book: Report of Development of New Media in China, Social Science Publisher, 7th Oct. 2012 http://news.163.com/12/1007/10/8D75TRRN00014JB5.html 2012
14. Xu Bing. "Regarding *Book From the Ground*." Chinese Contemporary Art – Yishu Dangdai. April 2012.

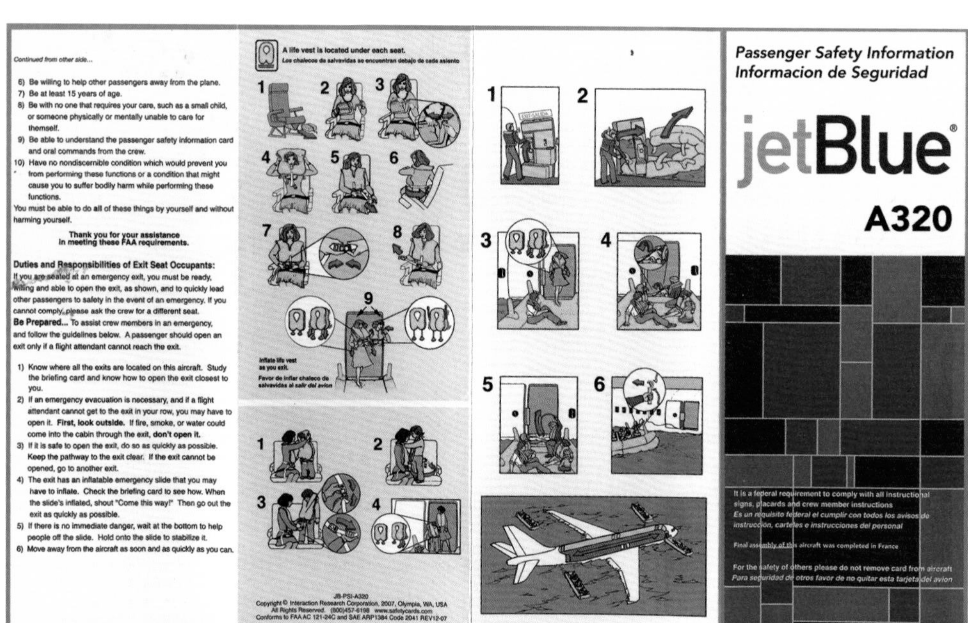

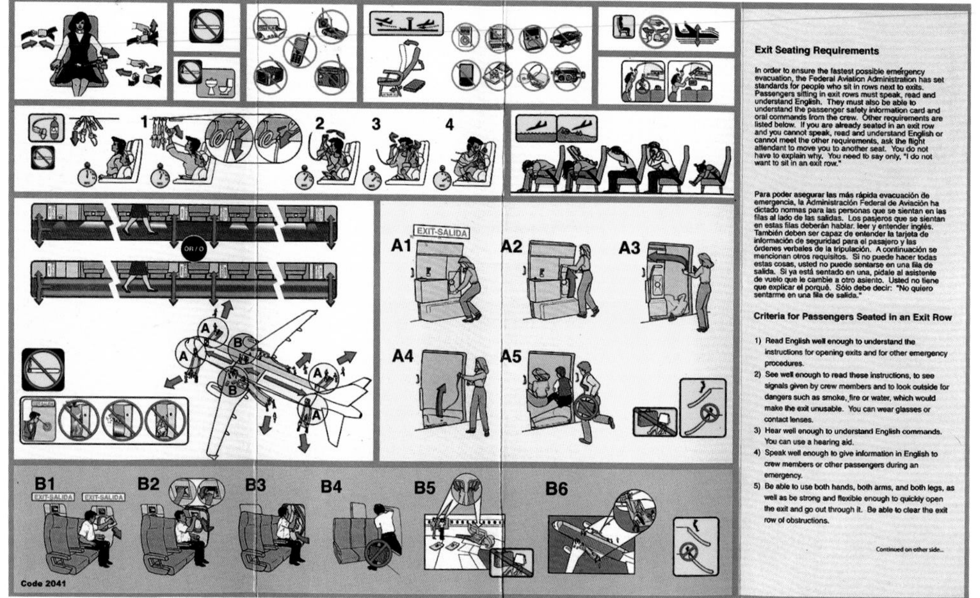

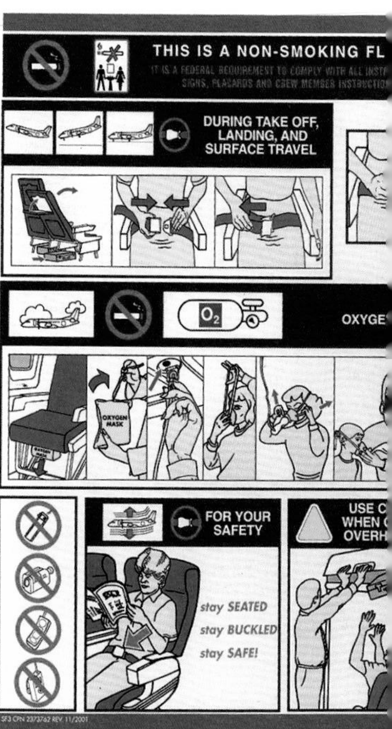

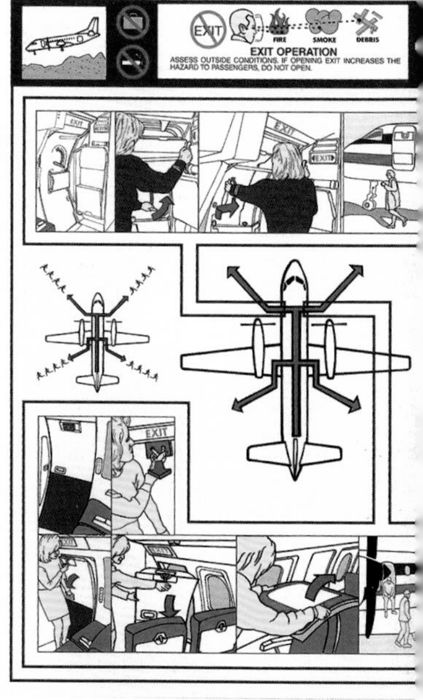

Airport Safety Cards collected by Xu Bing showing that from 1990 standard language has been slowly replaced by pictographs.

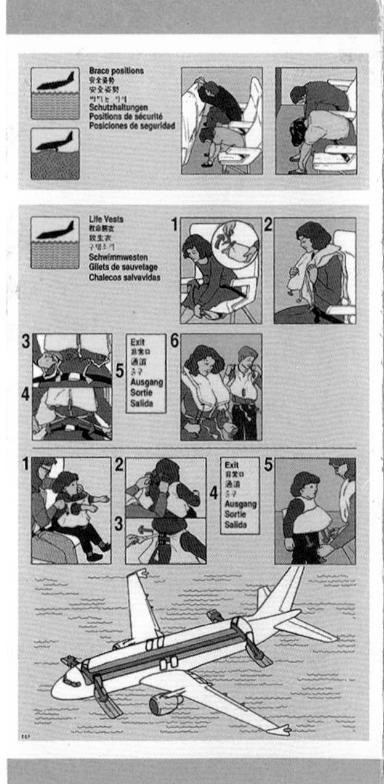

Safety A320

Final assembly of this aircraft was completed in France.

If you are sitting in an exit row please identify yourself to a crewmember to allow for reseating if: You lack the ability to read, speak, or understand the language, or the graphic form, or the ability to understand oral crew commands in the language specified by the airline.

安全 もしお客様が非常口付近にお座りで、機内で使われる言葉を読んだり 話したり理解できない場合や、絵の説明や航空会社の使用する言語での乗務員による口頭での指示が理解できない場合は、お座席を替わって頂くこともございますので、乗務員までお申し出下さい。

安全 如果您不懂我們的文字(圖和說)，或不懂示意圖，或不明白乘務員用航空公司指定語言作的口頭指示，但被安排在出口通道的座椅上，請告訴乘務員您的顧慮，讓我們重新安排您的座位。

안전

Sicherheit Wenn Sie in einer Reihe von Sitzen neben einem Notausgang sitzen, müssen Sie die Flugzeugbesatzung verständigen, damit diese Ihnen einen neuen Platz zuteilen kann, sollten Sie: die Sprache nicht sprechen, lesen oder verstehen können, oder die grafischen Darstellungen nicht verstehen, oder sollten Sie die mündlichen Anordnungen der Flugzeugbesatzung nicht verstehen.

Sécurité Si vous êtes assis sur une rangée située près d'une sortie veuillez vous identifier à un membre de l'équipage afin que l'on puisse vous attribue un autre siège si: vous ne pouvez pas lire, parler ou comprendre l'anglais, ou les illustrations graphiques, ou bien si vous ne pouvez pas comprendre les instructions orales de l'équipage.

Seguridad Por favor identifíquese con un tripulante para ser cambiado de asiento si usted está sentado en una de las hileras de la salida, y si tiene problemas para: leer, entender el idioma, instrucciones gráficas o la dificultad para entender ordenes verbales de la tripulación en el idioma utilizado por la aerolínea.

Exit Row Seating Selection Criteria: U.S. Federal Aviation Administration regulations specify procedures U.S. air carriers must follow concerning exit row seating. No air carrier may seat a person in an exit seat if it is determined that it is likely that the person would be unable to perform one or more of the applicable functions listed below or depicted on this safety card because the person:

1) Lacks sufficient mobility, strength, or dexterity in both arms and hands, and both legs to: a) reach upward, sideways, and downward to the location of emergency exit and exit-slide operating mechanisms; b) grasp and push, pull, turn, or otherwise manipulate those mechanisms; c) push, shove, pull, or otherwise open emergency exits; d) lift out, hold, deposit on nearby seats, or maneuver over the seatbacks to the next row objects the size and weight of over-wing window exit doors; e) remove obstructions similar in size and weight to over-wing exit doors; f) reach the emergency exit expeditiously; g) maintain balance while removing obstructions; h) exit expeditiously; i) stabilize an escape slide after deployment; or j) assist others in getting off an escape slide;
2) Is less than 15 years of age or lacks the capacity to perform one or more of the applicable functions without the assistance of an adult companion, parent, or other relative;
3) Lacks the ability to read and understand instructions related to emergency evacuation provided by the air carrier in printed or graphic form or the ability to understand oral crew commands;
4) Lacks sufficient visual capacity to perform one or more of the applicable functions without the assistance of visual aids beyond contact lenses or eyeglasses;
5) Lacks sufficient aural capacity to hear and understand instructions shouted by flight attendants, without assistance beyond a hearing aid;
6) Lacks the ability adequately to impart information orally to other passengers; or,
7) Has: a) a condition or responsibilities, such as caring for small children, that might prevent the person from performing one or more of the applicable functions; or b) a condition that might cause the person harm if he or she performs one or more of the applicable functions.

Functions to be performed: In the event of an emergency in which a crewmember is not available to assist, a passenger occupying an exit row seat may be called upon to perform the following functions:

1) Locate the emergency exit;
2) Recognize the emergency exit opening mechanism;
3) Comprehend the instructions for operating the emergency exit;
4) Operate the emergency exit;
5) Assess whether opening the emergency exit will increase the hazards to which passengers may be exposed;
6) Follow oral directions and hand signals given by a crewmember;
7) Stow or secure the emergency exit door so that it will not impede use of the exit;
8) Assess the condition of an escape slide, activate the slide, and stabilize the slide after deployment to assist others in getting off the slide;
9) Pass expeditiously through the emergency exit; and
10) Assess, select, and follow a safe path away from the emergency exit.

The passenger must identify himself or herself to allow reseating if he or she: a) Cannot meet the selection criteria listed above; b) Has a nondiscernible condition that will prevent him or her from performing the applicable functions; c) May suffer bodily harm as the result of performing one or more of those functions; or d) Does not wish to perform those functions (no reason needs to be given).

Federal Regulations Require All Passengers:

- **Regardless of where they are sitting or their physical condition, to review this card for their safety;**
- **To comply with these instructions, instructions of our crew or authorized employees, and all posted and lighted signs.**

When finished reviewing this card please return it to the seat pocket for our next customer.

UNITED

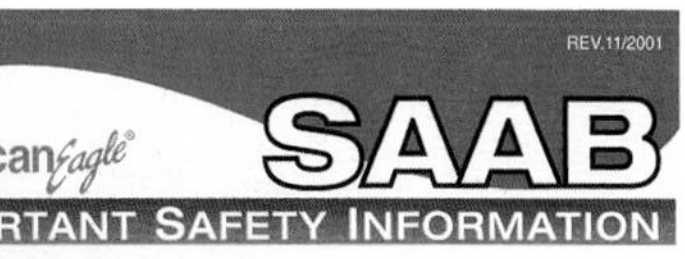

E SEATED IN AN EXIT ROW AND CANNOT UNDERSTAND CREW COMMANDS OR THE INFORMATION ON THIS CARD, IGHT ATTENDANT.

ÊTES ASSIS PRÈS D'UNE ISSUE DE SECOURS ET NE COMPRENEZ PAS LES INSTRUCTIONS DE FORMATIONS QUI SE TROUVENT SUR CE FORMULAIRE, VOUS ÊTES PRIÉS DE BIEN VOULOIR VOUS AVEC LE PERSONNEL DU BORD.

H IHR SITZ IN EINER REIHE AN EINEM DER AUSGÄNGE BEFINDET UND SIE SCHWIERIGKEITEN HABEN, DIE ESATZUNG ODER DIE INFORMATIONEN AUF DIESER KARTE ZU VERSTEHEN, SETZEN SIE SICH BITTE MIT EINEM RBINDUNG.

ESTÁ SENTADO EN UNA FILA DE SALIDA Y NO ENTIENDE LAS INDICACIONES DE LA TRIPULACIÓN O LA INFORMA-A, POR FAVOR PÓNGASE EN CONTACTO CON ALGUIEN DE LA TRIPULACIÓN DE SERVICIO.

emergency, if you are seated in an exit row you may be called upon to open the exit and engers in exiting the aircraft *if a crew member is not available to do so*. Please review the tion carefully.

3. You lack the ability to read and understand instructions related to emergency evacuations provided on this card in printed or graphic form or you lack the ability to understand oral crew member commands.
4. You lack sufficient visual capacity to perform one or more of the applicable functions without the assistance of visual aids other than contact lenses or eye glasses.
5. You lack sufficient hearing capacity to hear and understand instructions shouted by crew members without assistance other than a hearing aid.
6. You lack the ability to adequately communicate information orally to other passengers, or
7. You have a condition or responsibilities, such as caring for small children, that might prevent you from performing one or more of these functions, or
8. You have a condition that might cause you harm if you perform one or more of these functions.
9. You have a condition that is unrecognizable to others that will prevent you from performing the functions listed above or which might result in harm to you if you perform one of these functions, or
10. You do not wish to perform these functions.

Exit Row Responsibilities:

Please read the following information carefully. In the event of an emergency, you may be called upon to open the exit and assist fellow passengers in exiting the aircraft *if a crew member is not available to do so.*

- Follow oral directions and hand signals given by crew members.
- Locate the emergency exit.
- **ASSESS OUTSIDE CONDITIONS – IF OPENING EXIT INCREASES THE HAZARD TO PASSENGERS, DO NOT OPEN.**
- Recognize the emergency exit opening handle.
- Follow the instructions provided on the exit for proper operation.
- Operate the emergency exit.
- Stow or secure the emergency exit door so that it will not impede use of the exit.
- Pass quickly through the emergency exit.
- Assess, select, and follow a safe path away from the emergency exit.

ATION: ASSESS OUTSIDE CONDITIONS-IF OPENING EXIT INCREASES THE HAZARD TO PASSENGERS, DO NOT OPEN.

Please Do Not Remove This Card From Airplane

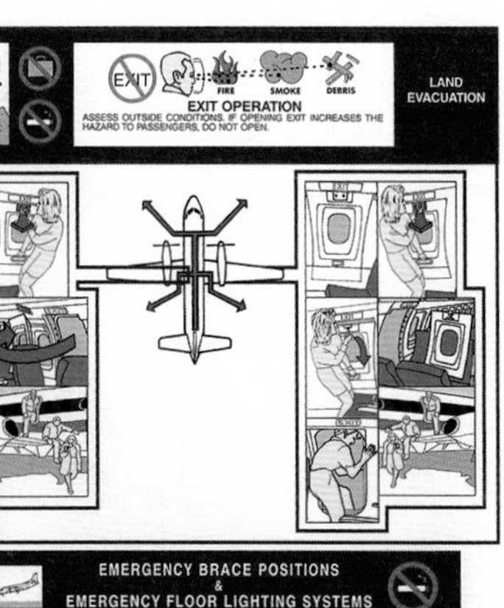

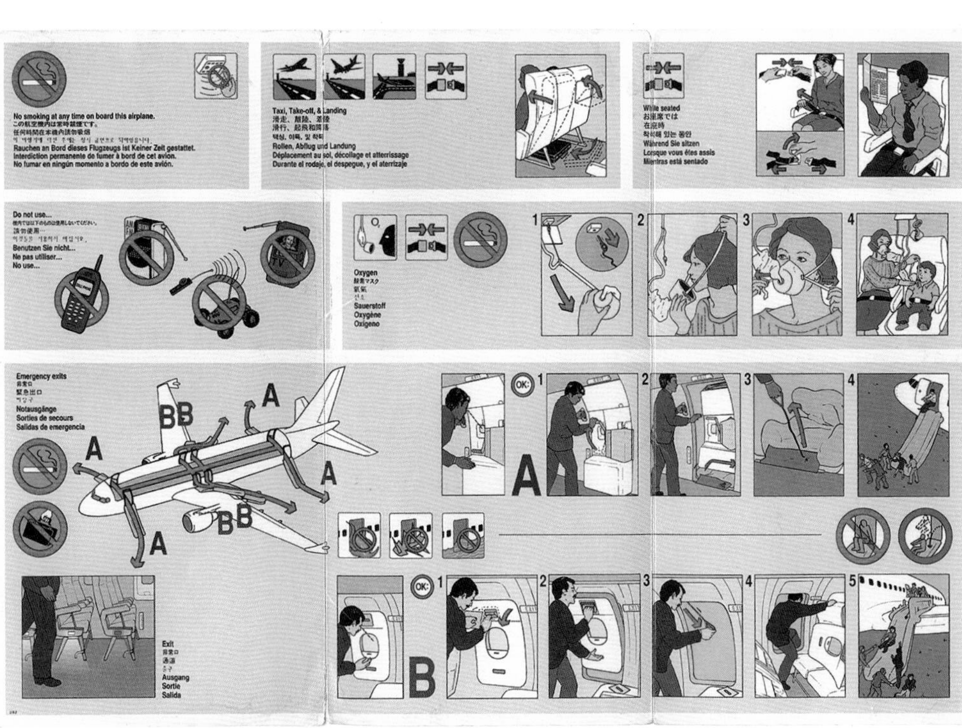

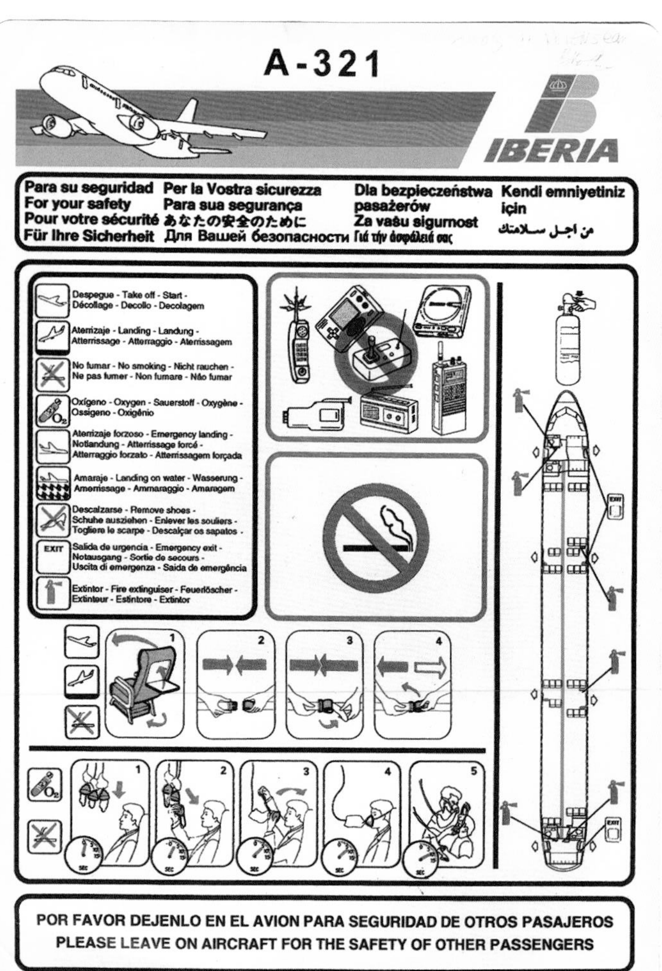
A-321
IBERIA
Para su seguridad
For your safety
Pour votre sécurité
Für Ihre Sicherheit
Per la Vostra sicurezza
Para sua segurança
あなたの安全のために
Для Вашей безопасности
Dla bezpieczeństwa pasażerów
Za vašu sigurnost
Για την ασφάλειά σας
Kendi emniyetiniz için
من اجل سلامتك
Despegue - Take off - Start - Décollage - Decollo - Decolagem
Aterrizaje - Landing - Landung - Atterrissage - Atterraggio - Aterrissagem
No fumar - No smoking - Nicht rauchen - Ne pas fumer - Non fumare - Não fumar
Oxígeno - Oxygen - Sauerstoff - Oxygène - Ossigeno - Oxigênio
Aterrizaje forzoso - Emergency landing - Notlandung - Atterrissage forcé - Atterraggio forzato - Aterrissagem forçada
Amaraje - Landing on water - Wasserung - Amerrissage - Ammaraggio - Amaragem
Descalzarse - Remove shoes - Schuhe ausziehen - Enlever les souliers - Togliere le scarpe - Descalçar os sapatos
Salida de urgencia - Emergency exit - Notausgang - Sortie de secours - Uscita di emergenza - Saída de emergência
Extintor - Fire extinguisher - Feuerlöscher - Extincteur - Estintore - Extintor
EXIT
POR FAVOR DEJENLO EN EL AVION PARA SEGURIDAD DE OTROS PASAJEROS
PLEASE LEAVE ON AIRCRAFT FOR THE SAFETY OF OTHER PASSENGERS

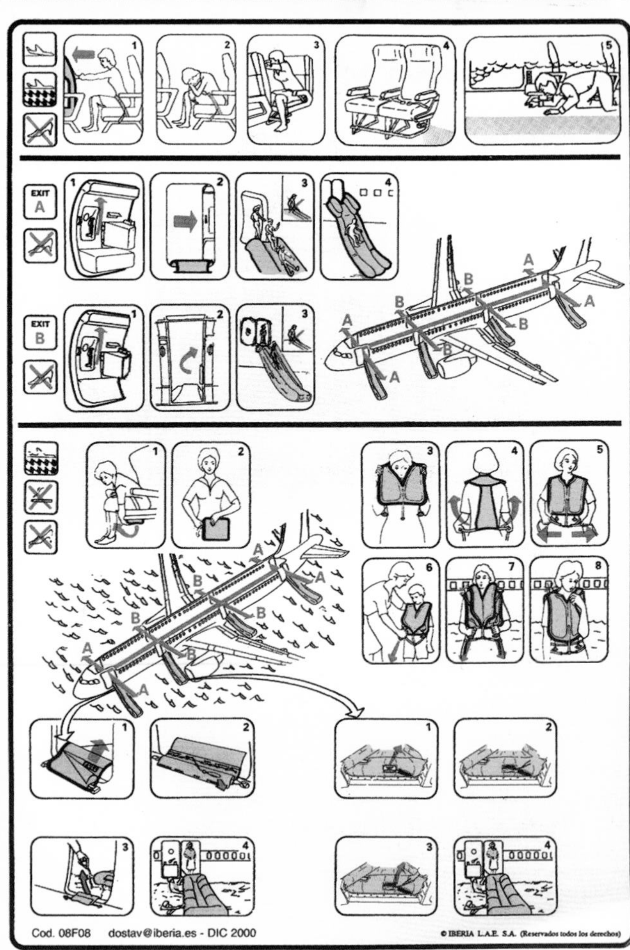
EXIT
A
EXIT
B
Cod. 08F08
dostav@iberia.es - DIC 2000
© IBERIA L.A.E. S.A. (Reservados todos los derechos)

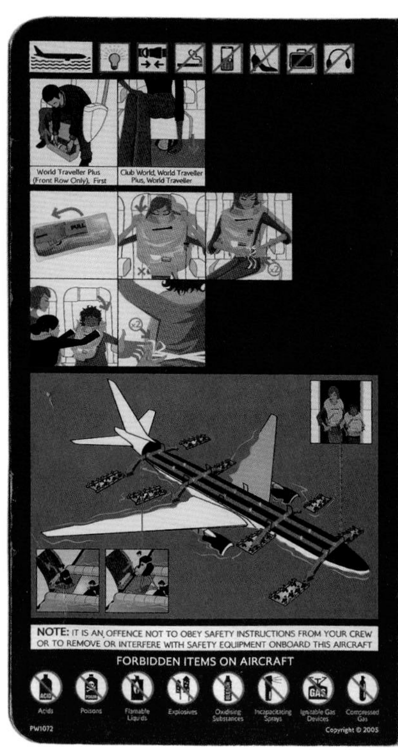
World Traveller Plus (Front Row Only), First
Club World, World Traveller Plus, World Traveller
NOTE: IT IS AN OFFENCE NOT TO OBEY SAFETY INSTRUCTIONS FROM YOUR CREW OR TO REMOVE OR INTERFERE WITH SAFETY EQUIPMENT ONBOARD THIS AIRCRAFT
FORBIDDEN ITEMS ON AIRCRAFT
Acids
Poisons
Flamable Liquids
Explosives
Oxidising Substances
Incapacitating Sprays
Ignitable Gas Devices
Compressed Gas
PW1072
Copyright © 2005

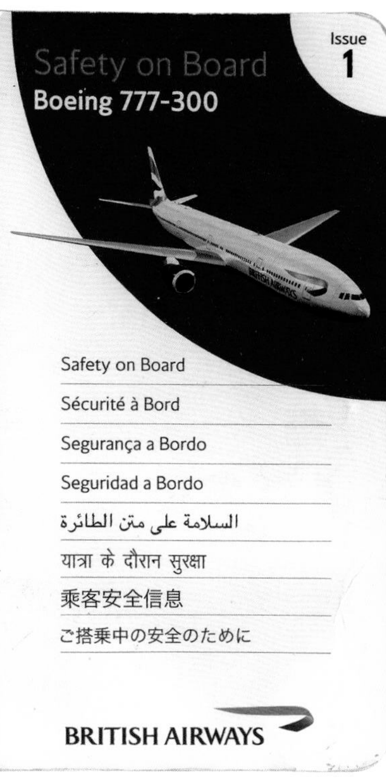
Issue
1
Safety on Board
Boeing 777-300
Safety on Board
Sécurité à Bord
Segurança a Bordo
Seguridad a Bordo
السلامة على متن الطائرة
यात्रा के दौरान सुरक्षा
乘客安全信息
ご搭乗中の安全のために
BRITISH AIRWAYS

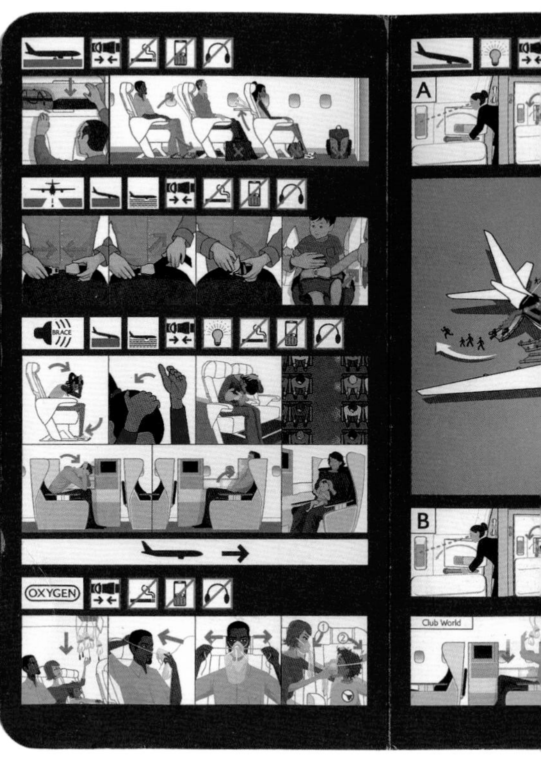
BRACE
OXYGEN
A
B
Club World

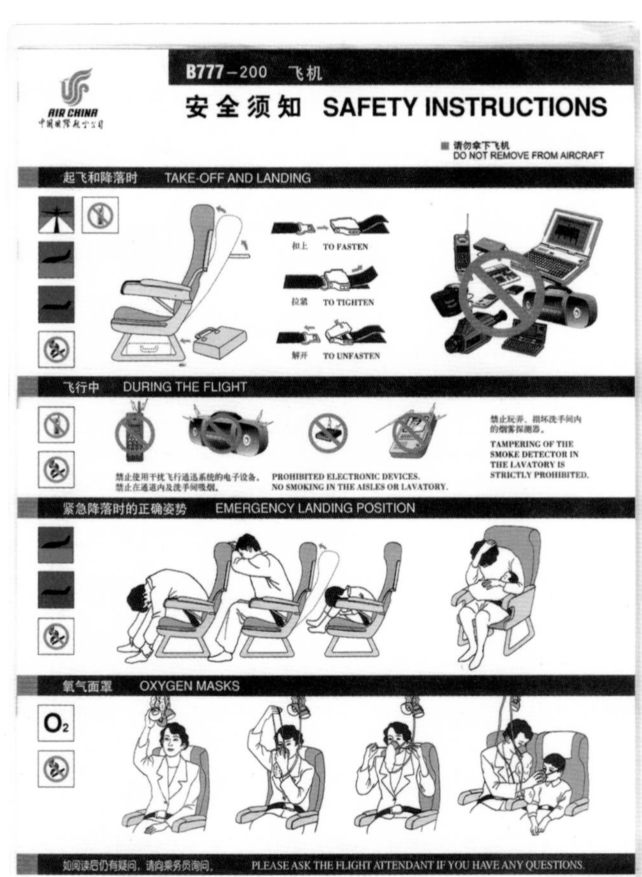

AIR CHINA
中国国际航空公司
B777-200 飞机
安全须知 SAFETY INSTRUCTIONS
请勿拿下飞机
DO NOT REMOVE FROM AIRCRAFT
起飞和降落时 TAKE-OFF AND LANDING
扣上 TO FASTEN
拉紧 TO TIGHTEN
解开 TO UNFASTEN
飞行中 DURING THE FLIGHT
禁止使用干扰飞行通迅系统的电子设备。 PROHIBITED ELECTRONIC DEVICES.
禁止在通道内及洗手间吸烟。 NO SMOKING IN THE AISLES OR LAVATORY.
TAMPERING OF THE SMOKE DETECTOR IN THE LAVATORY IS STRICTLY PROHIBITED.
紧急降落时的正确姿势 EMERGENCY LANDING POSITION
氧气面罩 OXYGEN MASKS
O_2
如阅读后仍有疑问，请向乘务员询问。 PLEASE ASK THE FLIGHT ATTENDANT IF YOU HAVE ANY QUESTIONS.

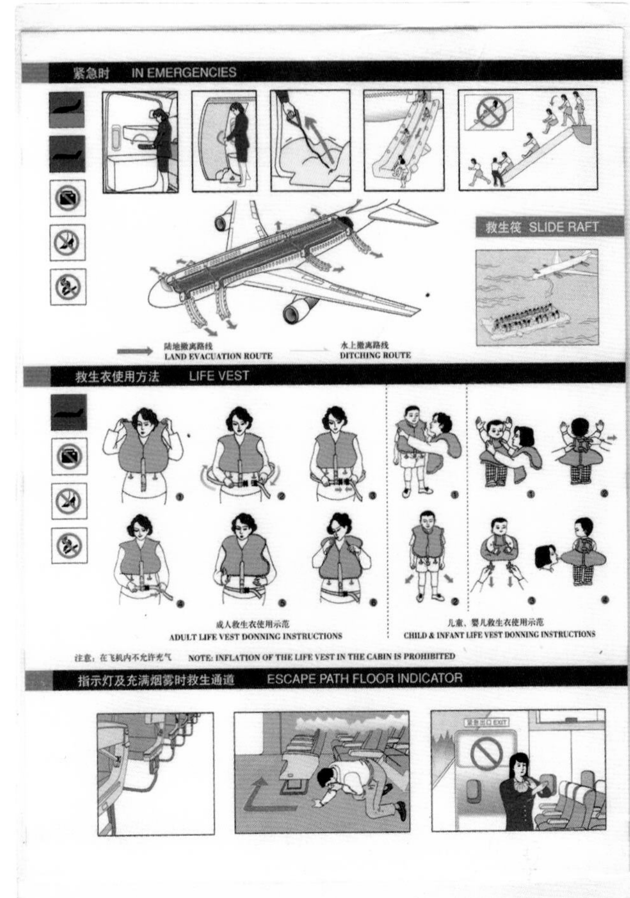

紧急时 IN EMERGENCIES
救生筏 SLIDE RAFT
陆地撤离路线 LAND EVACUATION ROUTE
水上撤离路线 DITCHING ROUTE
救生衣使用方法 LIFE VEST
成人救生衣使用示范 ADULT LIFE VEST DONNING INSTRUCTIONS
儿童、婴儿救生衣使用示范 CHILD & INFANT LIFE VEST DONNING INSTRUCTIONS
注意：在飞机内不允许充气 NOTE: INFLATION OF THE LIFE VEST IN THE CABIN IS PROHIBITED
指示灯及充满烟雾时救生通道 ESCAPE PATH FLOOR INDICATOR

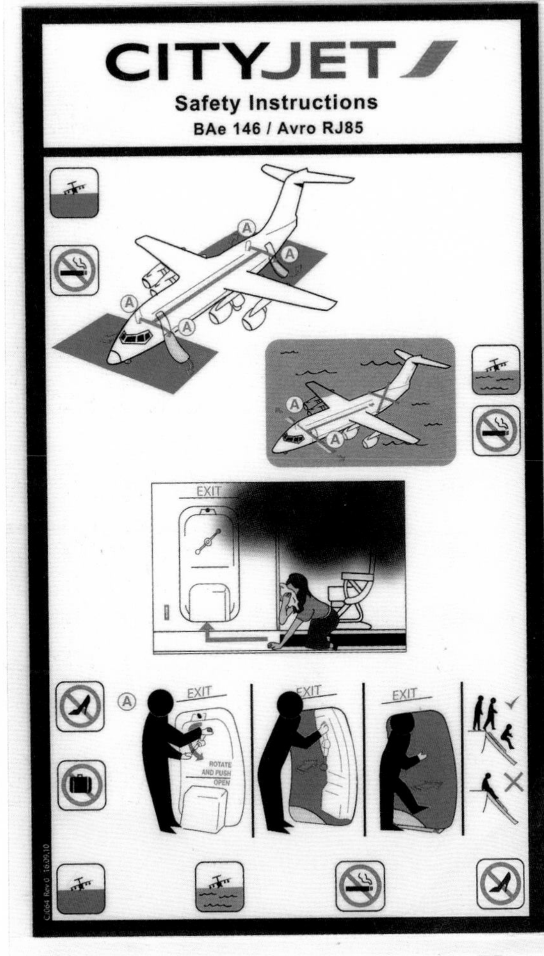

CITYJET
Safety Instructions
BAe 146 / Avro RJ85
EXIT
ROTATE AND PUSH OPEN

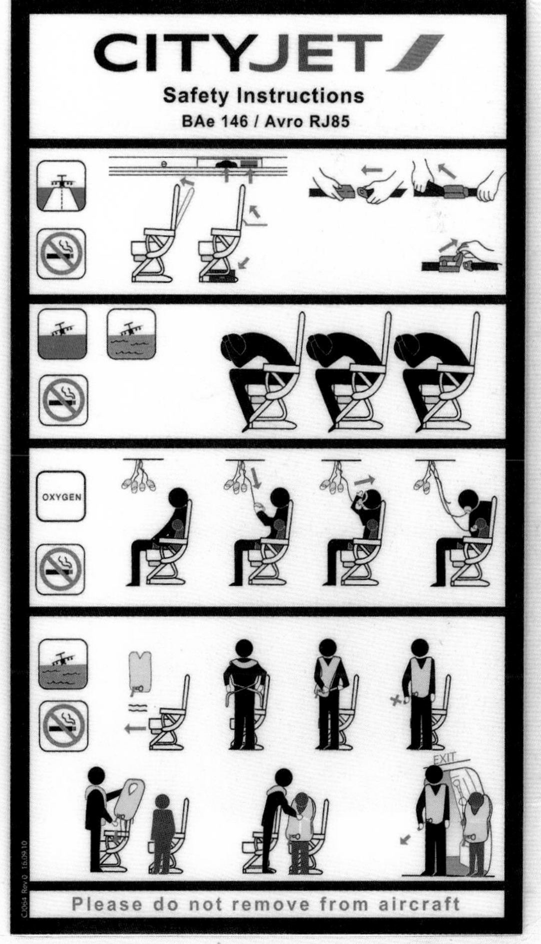

CITYJET
Safety Instructions
BAe 146 / Avro RJ85
OXYGEN
EXIT
Please do not remove from aircraft

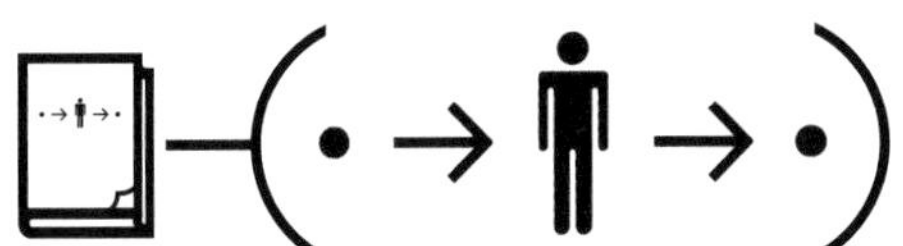

By Xu Bing

REGARDING *BOOK FROM THE*

This project is a result of my interest in signs and icons. It originated from airline-safety manuals. Since the 1990s I have spent countless hours in international airports and on board many different aircrafts and noticed that the design of airport signs and airline-safety manuals is based upon image recognition. Such diagrams and signs attempt to explain relatively complex matters with minimum words. This truly fascinated me. For years, I had been collecting hundreds of safety cards without having a clear goal. Then, in 2003, a sign printed on a chewing gum packet aroused my interest. The three simple images actually conveyed an important message: Please wrap the used gum and dispose of it into a trash bin. I came to realize that in addition to single icons being used to explain something simple, several icons together can be used to narrate a longer story. From then on, I began to collect and organize logos, icons, and signs from all over the world. I also began to research symbols employed in the specialized fields of mathematics, chemistry, physics, drafting, musical composition, choreography, and corporate branding, among others. In recent years, the rapid development of Internet and

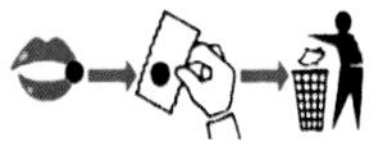

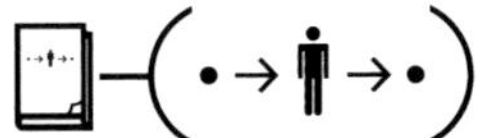

GROUND

digital technology has greatly expanded the field of icons. While my project of collecting these modern hieroglyphics has become an endless one, it makes me feel that my work is even more significant, and I am constantly reflecting on the issues that they present.

As early as 1627, the French theorist Jean Douet first suggested, in an essay titled "A Proposal to the King for a Universal Language," that Chinese was a potential model for an international language.[1] The word *model* is important here because Douet did not limit this "universal language" to the form of Chinese characters per se, instead he refers to the system of image recognition upon which the Chinese language is based. Today, nearly four hundred years have passed since the book was published, and human communication has indeed evolved in the direction predicted by Douet. We have come to sense that traditional spoken forms are no longer the most appropriate method for communication and, in response, great human effort has been concentrated on developing ways to replace traditional written languages with icons and images. For this reason, among others, humankind has entered the age of communicating through images.

Most languages take shape among a small group of people (a tribe or a village) sharing a similar set of vocalized expressions. As the scope of the group's activities expands, its language also develops into a regional mode of expression and eventually expands to the entire nation and, even, several nations. This is the millennia-long process of human-language evolution. Today, spurred by a trend of internationalization, the world is contracting, creating a "global village." However, this global "village" is distinct from the early villages out of which language first took shape. As citizens of the global village, we use a varied range of dialects and often employ mutually incomprehensible systems of symbols to express information in written form. We must, however, live and work together in the sense that we share information on a global scale. As a result, the inconvenience of miscommunication through language has become a significant burden in many of our lives. Our existing languages are based on geography, ethnicity, and culture (including the all-powerful English). Written languages now face an entirely unprecedented challenge. Today, the age-old human desire for a "universal script" has become a critical need. This predicament requires a new form of communication better adapted to the circumstances of globalization. Today the implications of the Tower of Babel can, all the more powerfully, be felt. Life is entirely different from what it was two thousand years ago, yet our current language and script are more or less the same. It is striking that our vernacular and written text have been developmentally left behind.

To some extent, human society today still contains elements of primitive civilizations. Yet there are constantly new social groups being formed, new tools being invented and also new technology being introduced into the world. Many of these changes happen so fast and suddenly that they challenge our acceptance of these new forms. The explosion of information and knowledge demands that we process new information quite rapidly. Today, most of us hardly have enough time and patience to consume and understand all the textual information that confronts us. We need a much more direct and faster way of grasping it. Our traditional way of comprehending is gradually being replaced by "image reading." In a way, an era of new pictograms is just dawning. A new model of learning based on images is emerging as if we are returning to the primeval civilization when written language was initially formed through the replication of images.

In relation to this, an analysis of some existing phenomena is informative:

The broadening range and increasing density of movement among peoples has impelled the rapid formation and use of a system of international icons. These symbols are most commonly found in areas of concentrated human density and diversity, and so it follows that the airport was among the first locales to make wide use of them. It could be said that along with airline-safety cards, airport signs were the first "common-reader" texts. The airport epitomizes the global village and, unconsciously, these texts have come to form an effective visual system that transcends the written word.

The continued standardization of transnational products, consumer lifestyles; the growth of pluralism, conterfeit culture, and the overall homogenization of diverse lifestyles brought on by globalization have rendered the visual form of ideas more recognizable. The explosion of international media has further strengthened the recongizability of these symbolic images. For example, the logo of the 2008 Beijing

2008 Beijing Olympics logo

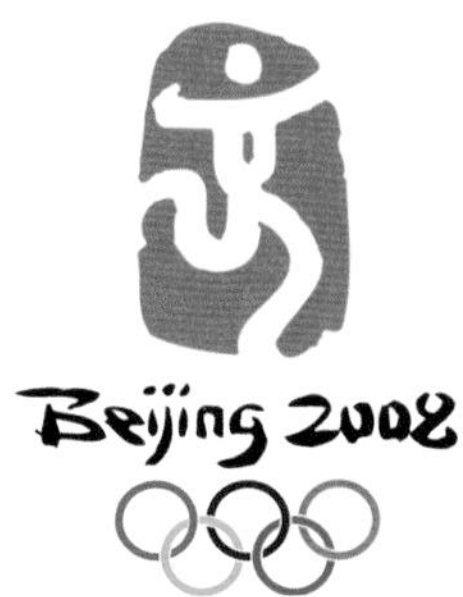

Coco-Cola logo

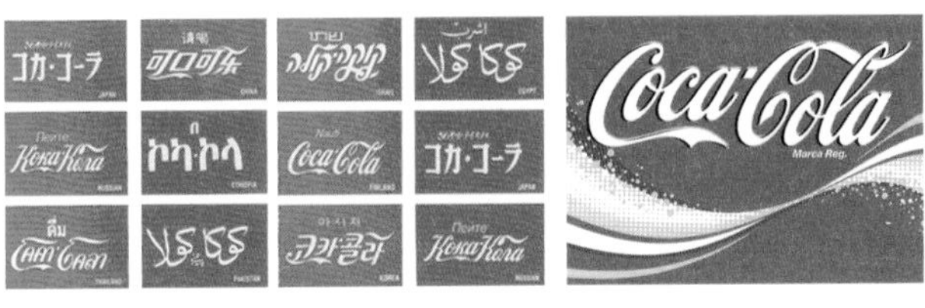

Olympics conveyed the significance, location, and spirit of the games through a simple, universal icon. To a certain degree, this phenomenon has begun to reduce illiteracy on a global scale by making it much easier to reach a common understanding.

It can be said with certainty that anything aimed at a global audience today must make use of a quick and effective mode of recognition and dissemination. Economic globalization demands direct commercial communication. Consequently, companies and products must employ logos that possess clearly identifiable characteristics that will transcend language and regional differences. Early attempts to market products to a global audience utilized translation, but now multinational businesses are marketing in the direction of wordlessness. For example past Coca-Cola ad campaigns included text translated into the language of the customer. But three years ago, the Coca-Cola Company made a decision to present their brand name to the international market in the form of an image, not as a word.[2] From this, *Coca-Cola* became an image that requires no translation.

The personal computer has also been fundemental in turning a specialized vocabulary into an intuitive, visual one. By employing icons instead of traditional text or numeric inputs computers have significantly lowered the basic knowledge required to take advantage of a technology that previously required intensive training to use. Now virtually anyone can distinguish computer functions and operate its programs. While the computerization of the workplace has, on one hand, resulted in a degree of physical laziness and degeneration, on the other hand it has also created a group of people who have easily adapted to this pictographic age. This is reflected in a new generation of people who find themselves at loggerheads with traditional reading but who are captivated by intuitive graphics.

The ubiquity of the Internet and the convenience of ever faster transglobal communication and information sharing have further exposed the limitations of interlanguage conversation. As a result, social media and online gaming consisting primarily of pictographs and images have emerged in great volumes. This vocabulary is developing at lightning speed, of its own accord, and is not bound by the geographical confines of the past. One example

Public information symbols published by International Organization for Standardization (ISO)

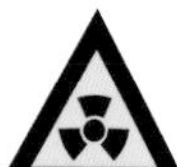

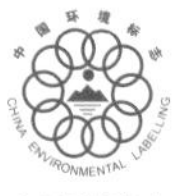

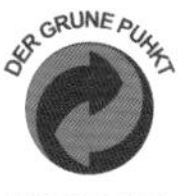

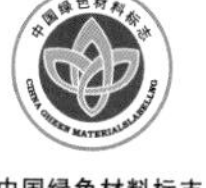

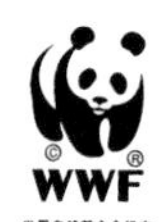

is "Mars language," used by Taiwanese youth. It combines pinyin, phonetic transliteration, punctuation, English letters, and Japanese words together with web emotional symbols or "emoticons." Many think such invented language has damaged the correctness of traditional language. In my opinion, the reason behind language transformation is the demand for a faster, easier, and more effective way of communication. Such invented language is the specific reaction of a new generation against the inconvenience of traditional language.

We easily overlook the fact that practitioners in such fields as mathematics, design, drafting, music, and dance already use their own "international languages" to communicate with one another. But the international language of "everyday life" has yet to be established. In 1990, the International Organization for Standardization (ISO) announced the final version of the first group of 55 "public information symbols." From 2001 to 2005, ISO separately published guidelines for the design of symbols — for example what visual elements an unambiguous symbol must possess or how to use these symbols — to the point of specifying the use of arrows.[3] This standardization can be seen as the embryonic steps toward a universal language for everyday life.

Copywriter and author, Michael Evamy states, "For now, the world's peoples must either be addressed in their own language, or by non-verbal means."[4] In that respect, a pictographic language not reliant upon phonics or specific characters has a special advantage. In the globalized world today, many scholars and scientists have already realized the advantage of image-based language compared with traditional language. One interesting example relates to the aftermath of an American nuclear test when scientists had to bury nuclear waste deep down in the Alabama desert. The danger of nuclear radiation from the waste can last up to ten thousand years. The scientists' problem was how to transmit this message to the generation living ten thousand years in the future. In the beginning, they wrote a warning text in English. Then they thought what if English does not exist after ten thousand years. Eventually, they chose to illustrate the warning message with signs and symbols. In fact, most languages die out in the evolution process. Only a small group of them survived and are still in use today. However, that does not mean that our languages have

     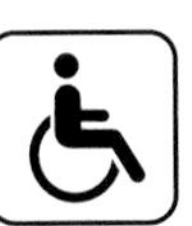 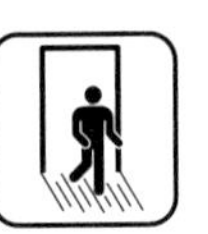   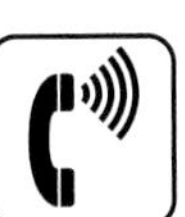

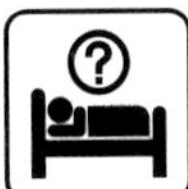   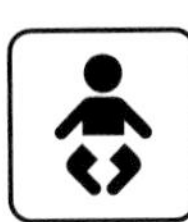      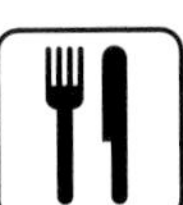

reached their paramount development. Languages will always adjust themselves and evolve in accordance with the progress of society.

Humankind has never abandoned the challenge of overcoming the obstacles of the written word; yet only under the conditions of the "global village" has a turning point been reached for such a system to emerge. The phenomena described above illustrates that there is not only a demand for a language model based fundamentally on images with the potential to surpass our current systems of writing, but that it has clearly emerged. I, myself, have come to realize this image-based language and its possibilities.

The sign language developed through *Book From the Ground* fits into this emergent language system mainly because the images collected and organized are already in use and have the ability to be easily recognized. When we began working on this, we had one principle: We did not engage in any subjective invention or fabrication but instead only collected, organized, and formatted existing signs and symbols. Generally speaking, subjective man-made symbols are personalized, lack common logic, and are not based upon a widely shared understanding. They cannot support a writing system that is easy to recognize and can be used repeatedly. This is why cartoons cannot be considered as a descriptive language. Every "word" in *Book From the Ground* has its own source or origin. The "grammar," including adjectives, person, tone, and prepositions, is similarly a collection of widely used and commonly recognized "representations," that we have analyzed and compiled according to their visual and psychological indicia. All of these elements already exist. They have only been collected and catalogued.

Visual communication is undoubtedly the most reliable means of communication and has the most potential to overcome cultural difference. Compared to other means, visual communication provides direct information based on common experiences. Therefore, signs and symbols that are based on direct experience are generally recognizable. For example, a sign with curving lines in front of a telephone receiver symbolizes sound coming from the telephone. Smooth waves mean a slow and calm voice while sharp waves indicate piercing noise. These visual experiences come from observations of nature; smooth waves look like the movement of water and smoke, while sharp waves resemble flashes of lightning. Humankind shares such visual experience regardless of language, geography, and cultural background. There are at least a hundred different signs for *coffee shop*. Our job is to organize and analyze them based on our psychological and visual habits. What we seek is the common visual elements that communicate the experience best. The core study is about visual communication.

To what degree can signs and symbols function as a language? This is my main interest in *Book From the Ground*. I hope my job has maximized the existing capacity of signs and symbols. Naturally, I understand the limitations of this visual language. Some ideas are easily expressed with this symbolic language while others are difficult, but I have a strong belief in how much this language actually can achieve. The story in *From Point to Point* would be a book with fourteen thousand characters when translated into standard Chinese. This was unthinkable before I started the project. We know that as a language, the ancient oracle script had only 260 characters. Today signs and symbols are already limitless and new signs and symbols keep on being invented. This means that they have already qualified as a language.

In certain respects, the language of icons transcends our structures of knowledge and the limitations of geographic and cultural specificity, it reflects the logic of real life and objects themselves rather than any preexisting, text-based knowledge. Comprehension is not contingent upon the readers level of education or knowledge of literature but instead stems from their experiences and way of life. Moreover, this language need not be taught or learned through traditional educational models. Regardless of your cultural background or mother tongue, you should be able to read this book as long as you have experience of the modern world. The educated and illiterate can equally enjoy the pleasures of reading.

In addition, after our computer program is perfected, writers of every language will be placed on equal footing. To a certain extent, this software will function as a point of transfer between dissimilar languages. These early results should not be dismissed, because they have the potential to expand into even larger arenas. The relationship between our new language and other, preexisting languages resembles the relationship between Mandarin and the many Chinese dialects: disparate pronunciations refer to identical characters. English cannot become a "global language," as its relationship to other languages is one of mutual exclusivity. As the use of English expands, other languages are lost.

The success of a language is in large part dependent on the power of its political and economic force.[5] Emperor Qin Shi eliminated the Six Kingdoms and unified the Chinese language; Mao popularized "standard" Mandarin characters through political means. Both revisions were undertaken with the aim of effectively communicating orders and unifying a country. This new system, the development of which I am now introducing to you, also draws its strength from political and economic factors but does not take the nation-state as its basic unit. It is rooted in the market rules of the global economy and world politics. Capital has become the new global language of power, but it must still undergo large-scale unification before it can more effectively control commerce.

It would be reasonable to expect me to write an introduction using this new icon-based "language." Unfortunately, this is not yet possible. However, all languages begin at the most elementary level of communication and only later develop into a medium suitable for complex expression. In this process, major components of the original language are lost and only small portions survive to form the languages we recognize today. Undoubtedly, this new language has only reached the oracle-bone phase — the most rudimentary pictographic state. Yet one cannot judge its potential by solely looking at its current capacity. Instead, one should consider its possibilities as a language of the future and whether its linguistic DNA allows it to continue growing.

I have created many works that relate to language. Twenty years ago I made *Book From the Sky*. It contains a text legible to no one on this earth, including myself. In contrast, today I have used this new sign language to write a book that everyone can understand. Despite their apparent differences, these two texts actually share something in common: Regardless of your mother tongue or level of education, they strive to treat the reader equally. *Book From the Sky* was an expression of my doubts and alarm over existing written languages, whereas *Book From the Ground* expresses my opinion on the development of language and is my quest for the ideal of a universal script. Perhaps this project is too ambitious, but its significance rests in making the attempt. The discussions about *Book From the Sky*, including its fundamental idea, is always related to tradition and the physicality of the art work. *Book From the Ground*, however, is more like a boundless body of water spreading into the society in which we live today. It has no fixed form resembling traditional art. Perhaps the best form of *Book From the Ground* is its "non-art" appearance. I believe that the power of this work does not lie in its resemblance to art but in its ability to present a new way of looking at things.

Finally, I want to share with you the real inspiration behind *Book From the Ground*. Part of the software program for *Book From the Ground* was first exhibited in a show called "Automatic Update" in the Museum of Modern Art in New York. This exhibition investigated art after the dot.com boom and how artists living in the post–video art era reacted against high technology. My work was shown in this exhibition as an example of Western experimental art but, for me the true inspiration for this work is deeply rooted in my own cultural tradition. My sensitivity to sign language lies in the fact that I am bound to the picturesque tradition of the Chinese language, and I have grown a habit of image-reading in this culture.

1. Eco, Umberto. *The Search for the Perfect Language*, Cambridge: Blackwell, pp. 158-159. 1995
2. Evamy, Michael. *World Without Words*, London: Laurence King, p.12. 2007
3. *International Organization for Standardization, Public Information Symbols* ISO 7001: 1990; *Graphical symbols incorporating arrows - Synopsis* ISO/TR 10488: 1991; *Basic principles for graphical symbols for use on equipment - Part 1: Creation of symbol originals* IEC 80416-1: 2001; *Basic principles for graphical symbols for use on equipment - Part 2: Form and use of arrows* ISO 80416-2: 2001; *Basic principles for graphical symbols for use on equipment - Part 3: Guidelines for the application of graphical symbols* IEC 80416-3: 2002; *Basic principles for graphical symbols for use on equipment - Part 4: Guidelines for the adaptation of graphical symbols for use on screens and displays ISO* 80416-4: 2005.
4. ibid., p. 11.
5. Crystal, David. *English as a Global Language*, New York: Cambridge University Press, p. 5. 1997

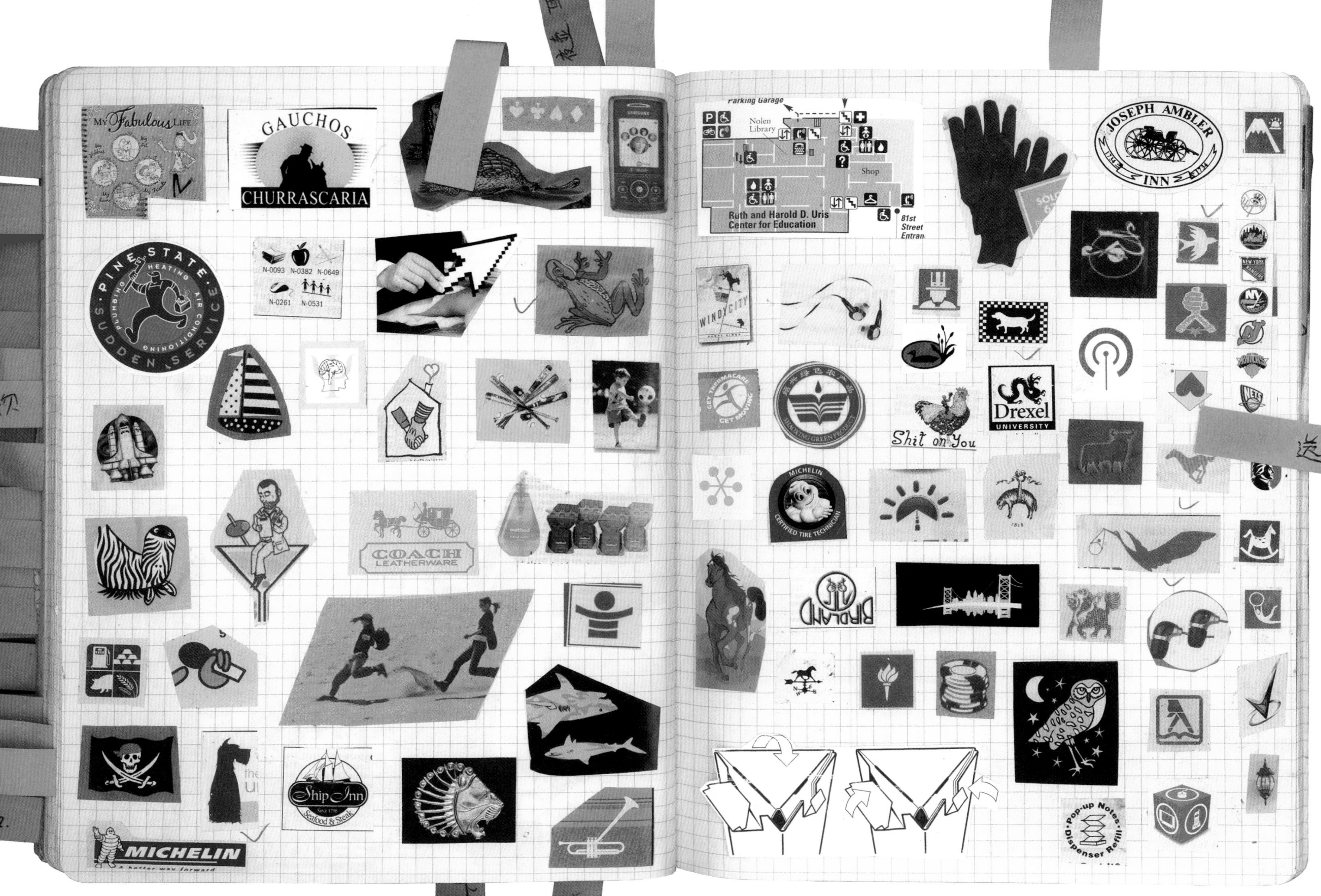
My Fabulous Life
GAUCHOS
CHURRASCARIA
PINE STATE
HEATING AIR CONDITIONING PLUMBING
SUDDEN SERVICE
N-0093 N-0382 N-0649
N-0261 N-0531
COACH
LEATHERWARE
Ship Inn
Seafood & Steak
MICHELIN
Parking Garage
Nolen Library
Shop
Ruth and Harold D. Uris Center for Education
81st Street Entran
JOSEPH AMBLER INN
WINDY CITY
GET THERMACARE GET MOVING
Shit on You
Drexel
UNIVERSITY
MICHELIN
CERTIFIED TIRE TECHNICIAN
BIRDLAND
Pop-up Notes Dispenser Refill

LES MISERABLES
WWW.LESMISNEWYORK.COM

The PHANTOM of the OPERA
The longest-running show in Broadway history.

Longwood Gardens

BROOKLYN BAR ASSOCIATION
JUSTICE
INTEGRITY
HONOR
COURTESY
1872

CHAIRMAN

Blue Diamond

1. 예 약
먼저, 탑승하시고자 하는 항공편을 예약하십시오.
이 때 반드시 보너스 사용임을 말씀해 주십시오.
2. 발 급

HARBOR MAGIC

May - June
April - June
March - May
February - May

POWDER
POWDER
POWDER
POWDER

CHINESE AMERICAN REAL ESTATE ASSOCIATION

OSPREY

THOMAS'

iPod ready

Transmitt

OXY

Water

KEYSCARIBBEAN

Fully Insured
FINISHING
Painting

WIN ZONE

RONALD McDONALD HOUSE CHARITIES

50 SHEETS

Teleflora

FTD

Ohio Knitting Mills
CLEVELAND, O.

MON

picholine

Treat yourself to a Black
www.blackbearinn
Black B
In

BRAND NEW!
1-4 People / Sun-Thurs
Weekends May Be Higher

RoomSaver
PA11043

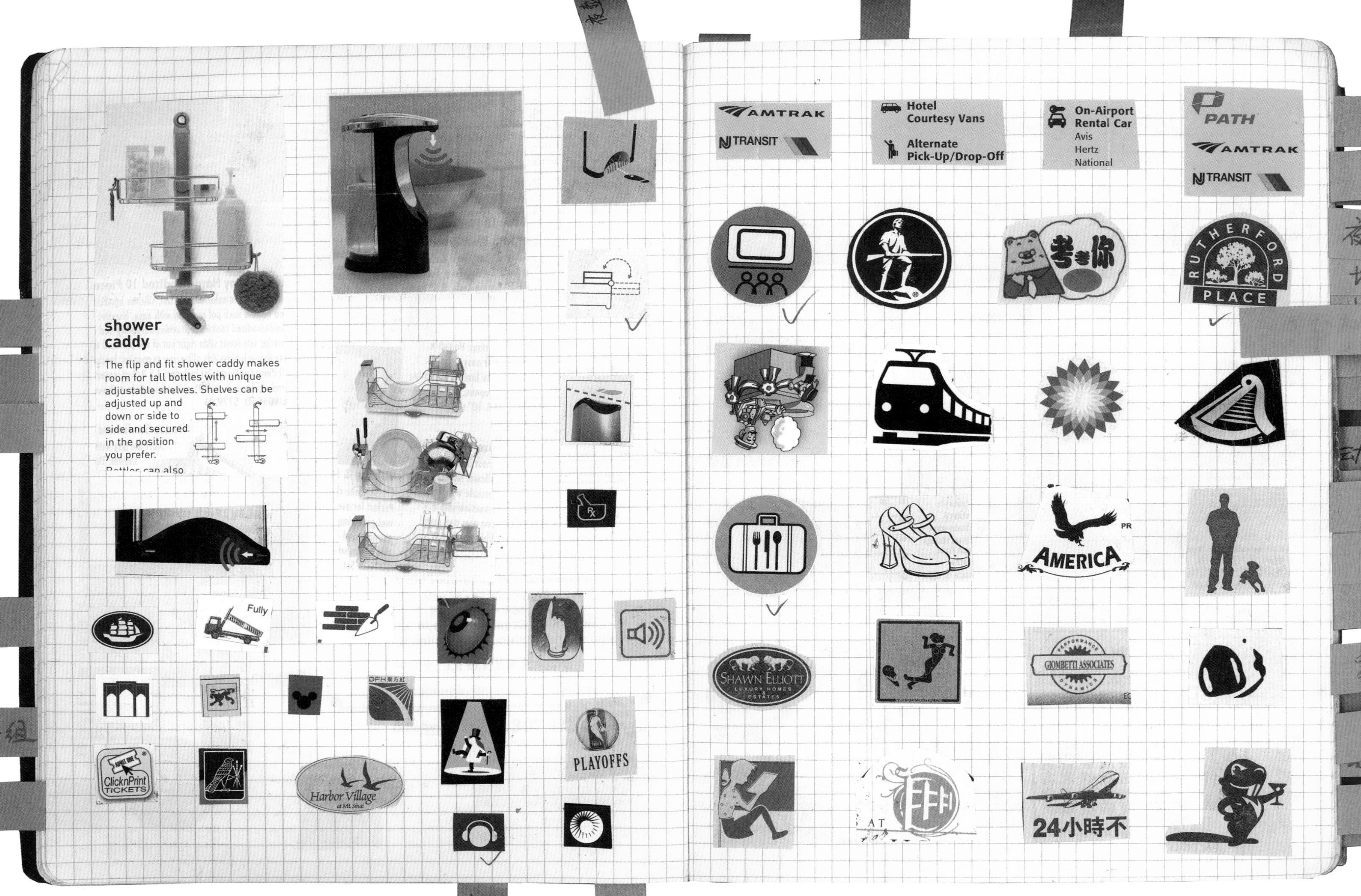
shower caddy
The flip and fit shower caddy makes room for tall bottles with unique adjustable shelves. Shelves can be adjusted up and down or side to side and secured in the position you prefer.
Fully
PLAYOFFS
ClicknPrint TICKETS
Harbor Village at Mt. Sinai
DFH
AMTRAK
NJ TRANSIT
Hotel Courtesy Vans
Alternate Pick-Up/Drop-Off
On-Airport Rental Car
Avis
Hertz
National
PATH
AMTRAK
NJ TRANSIT
考考你
RUTHERFORD PLACE
AMERICA
SHAWN ELLIOTT LUXURY HOMES & ESTATES
GIOMBETTI ASSOCIATES
PERFORMANCE DYNAMICS
24小時不

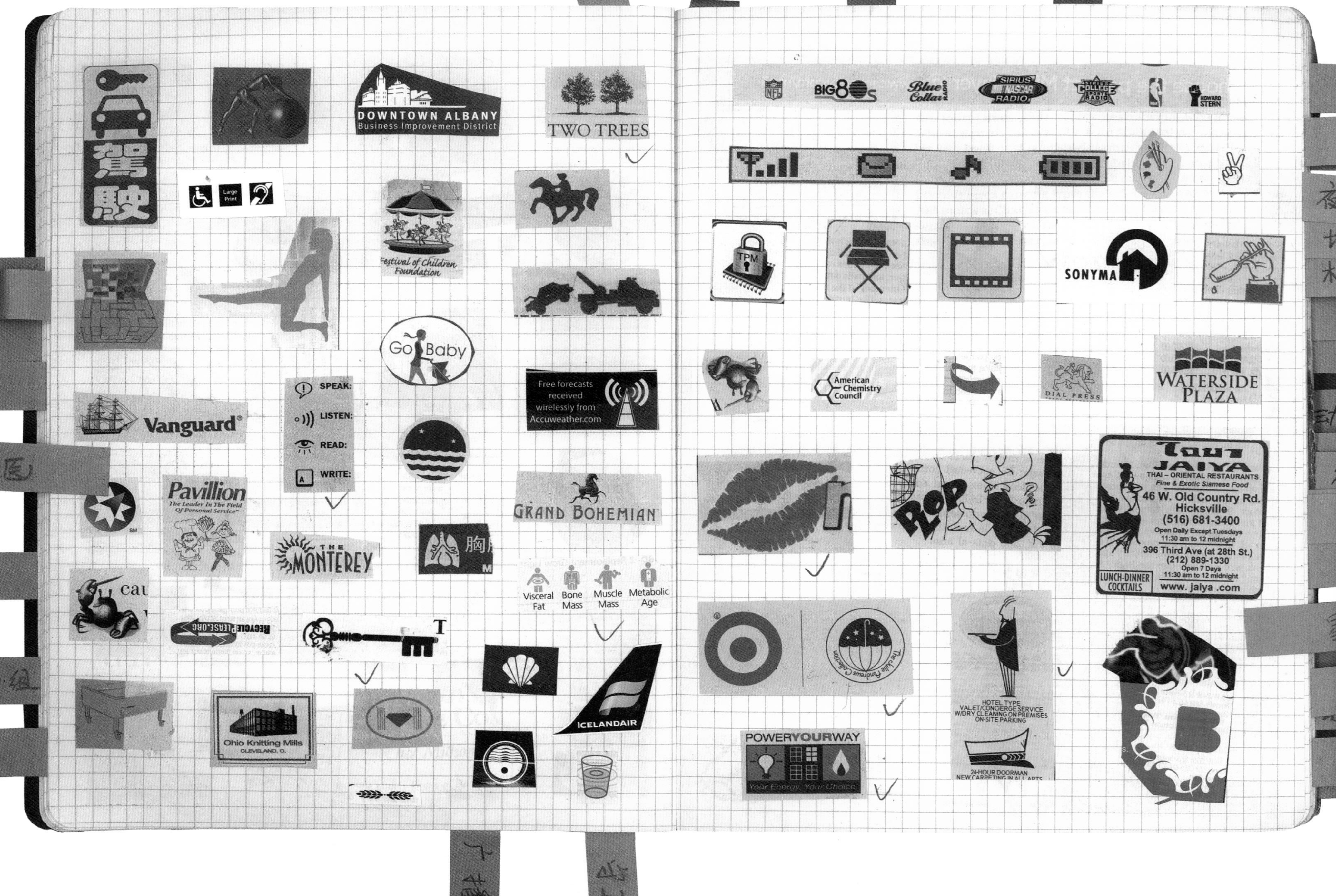

驾駛
Large Print
DOWNTOWN ALBANY
Business Improvement District
TWO TREES
Festival of Children Foundation
Go Baby
Vanguard
SPEAK:
LISTEN:
READ:
WRITE:
Free forecasts received wirelessly from Accuweather.com
Pavillion
The Leader In The Field Of Personal Service
GRAND BOHEMIAN
THE MONTEREY
Visceral Fat
Bone Mass
Muscle Mass
Metabolic Age
RECYCLEPLEASE.ORG
ICELANDAIR
Ohio Knitting Mills
CLEVELAND, O.
NFL
BIG 80s
Blue Collar RADIO
SIRIUS NASCAR RADIO
HOWARD STERN
TPM
SONYMA
American Chemistry Council
DIAL PRESS
WATERSIDE PLAZA
POP
JAIYA
THAI – ORIENTAL RESTAURANTS
Fine & Exotic Siamese Food
46 W. Old Country Rd.
Hicksville
(516) 681-3400
Open Daily Except Tuesdays
11:30 am to 12 midnight
396 Third Ave (at 28th St.)
(212) 889-1330
Open 7 Days
11:30 am to 12 midnight
LUNCH-DINNER COCKTAILS
www.jaiya.com
HOTEL TYPE
VALET/CONCIERGE SERVICE
W/DRY CLEANING ON PREMISES
ON-SITE PARKING
24-HOUR DOORMAN
POWERYOURWAY
Your Energy. Your Choice

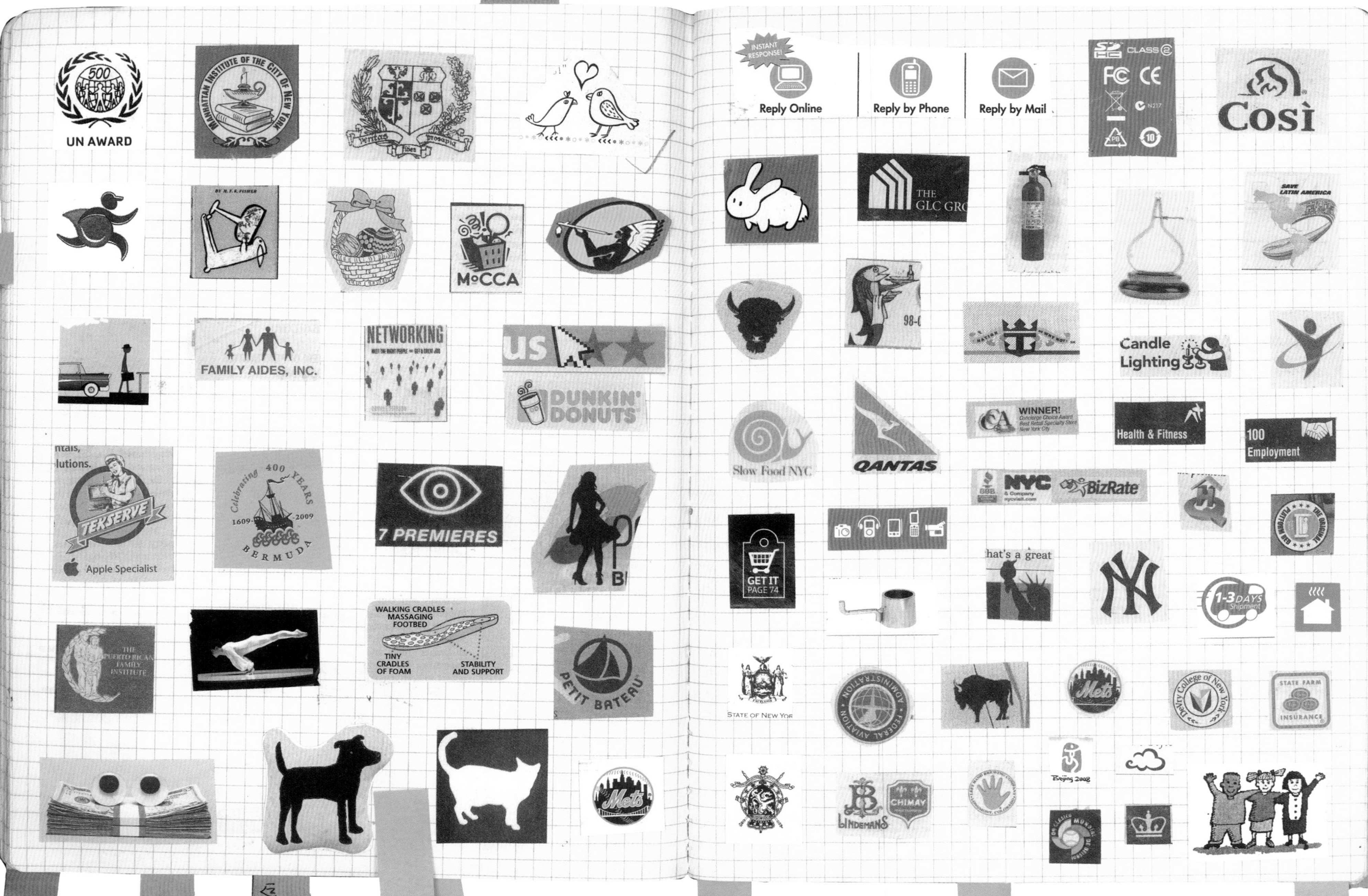
UN AWARD
MANHATTAN INSTITUTE OF THE CITY OF NEW YORK
INSTANT RESPONSE!
Reply Online
Reply by Phone
Reply by Mail
Così
MoCCA
THE GLC GR
SAVE LATIN AMERICA
FAMILY AIDES, INC.
NETWORKING
US
DUNKIN' DONUTS
Candle Lighting
WINNER!
Health & Fitness
100 Employment
Apple Specialist
TEKSERVE
Celebrating 400 YEARS 1609 2009 BERMUDA
7 PREMIERES
Slow Food NYC
QANTAS
NYC
BizRate
GET IT PAGE 74
hat's a great
1-3 DAYS Shipment
THE PUERTO RICAN FAMILY INSTITUTE
WALKING CRADLES MASSAGING FOOTBED
TINY CRADLES OF FOAM
STABILITY AND SUPPORT
PETIT BATEAU
STATE OF NEW YOR
FEDERAL AVIATION ADMINISTRATION
Mets
DeVry College of New York
STATE FARM INSURANCE
LINDEMANS
CHIMAY
Beijing 2008

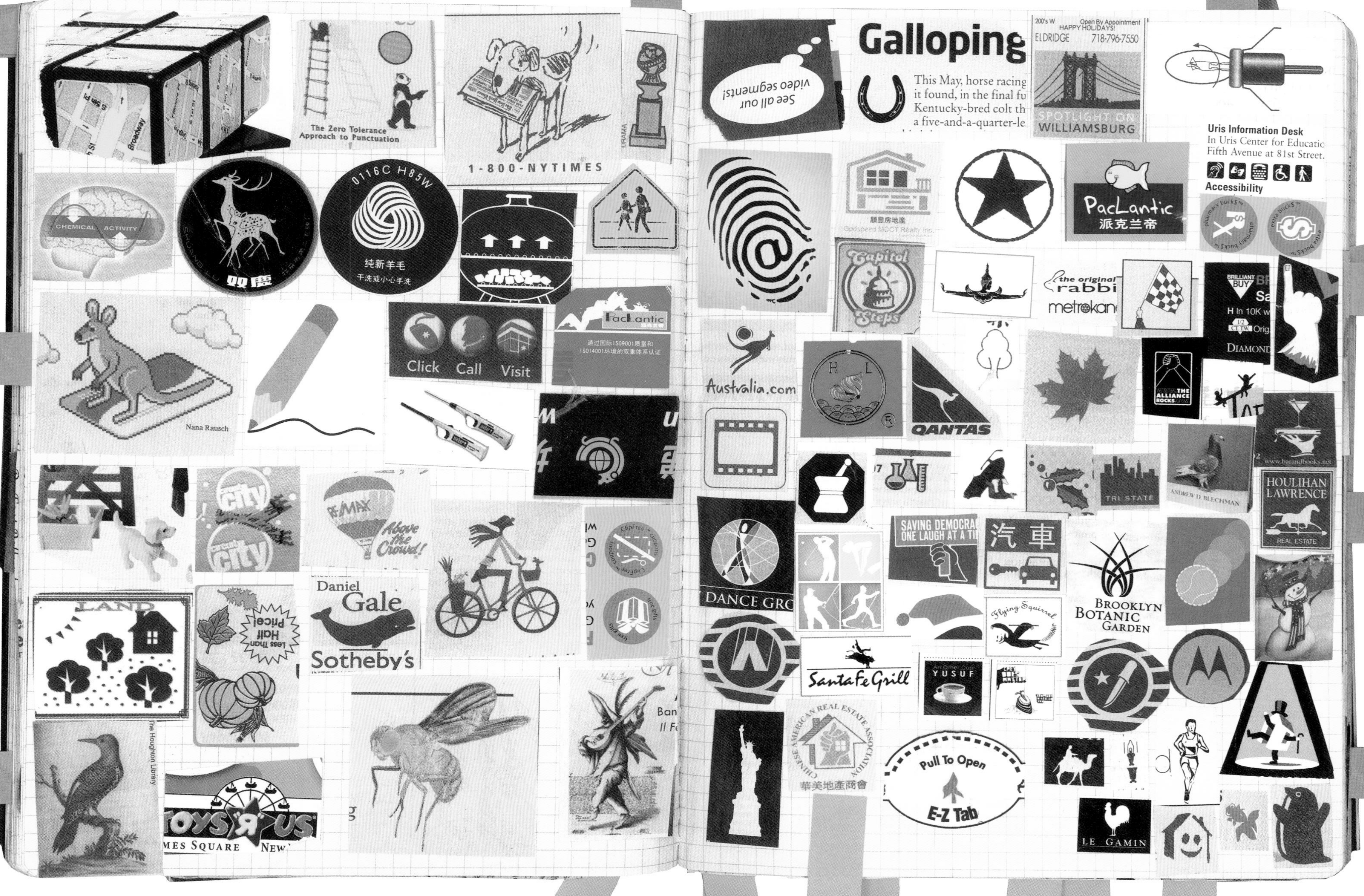

The Zero Tolerance Approach to Punctuation
1-800-NYTIMES
CHEMICAL ACTIVITY
0116C H85W
纯新羊毛
干洗或小心手洗
Click Call Visit
PacLantic
Nana Rausch
Above the Crowd!
Daniel Gale Sotheby's
Less Than Half Price!
LAND
The Houghton Library
TOYS"R"US
MES SQUARE
See all our video segments!
Galloping
This May, horse racing
it found, in the final fu
Kentucky-bred colt th
a five-and-a-quarter-le
ELDRIDGE 718-796-7550
HAPPY HOLIDAYS!
SPOTLIGHT ON WILLIAMSBURG
Uris Information Desk
In Uris Center for Educatic
Fifth Avenue at 81st Street.
Accessibility
PacLantic
派克兰帝
Capitol Steps
the original rabbi
metrokane
DIAMOND
Australia.com
QANTAS
THE ALLIANCE ROCKS
HOULIHAN LAWRENCE
REAL ESTATE
TRI STATE
ANDREW D. BLECHMAN
SAVING DEMOCRAC
ONE LAUGH AT A TI
汽車
BROOKLYN BOTANIC GARDEN
DANCE GRO
Flying Squirrel
Santa Fe Grill
YUSUF
CHINESE AMERICAN REAL ESTATE ASSOCIATION
華美地產商會
Pull To Open
E-Z Tab
LE GAMIN

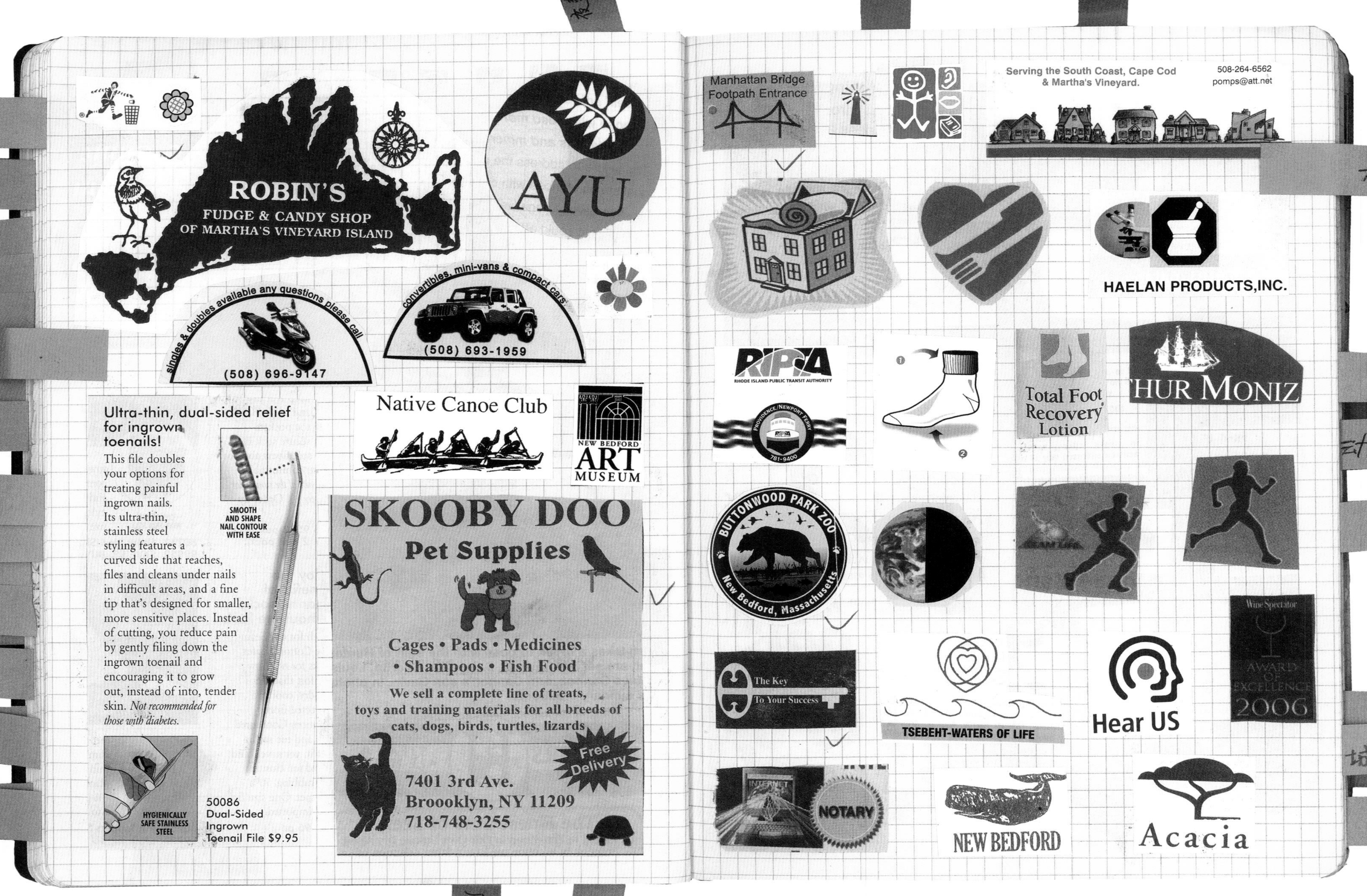
ROBIN'S
FUDGE & CANDY SHOP
OF MARTHA'S VINEYARD ISLAND
AYU
singles & doubles available any questions please call
(508) 696-9147
convertibles, mini-vans & compact cars
(508) 693-1959
Ultra-thin, dual-sided relief for ingrown toenails!
This file doubles your options for treating painful ingrown nails. Its ultra-thin, stainless steel styling features a curved side that reaches, files and cleans under nails in difficult areas, and a fine tip that's designed for smaller, more sensitive places. Instead of cutting, you reduce pain by gently filing down the ingrown toenail and encouraging it to grow out, instead of into, tender skin. Not recommended for those with diabetes.
SMOOTH AND SHAPE NAIL CONTOUR WITH EASE
HYGIENICALLY SAFE STAINLESS STEEL
50086
Dual-Sided
Ingrown
Toenail File $9.95
Native Canoe Club
NEW BEDFORD
ART
MUSEUM
SKOOBY DOO
Pet Supplies
Cages • Pads • Medicines
• Shampoos • Fish Food
We sell a complete line of treats, toys and training materials for all breeds of cats, dogs, birds, turtles, lizards
Free Delivery
7401 3rd Ave.
Brooooklyn, NY 11209
718-748-3255
Manhattan Bridge
Footpath Entrance
Serving the South Coast, Cape Cod
& Martha's Vineyard.
508-264-6562
pomps@att.net
HAELAN PRODUCTS,INC.
RIPTA
RHODE ISLAND PUBLIC TRANSIT AUTHORITY
PROVIDENCE/NEWPORT FERRY
781-9400
Total Foot
Recovery
Lotion
THUR MONIZ
BUTTONWOOD PARK ZOO
New Bedford, Massachusetts
The Key
To Your Success
TSEBEHT-WATERS OF LIFE
Hear US
Wine Spectator
AWARD OF EXCELLENCE
2006
NOTARY
NEW BEDFORD
Acacia

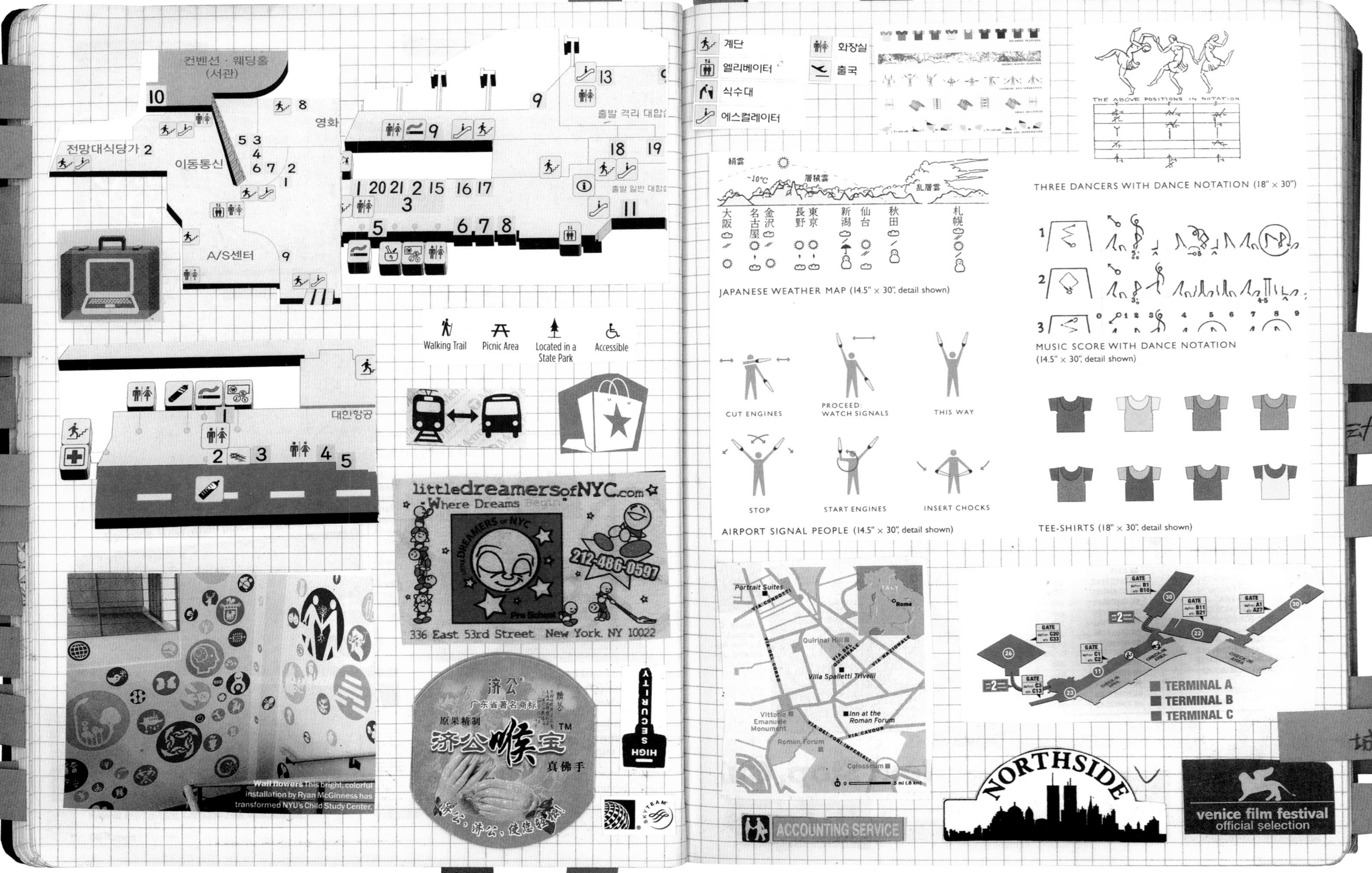

컨벤션 · 웨딩홀
(서관)

10

8

영화

전망대식당가 2

5 3
4
6 7 2
1

이동통신

A/S센터

9

9

9

13

출발 격리 대합

18 19

1 20 21 2 15 16 17
3

출발 일반 대합

11

5 6 7 8

대한항공

2 3 4 5

Walking Trail

Picnic Area

Located in a State Park

Accessible

littledreamersofNYC.com
Where Dreams Begin

DREAMERS of NYC

Pre School

212-486-0597

336 East 53rd Street New York, NY 10022

Wall flowers This bright, colorful installation by Ryan McGinness has transformed NYU's Child Study Center.

济公®
广东省著名商标
原果精制
济公猴宝 TM
真佛手

HIGH SECURITY

SKYTEAM

계단

엘리베이터

식수대

에스컬레이터

화장실

출국

THE ABOVE POSITIONS IN NOTATION

巻雲

~10°C

層積雲

乱層雲

大阪 名古屋 金沢 長野 東京 新潟 仙台 秋田 札幌

JAPANESE WEATHER MAP (14.5" × 30", detail shown)

THREE DANCERS WITH DANCE NOTATION (18" × 30")

MUSIC SCORE WITH DANCE NOTATION
(14.5" × 30", detail shown)

CUT ENGINES

PROCEED: WATCH SIGNALS

THIS WAY

STOP

START ENGINES

INSERT CHOCKS

AIRPORT SIGNAL PEOPLE (14.5" × 30", detail shown)

TEE-SHIRTS (18" × 30", detail shown)

Portrait Suites

VIA CONDOTTI

ITALY

Rome

Quirinal Hill

VIA DEL QUIRINALE

VIA NAZIONALE

VIA DEL CORSO

Villa Spalletti Trivelli

Vittorio Emanuele Monument

Inn at the Roman Forum

Roman Forum

VIA DEI FORI IMPERIALI

VIA CAVOUR

Colosseum

GATE B1 B10

GATE B11 B21

GATE A1 A27

GATE C20 C33

GATE C1 C2

GATE C3 C13

TERMINAL A
TERMINAL B
TERMINAL C

ACCOUNTING SERVICE

NORTHSIDE

venice film festival
official selection

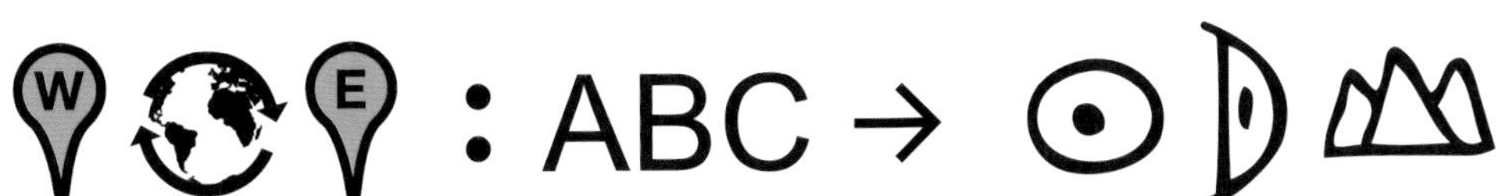
W
E
: ABC →

By Haytham Nawar

CROSS-CULTUR
FROM ALPHABE
PICTOGRAPHS

ABC →

AL SHIFT: S TO

In today's world, there are more than five thousand languages and dialects in use, of which only a hundred may be considered of major importance. Inter-communication among them has proved not just difficult but often impossible.[1] A universal language would be the solution to this problem. In fact over the last thousand years more than eight hundred attempts have been made to develop an official second language that in time could be adopted by all major countries[2]. Some of the most recognized examples are Esperanto, Interlingua, Ido, and Volapuk. However, all of them combine elements of existing languages and rely on the Roman alphabet, which reduces their applicability in certain regions of the world. The aim of this essay is to explore the possibility of developing an effective system for conveying information/knowledge on a universal scale with pictographic communication. Potentially this could bridge linguistic and cultural gaps, thereby creating a broader platform for multiculturalism.

The majority of current living languages are dependent on alphabets, however, historically this was not the case. Languages were often initiated with pictographic references, Egyptian hieroglyphs being one of the best examples, and later evolved into alphabetic languages. While there are many examples of this transformation, Chinese is one language that resisted becoming alphabetized and still retains its pictographic roots.

PICTOGRAPHIC / SEMANTOGRAPHIC SYSTEMS

The notion of *semantography*, from the Greek words *semanticos*, indicating "significant meaning," and *graphin*, "to write" is somewhat useful in the pursuit of an international language. Charles K. Bliss coined the term in 1947 to define his development of a nonalphabetic writing system based on the principles of ideographic writing and chemical symbolism. *Semantography* was also the name of Bliss' 1949 book, which outlined the tenets of the Blissymbolic communication system.[3] The majority of written systems are derived from ideographic languages, but pictographic languages seem to be a more recent invention. Some of these more recent examples are described below.

ISOTYPE

"Pictures are a better means of communication than words." — Otto Neurath[4]

In the 1930s, Otto Neurath (1882-1945) created Isotype, also known as the Vienna Method of Pictorial Statistics (*Wiener Methode der Bildstatistik*). It is a communication system developed at the Social and Economic Museum of Vienna (Gesellschafts- und Wirtschaftsmuseum in Wien) that uses a pictorial form within a two-dimensional syntax to show social, technological, biological, and historical connections.

Among Neurath's pictographs are those that represent different industries and forms of communication. These pictorial "world supplements" (Fig. 1), while being completely understandable themselves, can assume other meanings in combination with other symbols or through other forms of manipulation.

Neurath introduced two basic rules for his system. The first is related to the presentation of statistics by means of icons and claims that an icon represents a certain quantity of things, with more icons representing a greater quantity. The second was a general rule that perspective should not be used. The graphic treatment for all Neurath's pictures was based on what the observer actually saw, rather than the spoken or written words associated with what was seen. The picture had to present the important characteristics first, followed by less important details. Isotype grammar could further impact meaning either through the use of color and texture or by the addition of pictographs.

"Visual education" was always the prime motive behind Isotype, which was commonly implemented through exhibitions and books designed to inform ordinary citizens (including schoolchildren) about their relationship to the world. It was never intended to replace verbal language but instead was conceived as a "helping language" that was accompanied by verbal elements. Neurath realized that it could never be a fully developed language and instead referred to it as a "language-like technique."[5]

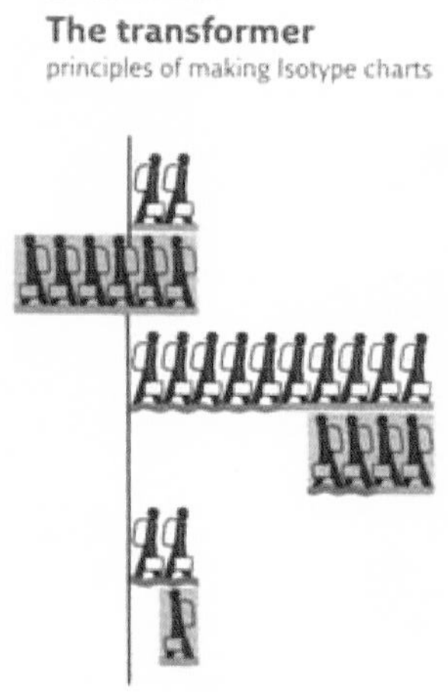

1

BLISSYMBOLICS

"In 1942 I named my symbols World Writing; then in 1947 chose an international scientific term, Semantography... My friends argued that it is customary to name new writing systems after the inventor, so I called it Blissymbolics or Blissymbols or simply Bliss."[6] — Charles K. Bliss

Blissymbolics is a communication system that was originally developed in the 1950s by Charles K. Bliss (1897–1985). It consists of about a hundred basic pictorial symbols each representing different concepts. These symbols can then be combined together with others to generate new concepts.

The 30 symbols shown in Fig. 2 are already used internationally. By putting a small action indicator on top of these symbols, the verbs *to hear*, *to see*, *to write*, *to feel*, and *to reason* are formed. The 'line letters' form combinations of outlined symbols, which are shown in (Fig. 3.)

Blissymbols can be sequenced grammatically to form many different sentence types. The grammar of Blissymbols is based on a certain interpretation of nature, dividing it into matter (material things), energy (actions), and human values (mental evaluations). In an ordinary language, these would give way respectively to substantives, verbs, and adjectives. Simple shapes make Blisssymbols easy to draw, and since both abstract and concrete concepts can be represented, they are employable by both children and adults. Therefore they are an appropriate tool for a wide range of intellectual abilities. In fact, Blissymbolics has been used as a way to help developmentally impaired children at the Holland Bloorview Kids Rehabilitation Hospital in Canada.

The Blissymbolics Communication International Authorized Vocabulary (BCI-AV) represents the latest set of formally approved Blissymbols that appears in Bliss dictionaries. The BCI standard Blissymbolics language structure and vocabulary is based on and derived from Bliss's *Semantography*. BCI develops Blissymbolics in accordance with the needs of its users, who have embodied national, cultural, and developmental differences; the maintenance of the logic of the system and of Blissymbolics as a multicultural language; and sensitivity to the pragmatic needs for communication.[7]

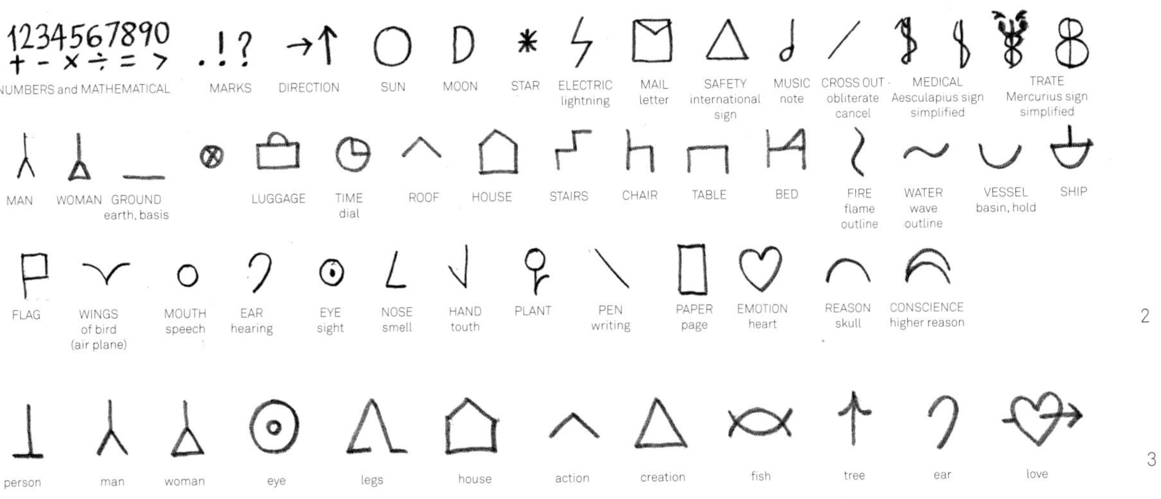

2

3

NOBEL UNIVERSAL GRAPHICAL LANGUAGE

Nobel Language was created in 2010 by Milan Randić, professor emeritus in the Department of Mathematics and Computer Science at Drake University in Des Moines, Iowa. Named after the chemist Alfred Nobel, this pictographic language is based on 120 basic signs that are combined with many different-shaped arrows. Its main purpose is to facilitate communication between speakers who do not share a common language. Curiously, after spending several weeks in Japan, Randić became intrigued by Chinese characters and Japan's kanji as a model for a universal script.

Nobel Language is designed based on the following requirements (Fig. 4).

(1) A small number of basic signs
(2) Signs that are easy to recognize
(3) Signs that are easy to reproduce
(4) Sign combinations being limited to three signs
(5) Signs that are complementary in that they closely resemble their meanings.

There are many signs that are easily recognized but in order to be acceptable for Nobel, they also needed to be easily reproduced to facilitate communication. In addition, when making combinations of signs, one has to limit the amount of symbols in order to maintain clarity: No more than three signs should be combined into a single word. Finally, the last requirement was to produce signs that facilitate one's ability to remember and learn them easily. Randić states "To learn sixty words of a new language is not much, but to learn them in 15 minutes illustrates the important quality of Nobel — the very close relationship, either pictographic or ideographic, between the signs and their meaning." [8]

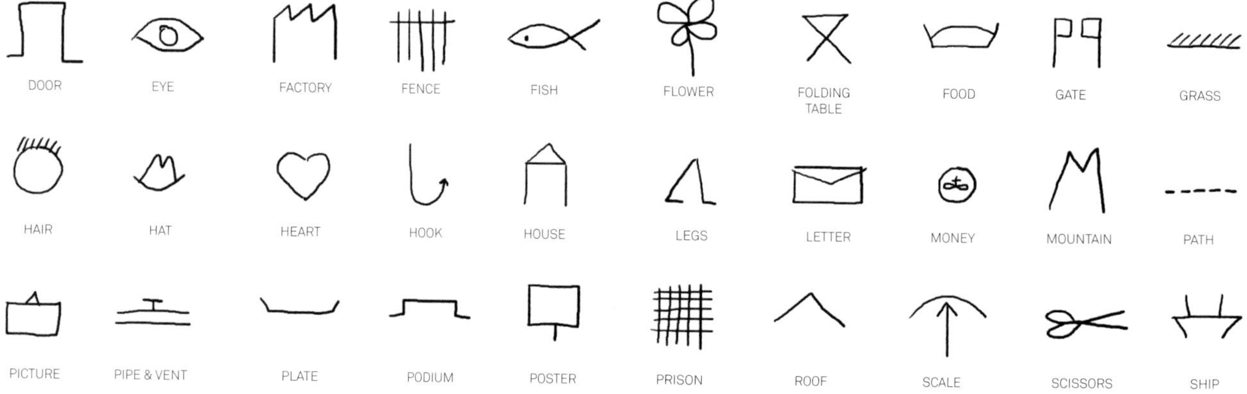

ICONJI

In 2010, Kai Staats, founder and former CEO of Terra Soft Solutions, and his team created a new Short Message Service (SMS) communication system that combined the speed, variety, and linguistic richness of a global art project. iConji is a pictographic communication system based on an open, visual vocabulary of characters with built-in translations of 12 languages. Its symbols are delivered electronically to computers, phones, tablets, and other similar electronic devices.

In May 2010, iConji Messenger was released with support for Apple iOS (Fig. 5) and most Web browsers. In December 2010, iConji Social was released as a Web application only, with support for Facebook and Twitter as broadcast medium.

iConji Messenger consists of 1,183 characters, known as the lexiConji vocabulary. It contains base words commonly used in daily communication—word frequency lists, frequently used mathematical and logic symbols, punctuation symbols, and flags of all nations. The process of assembling a message from iConji characters is called iConjisation.

In February 2011, iConji launched its artist search, where users are encouraged to create and submit designs for new characters or better versions of existing ones. There are several criteria for accepting a submitted character, but the process is made simple by using available online graphic templates, instructions, and examples.[9]

iConji is popular in electronic communications used in Japan but supports online translation into many languages including Swahili and Chinese. Emoji icons are heavily slanted towards conveying emotional "punctuation" and are more useful in augmenting SMS than in communicating complete stand-alone messages.

How to Use iConji Messenger for iPhone OS

This application is not maintained at this time.

1. Search for an iConji character (Search Tips).
2. Select the Recipient of your Message.
3. Compose a Message:
    - From one of the 8 keyboard Panels (below), select a character to add to your Message.
    - Tap any character already in your Message to add Notes, add a Location tag, or modify the character to be a verb, adverb, or adjective.
    - To remove, select and hold for a moment, then drag back to the keyboard panel below.
4. Select a Character for your Message; or Customize your Keyboard:
    - Select a character to add to your Message; or
    - Press and hold (until all the characters shake), and then move to another location on the same keyboard panel or to another panel.
    - To make room for characters in full keyboard panels, first move one or more unwanted characters out of the full panel into the Bottomless Bucket (far right).
    - Tap any character again to stop them from shaking.
    - Any changes you make to the keyboard are remembered so every time you log in, from your iPhone, Facebook, or Web app, your keyboard will be as you like it.
5. Select a Keyboard Panel:
    - Panels 1-7 contain a maximum of 54 characters each.
    - The 8th is the Bottomless Bucket and holds all the characters you do not use on a regular basis.

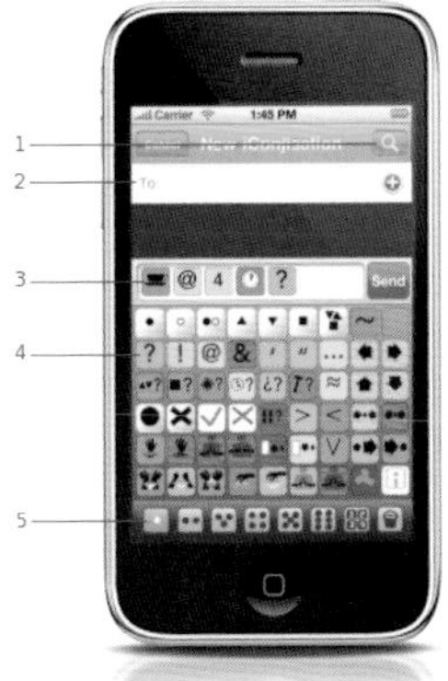

5

THE NOUN PROJECT

Edward Boatman initiated the Noun Project as a Kickstarter campaign in 2011. It is a website created to build an accessible and free collection of symbols. These are applicable and downloadable for all types of design projects, including websites, user interfaces, and print design. Each symbol comes with a title and credit line. The Noun Project aims to create a single, free online library of symbols that are commonly used throughout the world in order to foster shared design resources through the platform of the Internet. It is hoped that with sufficient financial backing and participation, The Noun Project website will grow into a user-friendly, symbol database (Fig. 6).

There has been much debate about the project's legality because symbols are made available for free. Boatman maintains that the symbols on the site are licensed under the Creative Commons Attribution, or they are already used in the public domain. The Noun Project features symbols from many collections including the U.S. National Park Service (including map and pedestrian symbols), AIGA (American Institute of Graphic Arts), Modern Pictograms (an icon-based typeface for interface designers and programmers) and health care symbols from the Robert Wood Johnson Foundation.

6

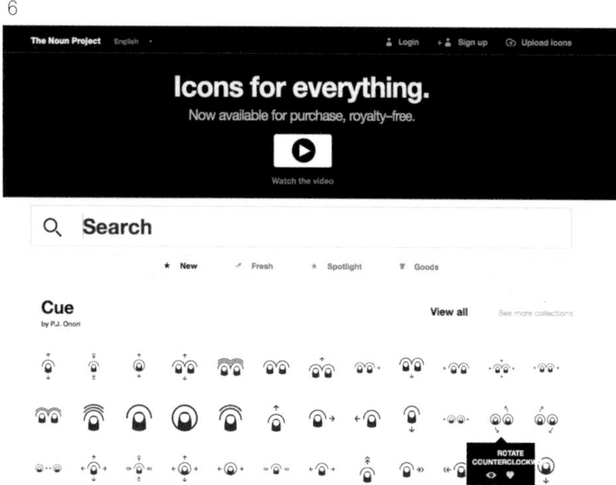

XU BING'S *BOOK FROM THE GROUND*

Pictographs are still in use as the main medium of written communication in some nonliterate cultures, and are often used as simple symbols in most contemporary cultures. Examples of ideograms include directional signage systems, such as in airports and other environments where people may not be familiar with the language yet are obliged to communicate, as well as Arabic numerals and mathematical notations, which are used worldwide regardless of their different spoken signfiers.

One contemporary example of an ideographic language is the *Book From the Ground* project by Chinese artist Xu Bing. Inspired by airport signage, the book is an attempt to create a universal pictographic language to tell stories that can be comprehended regardless of the reader's cultural background.

Book From the Ground is a collection of thousands of informational and instructional pictographs culled from the fields of mathematics, chemistry, music, and from the Internet. These pictographs represent the structural components of a communication system based on translatable pictures rather than alphabets.

Modern culture has levelled the global symbolic landscape to the point where we all know the sign for *man, alarm-clock,* and *airplane*. We do not need a dictionary to recognize these symbols. Xu Bing emphasizes this homogenization of language with the example of Coca-Cola, which stopped printing its labels in other languages.[10] *Coca-Cola* is now a universally recognized symbol, more than it is an actual word. Even IKEA includes a universal set of instructions composed in the language of symbols and signs with every piece of furniture purchased.[11]

These examples show that there are advantages to a visual communication method based on a pictographic system compared to an alphabetic one. Relatively small numbers of pictographic symbols are needed to express a complex idea in contrast to many words or sentences, and our ability to comprehend and recall a sign is enhanced because we do not need to learn its precise meaning. Furthermore, the ability to use a visual-communication method does not depend on the alphabetic languages we already know, which means that pictographic communication systems may overcome the problem of linguistic diversity.

Symbols have already evolved to the point of universal acceptance in such areas as music and mathematics. Xu's project is an effort to raise the idea of a universal pictographic language to a broad level. It would be bold to imply that standardizing a pictographic language would result in perfect intercultural communication. However, the first step toward solving the quandary of a global language is establishing that it is vital for humans to be able to communicate on a universal scale. This notion of intercultural communication is also the foundation for the rise of the global citizen of todays' planet.

Generally speaking, while all people are to some extent culturally bound, the flexibility of the global citizen allows for adaptability and adjustment. These adjustments and adaptations, however, must always be dependent on some constant factors and common ground. Bearing in mind that every culture or system has its own internal coherence, integrity, and logic, and that all cultural systems should be equally valid as variations on the human experience, a proposed multicultural communication system or language should utilize commonalities and avoid cultural differences and conflicts.

1. Dreyfuss, H. (1972) *Symbol Sourcebook: An Authoritative Guide to International Graphic Symbols*, New York: John Wiley and Sons.
2. Okrent, A. (2009) *In the Land of Invented Languages*, New York: Spiegel & Grau, Random House, Inc.
3. Bliss, C. K. (1949) *Semantography, a non-alphabetical symbol writing, readable in all languages; a practical tool for general international communication, especially in science, industry, commerce, traffic, etc., and for semantical education, based on the principles of ideographic writing and chemical symbolism*, Sydney: Institute for Semantography.
4. Neurath, O. ([1936] 1998), *International Picture Language*, University of Reading, Reading & Language Information Centre, Reading, Berkshire, UK p. 13.
5. Neurath, O. ([1936] 1998), *International Picture Language*, University of Reading, Reading & Language Information Centre, Reading, Berkshire, UK p. 13.
6. Bliss, C. K. (1965), *Semantography (Blissymbolics)*, 2d enlarged ed., Sydney: Semantography (Blissymbolics) Publications.
7. Blissymbolics Communication International. (2012), *Blissymbolics Communication International*. http://www.blissymbolics.org/. Accessed 21 February 2012.
8. Randic, M. (2010) *Nobel Universal Graphical Language*, USA: Xlibris Corp. p. 26.
9. Staats, K. (2010), iconji. http://www.iconji.com/community/artist/. Accessed 25 February 2012.
10. Xu Bing, (2012) 'Regarding *Book From the Ground*' Art China - Yishu Dangdai, April Issue.
11. Pinkert, A. (2008) Xu Bing: The Future of Art and New Media, http://www.stillindie.com/2008/11/xu-bing-future-of-art-and-new-media.html Accessed 25 November 2011.

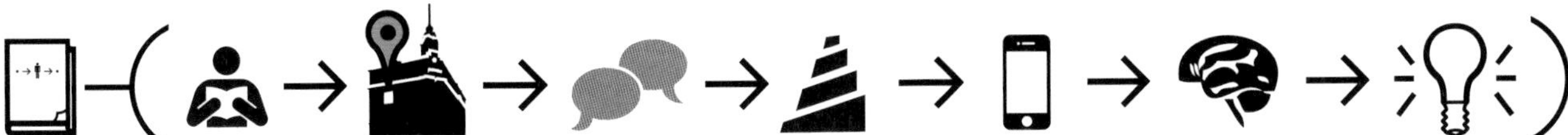

By Mathieu Borysevicz

EXTENSION FRO EXHIBITION, ETC

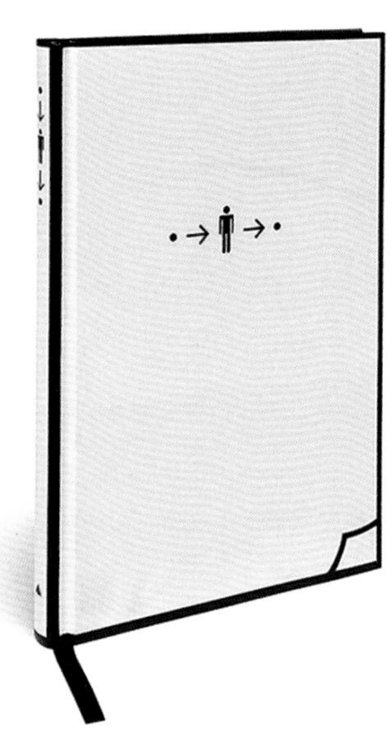

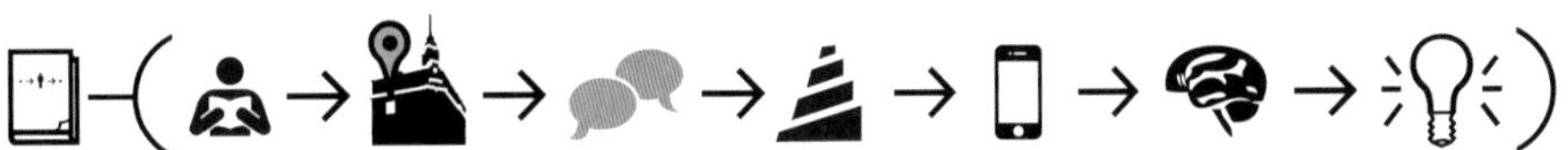

M THE GROUND—

Book From the Ground is an extensive project that culminates in the publication, *From Point to Point*, yet it isn't where it ends. *Book From the Ground* is a vehicle, an extension of the artist's mind that also has a life of its own. It is a living language, a global phenomenon, and a constantly expanding artistic project. Xu Bing's linguistic, imagistic enterprise is growing even as you read this. At the time of writing this essay *From Point to Point* has been published in four different countries on three different continents and presented countless times across the rest of the world, and there are many more plans in the works.

However, it still is a book and as such poses some obvious curatorial problems when presenting it as a full-scale art exhibition. Even Xu Bing's favorite part of the project is it's "non-art appearance." So how to fill a one thousand square meter art gallery with a simple one hundred and twelve page book? This, of course, is no ordinary book. It is a quite visual — composed entirely of pictographs, symbols, and logos — yet still, rather small, book. How to present this extraordinary publication and the project that gave rise to it in a way that adequately captures the colourful, icon-driven, and user-friendly content of the work itself?

Just how does one relay the significance of Xu Bing's new language and its relationship to our homogenized cultural terrain through a physical manifestation?

From Point to Point's story — a day in the life of Mr. Black — is laced with corporate logos and Internet chatter, so it became clear that the one identity we all share in the age of globalization is that of the 'consumer'. Hence one of the first components that we began to develop for the exhibition was the idea of a "book launch". Bookstores around the world employ the 'book launch' a marketing event to promote their new releases. The occasion for this exhibition was the release of *From Point to Point* in mainland China, so our event became an exhibition masquerading as a book launch or vice versa. Usually a book launch is promoted with a poster of the author's portrait flanked by tables stacked with volumes of the newly released publication. *The Tower of Babel* installation, composed of over 2000 copies of *From Point to Point*, was our stack of books, which both completed the 'book launch' mise-en-scene as well as functioned as an independent installation work, nodding to the mythological spire of miscommunication from which it borrows its title. The tower was shown in tandem with a poster of the author's image that had been reduced to a symbol, and propped up on a painting easel. In this way, Xu's simplified portrait, complete with his signature spectacles and long wavy hair, greeted every visitor to the show, as if he was behind the scenes getting prepared for a public reading and signing.

Another idea inspired by the consumer aspect of *From Point to Point*'s story was the pop-up store. In this day and age, a book in itself is not enough, the consumer wants merchandise as well. This "store" went through many configurations during the planning of the show. The end result not only presented a dramatic, interactive consumer experience, which proved to be quite popular and lucrative, but also an entire installation that was indeed the three-dimensional manifestation of the symbol for *store*. This *Book From the Ground Concept Store* carried something for everyone including shirts, newspapers, jewelry, chocolates, umbrellas, placemats, and other random household items.

Shown together with these lighthearted works that were created especially for the exhibition was more traditional print and drawing work, a site-specific animation film that mimicked tourist activity along Shanghai's Bund and was projected onto a wall that lies parallel to the actual view, and archival material. Previous renditions of the book were displayed in museum cases to illustrate the project's evolution from conception through birth. The earliest incarnations were essentially handmade catalogues of clippings from magazines, newspapers, and books. Later, this collection of icons slowly evolved into a disjointed narrative with rudimentary illustrations that were bound in covers; and eventually into the final published draft of *From Point to Point*, which still continues to be amended with each new printing. There is also a mock-up installation of Xu's studio, complete with computers, fax machines, furniture, and a ton of the artists' reference material — cell phone photos of signs in public spaces, books about symbols, hundreds of airport safety manuals, as well as montage 'artworks' — all displayed in a beautiful mess typical of any working art studio. Then there is the computer chat software that translates Chinese and English into an intermediate language of icons, which was invented in 2006 and has been updated many times since, plus the recent addition of a dictionary software program that allows users to translate and edit icon text.

Book From the Ground is a six-year old and still ongoing project. Some of the research material and works in progress have had previous exposure in "Piktogramme-die Einsamkeit der Zeichen/ Pictograms: The Loneliness of Signs", Kunstmuseum Stuttgart, Germany (2006); "Automatic Update", Museum of Modern Art, New York (2007), and "Xu Bing: From Book From the Sky to Book From the Ground", Eslite Gallery, Taipei (2012), which traced the evolution of the project since Xu Bing's early groundbreaking work *Book From the Sky*. In April 2012, Guangxi Normal University Publishing House published *From Point to Point* in mainland China. As I write this, the Hong Kong version of *From Point to Point* is being launched while another version is being published in France and documentary elements are being exhibited at Massachusetts Museum of Contemporary Art, USA and other venues throughout the world.

The following pages illustrate Xu Bing's first solo show in eight years in Shanghai held at Three on the Bund on the occasion of the mainland Chinese publication in the Spring of 2012. The exhibition — a literal extension of *From Point to Point* — celebrates and brings to life the milestone accomplishment of the book, and the result of Xu's intensive, long-term research. It also shows the artist's ingenuity in implementing this exuberant material. Furthermore, the exhibition attempts to manifest the phenomenon of modern hieroglyphics through easy-to-comprehend forms and illuminate the significance, scope, and potential that this language has in our world today.

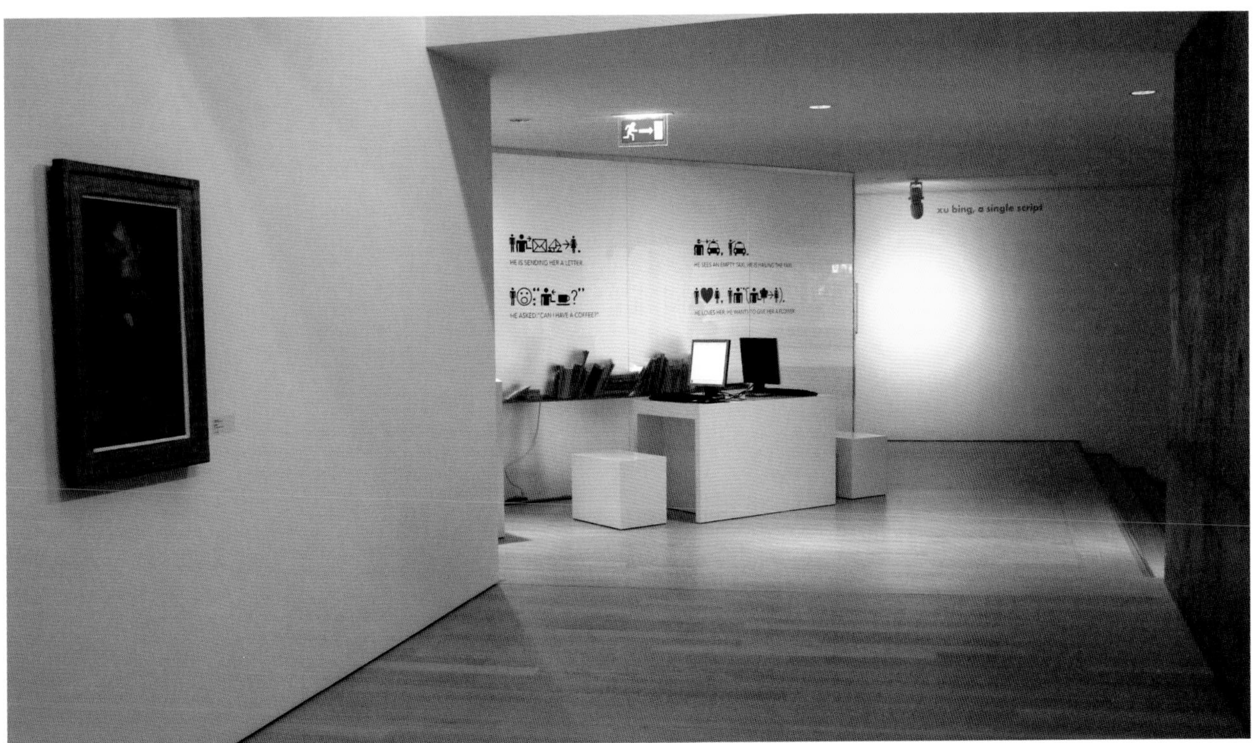

"Pictograms: The Loneliness of Signs",
Kunstmuseum Stuttgart.Germany, 2006.
Book From the Ground installation view.

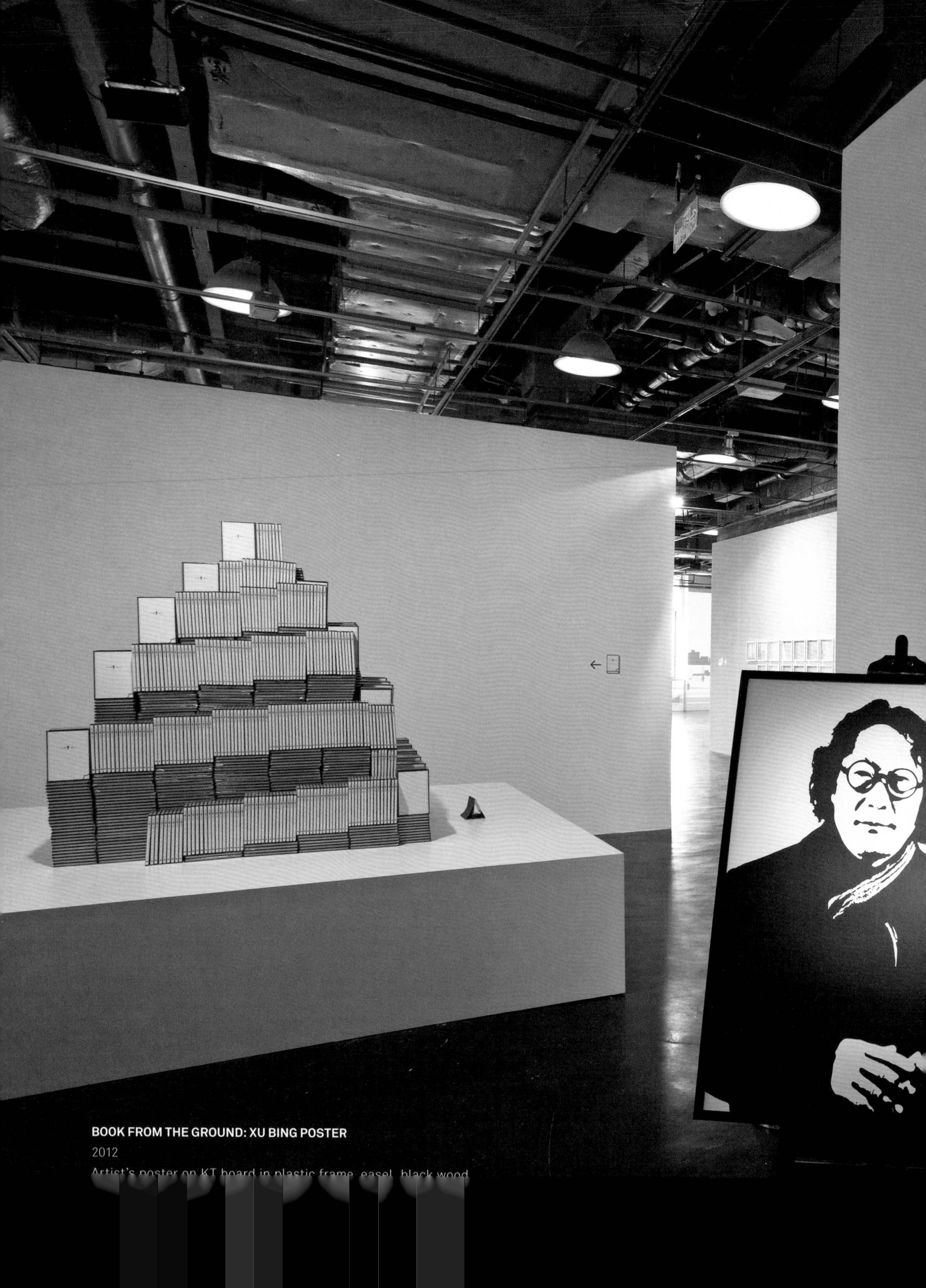

BOOK FROM THE GROUND: XU BING POSTER

2012

Artist's poster on KT board in plastic frame, easel, black wood

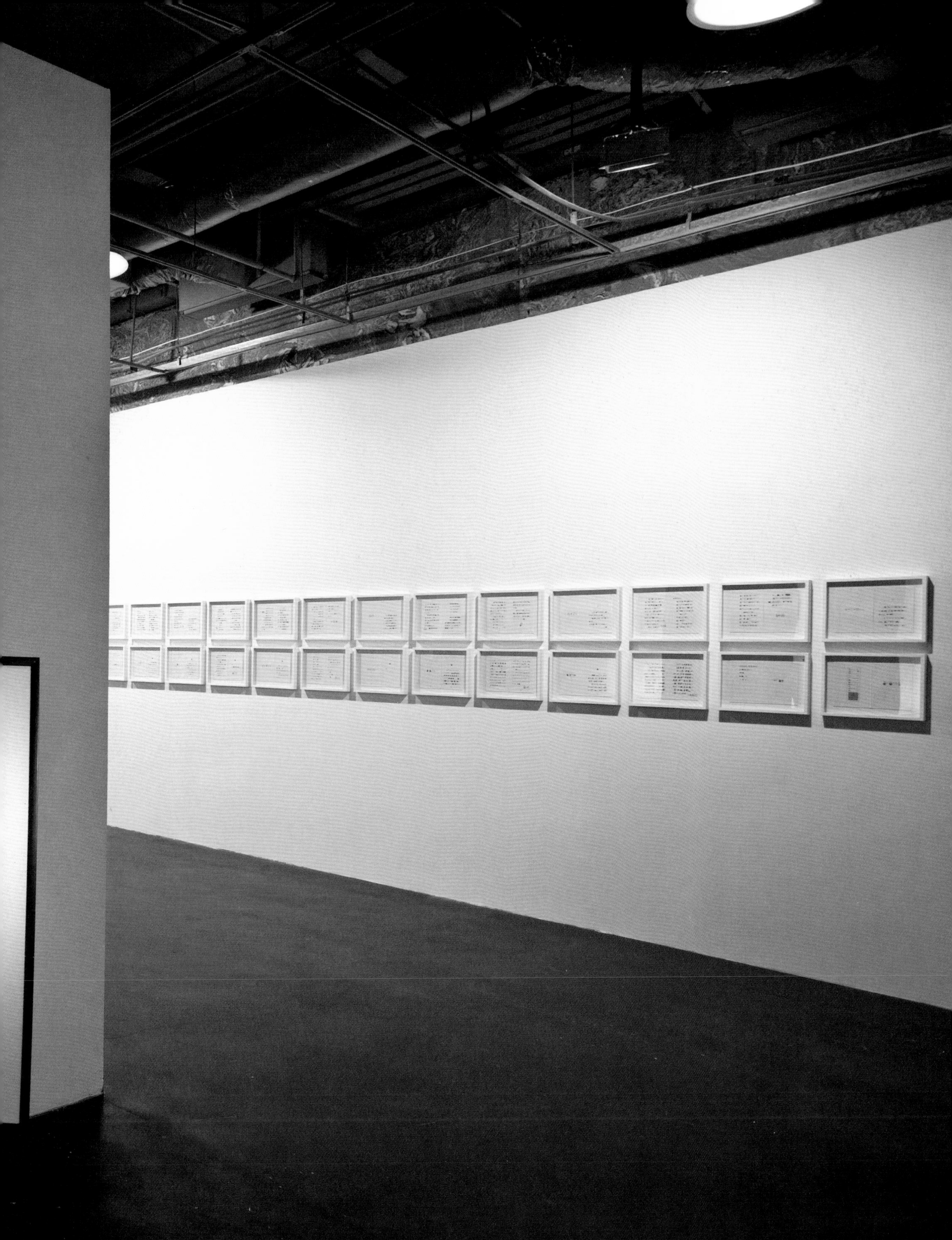

TOWER OF BABEL.

2012

books, paper, and wood

dimensions variable

2400 copies of *From Point to Point* are stacked together to form a *Tower of Babel* at the entrance to the exhibition hall. With a direct reference to the Bible tale of the same name, Xu Bing illustrates the root of human miscommunication and the innate human desire to remedy it.

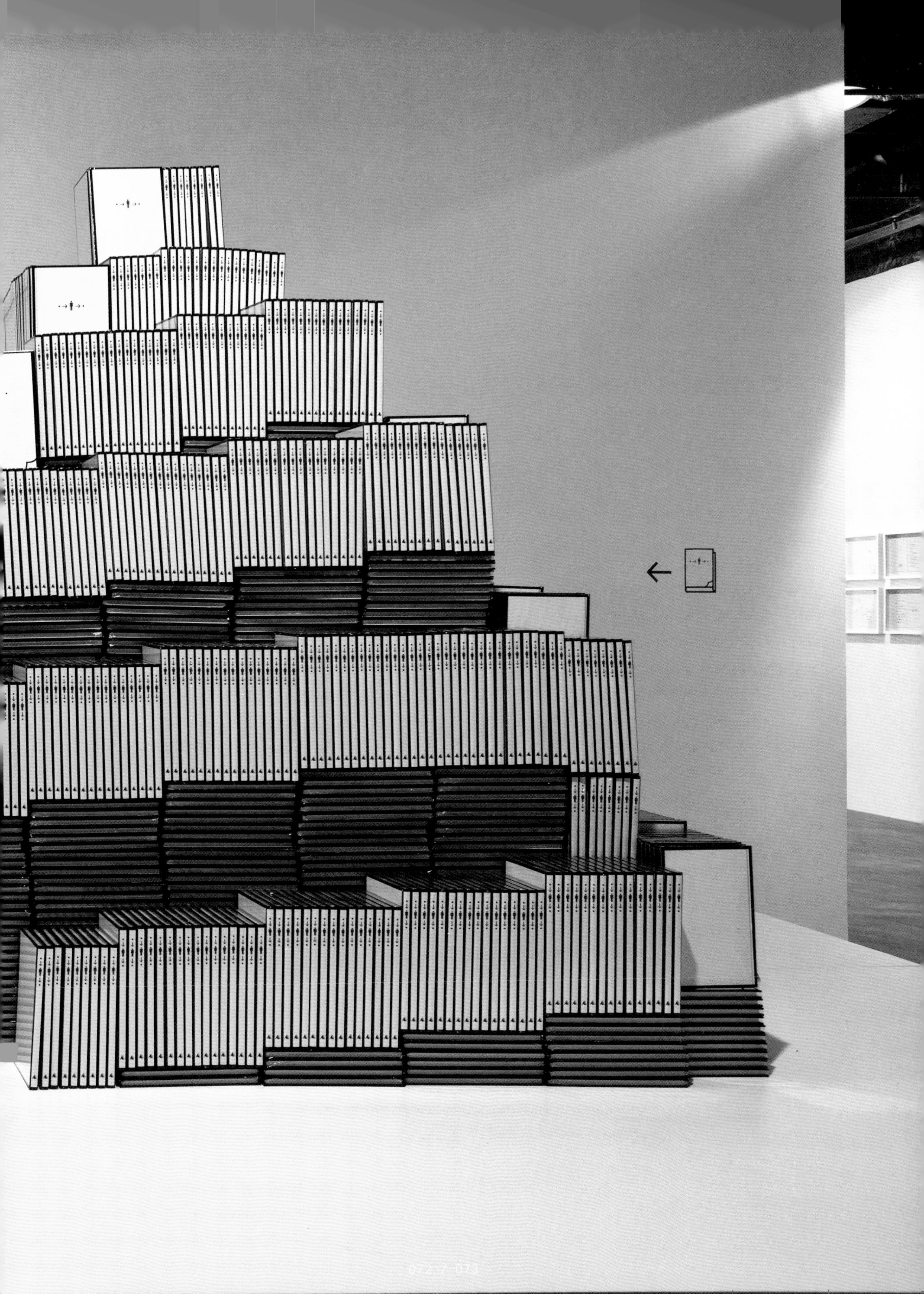

FROM POINT TO POINT, MAINLAND CHINA EDITION

2012

permanent marker on 60 double page spreads of mainland Chinese edition of *From Point to Point*

148 x 440mm, 63 pieces

Sixty page spreads from *From Point to Point* are framed and installed in two long rows. On each spread a singular icon has been hand drawn by Xu Bing with a colored marker. These hand-drawn icons in sequence form their own story over the existing narrative of the book.

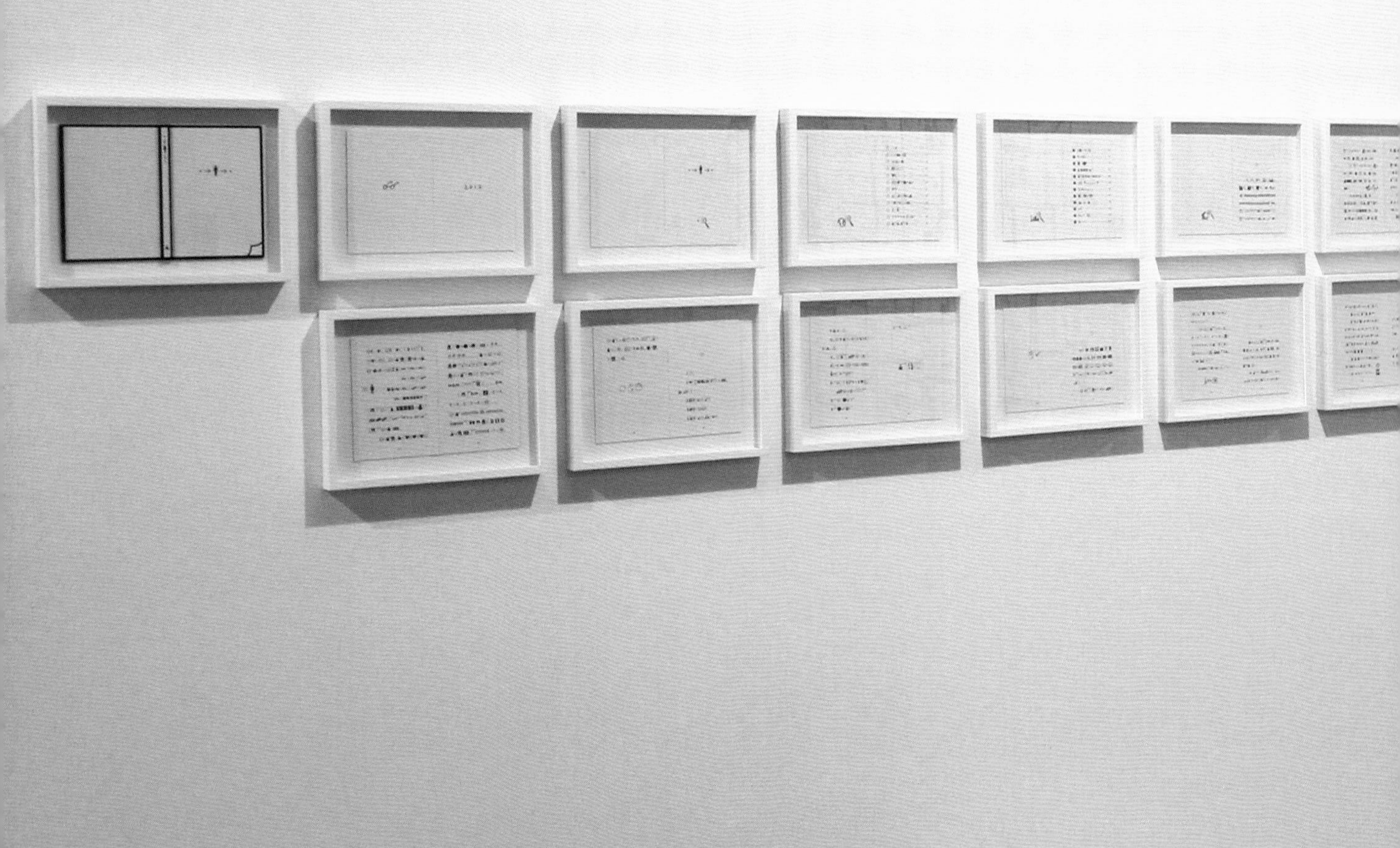

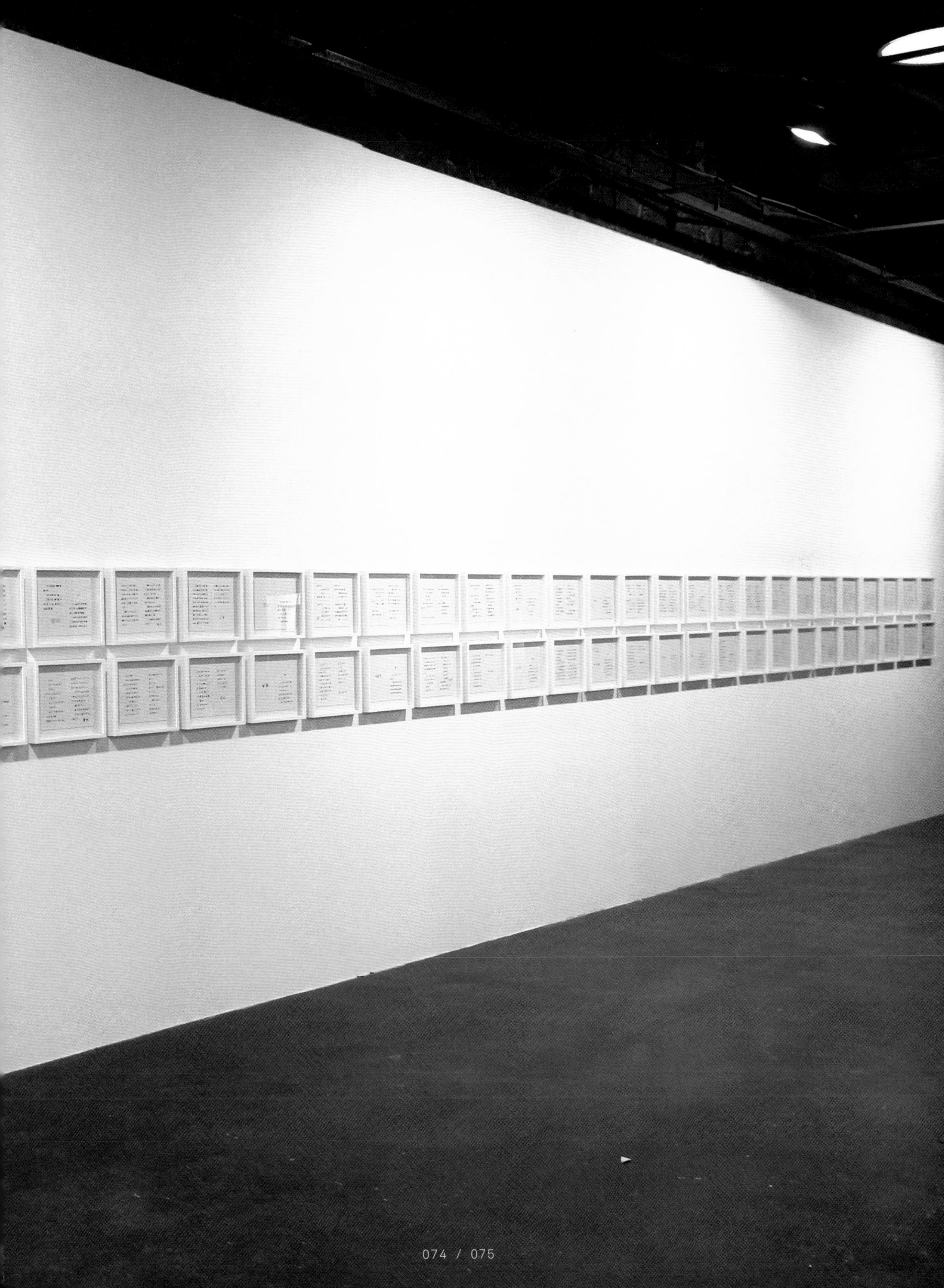

4

5

= $$$ ...... ✗

= $$$ ...... ✗

= $$$$...... ✗

= $$ ...... ✓,

44

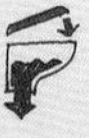

45

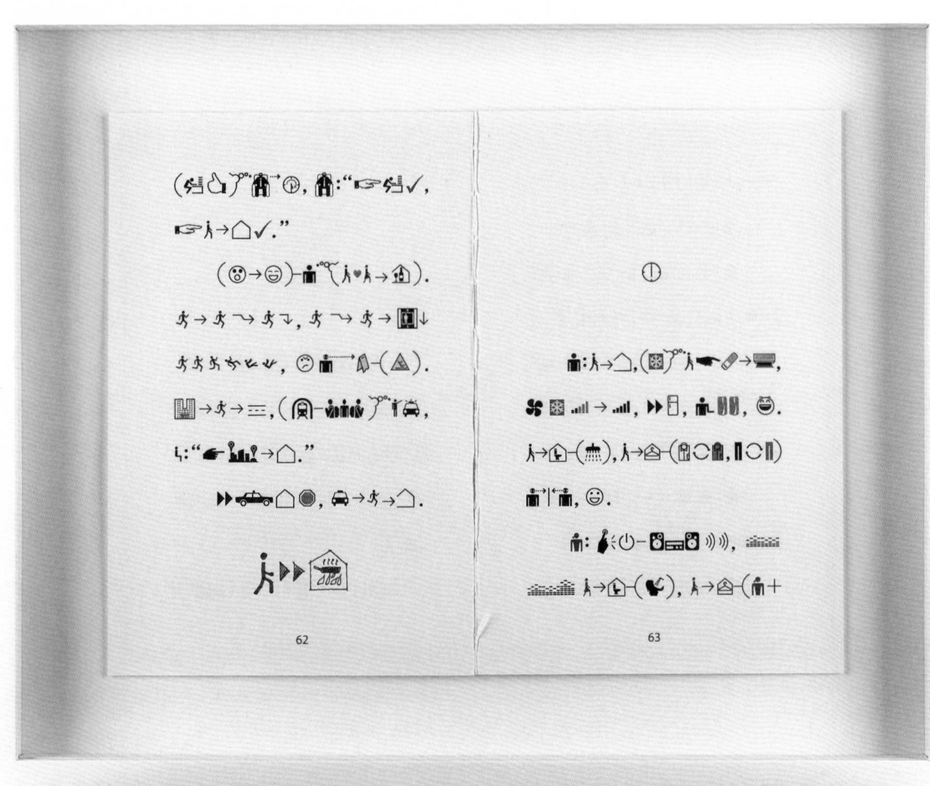

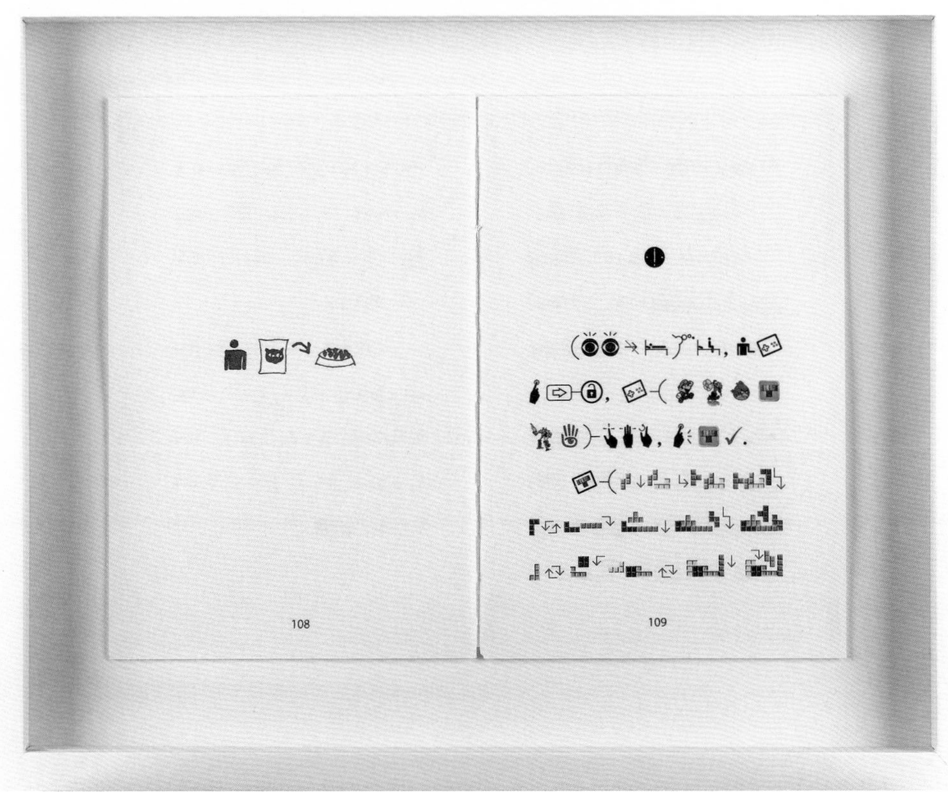

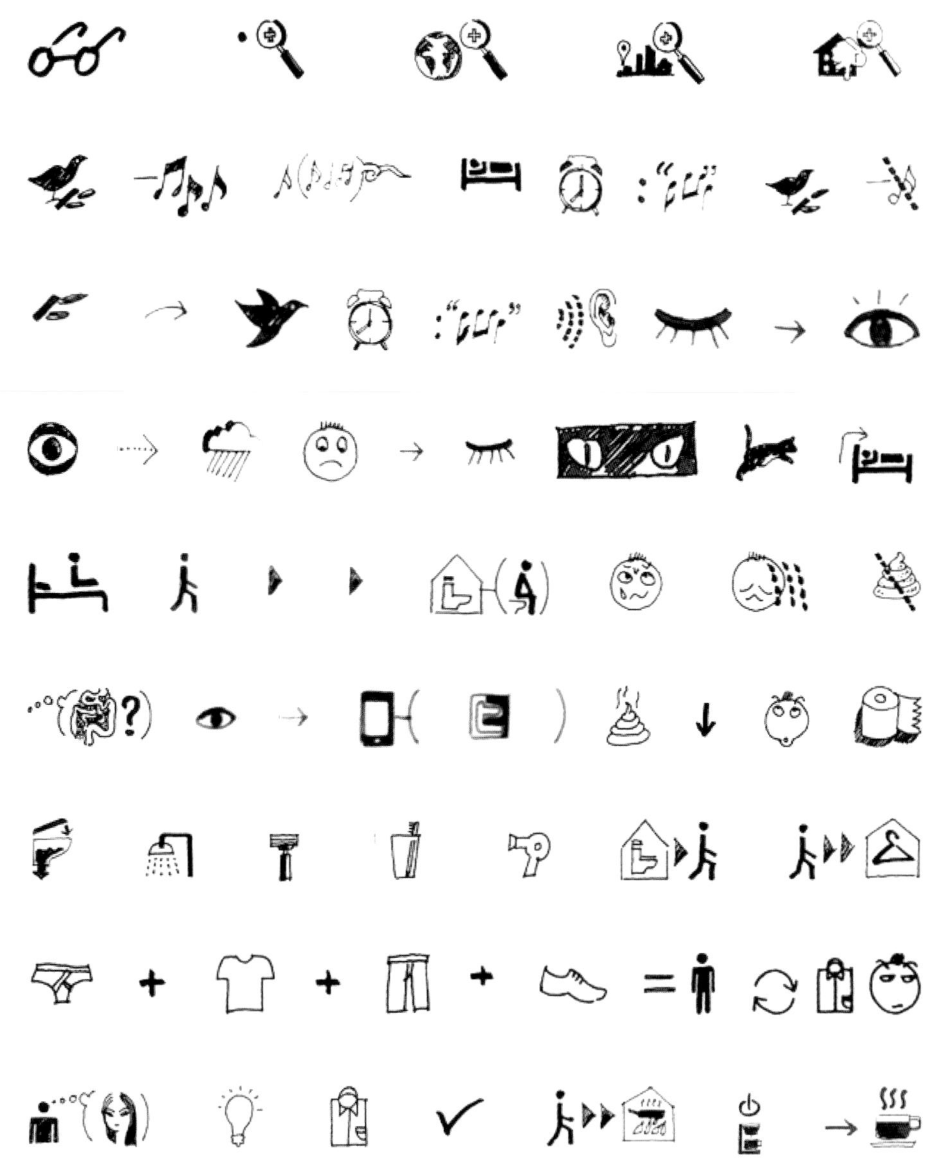

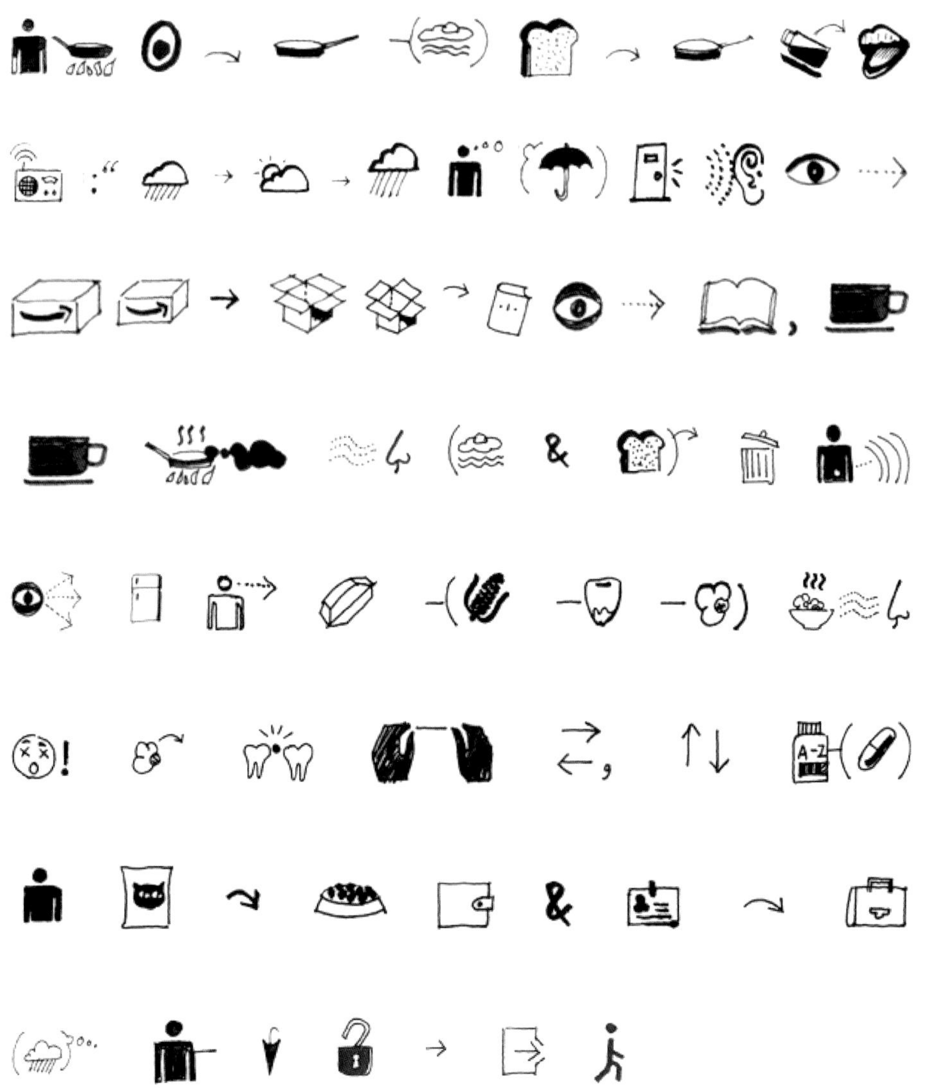
A-Z

BOOK FROM THE GROUND: *FROM POINT TO POINT* PAST VERSIONS

2003–2012
binders, books, mixed media
dimensions variable

Book From the Ground started in 2006. Presented in a museum case are seven volumes lined up from left to right to represent the significant evolutionary steps of this project. The first books are simple binders filled with logos and symbols that were clipped out of magazines and newspapers then catalogued together as reference material. Later books depict the initial development of Mr. Black's narrative in a large dark binding full of notations and corrections. Last we see the first published version (Taiwan, 2011) also with pencil marked emendations, and, finally, the present mainland China version of *From Point to Point*.

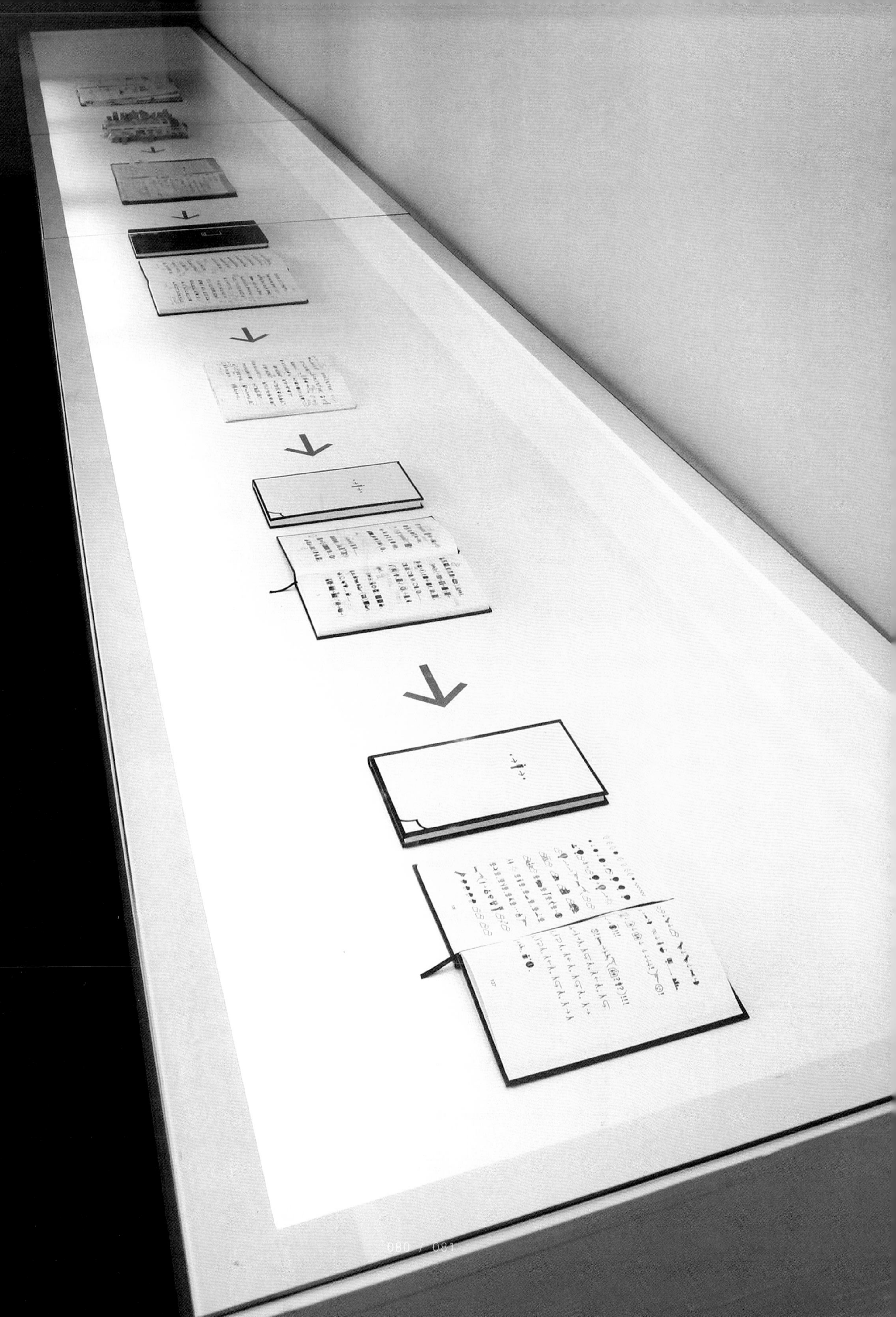

动词

对话, 对讲 (DELL广告)

talking, chatting, conversation

reading, reading newspaper

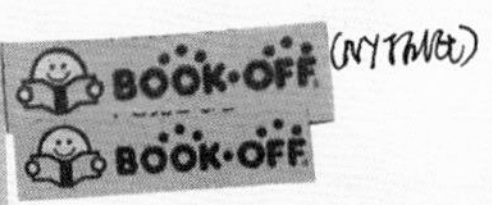

(NYT广告)

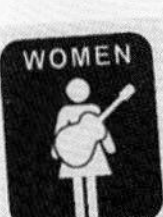

弹奏

sky magazine

play music

sky magazine

shipping, moving, moving fragile items

walking upstairs

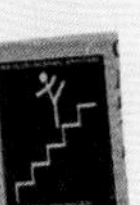

hear, listen, ear (delta)

cut here, perforate, remove

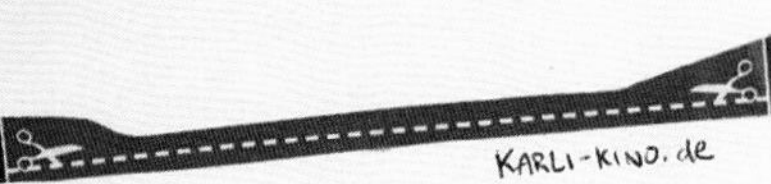

KARLI-KINO.de

take elevator, ascend/descend

KARLI-KINO.DE

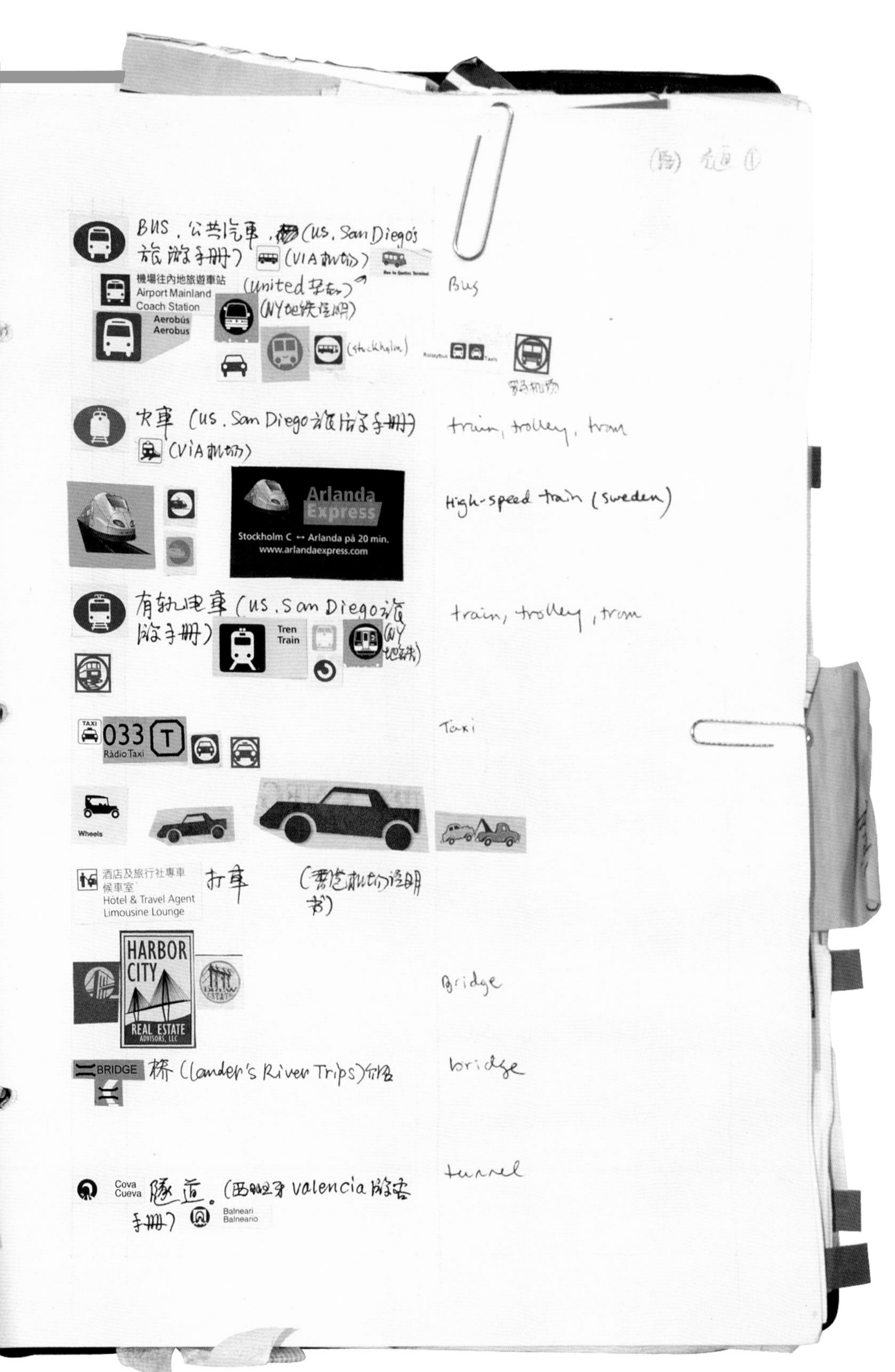

機場往內地旅遊車站
Airport Mainland
Coach Station
Aerobús
Aerobus
Bus
Arlanda
Express
Stockholm C ↔ Arlanda på 20 min.
www.arlandaexpress.com
High-speed train (sweden)
train, trolley, tram
Tren
Train
TAXI
033
Ràdio Taxi
Taxi
Wheels
酒店及旅行社專車
候車室
Hotel & Travel Agent
Limousine Lounge
HARBOR
CITY
REAL ESTATE
ADVISORS, LLC
Bridge
BRIDGE
bridge
Cova
Cueva
Balneari
Balneario
tunnel

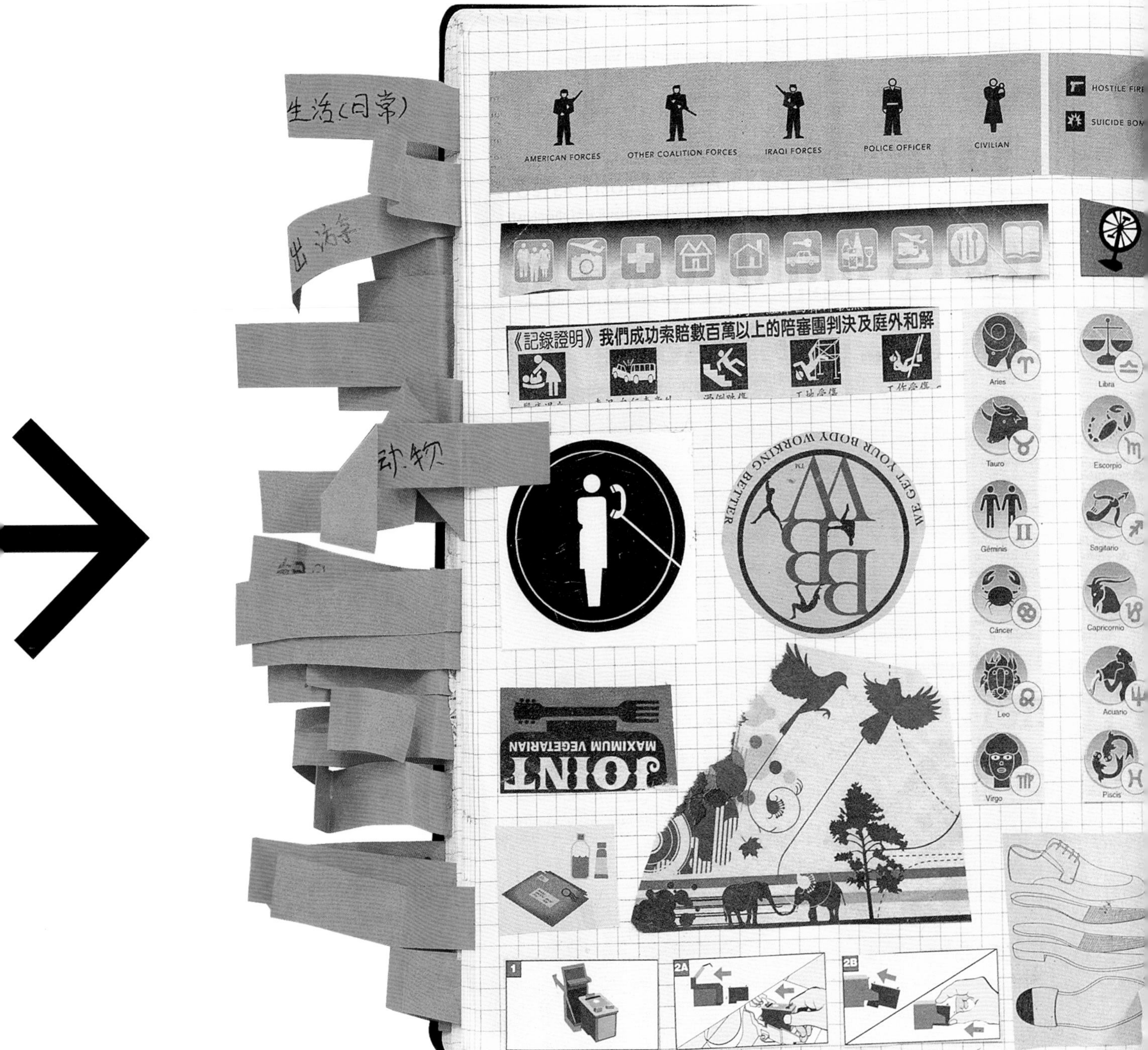

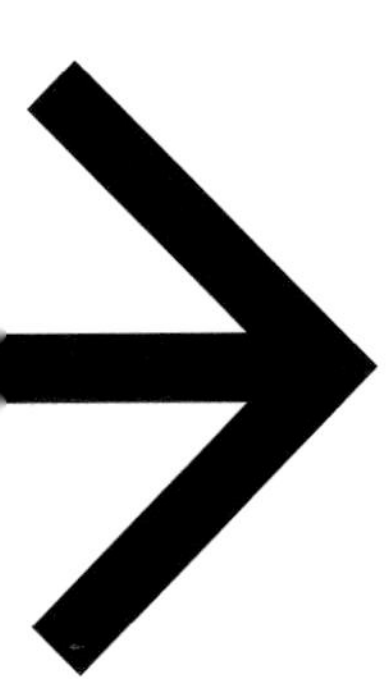

生活(日常)
动物
AMERICAN FORCES
OTHER COALITION FORCES
IRAQI FORCES
POLICE OFFICER
CIVILIAN
《記錄證明》我們成功索賠數百萬以上的陪審團判決及庭外和解
WE GET YOUR BODY WORKING BETTER
JOINT
MAXIMUM VEGETARIAN
Aries
Tauro
Géminis
Cáncer
Leo
Virgo
Libra
Escorpio
Sagitario
Capricornio
Acuario
Piscis
1
2A
2B

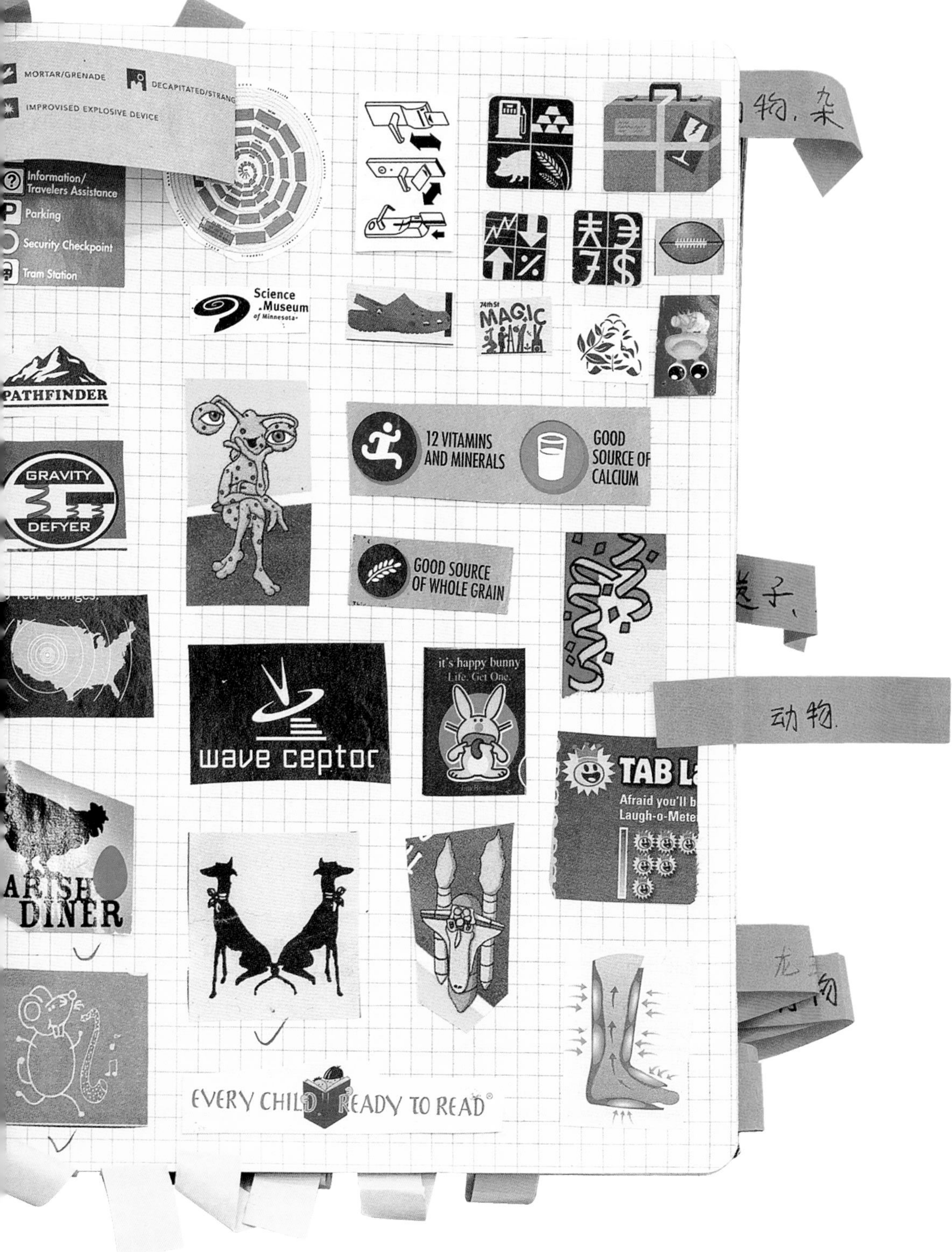
MORTAR/GRENADE
IMPROVISED EXPLOSIVE DEVICE
Information/
Travelers Assistance
Parking
Security Checkpoint
Tram Station
Science Museum of Minnesota
PATHFINDER
MAGIC
GRAVITY
DEFYER
12 VITAMINS AND MINERALS
GOOD SOURCE OF CALCIUM
GOOD SOURCE OF WHOLE GRAIN
wave ceptor
it's happy bunny
Life. Get One.
DINER
EVERY CHILD READY TO READ
物, 杂
动物.

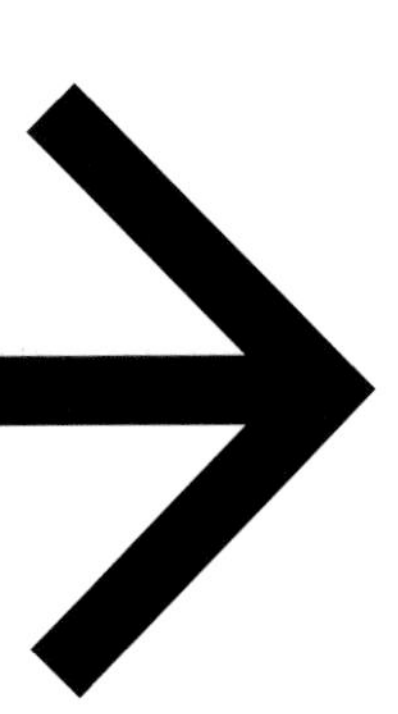

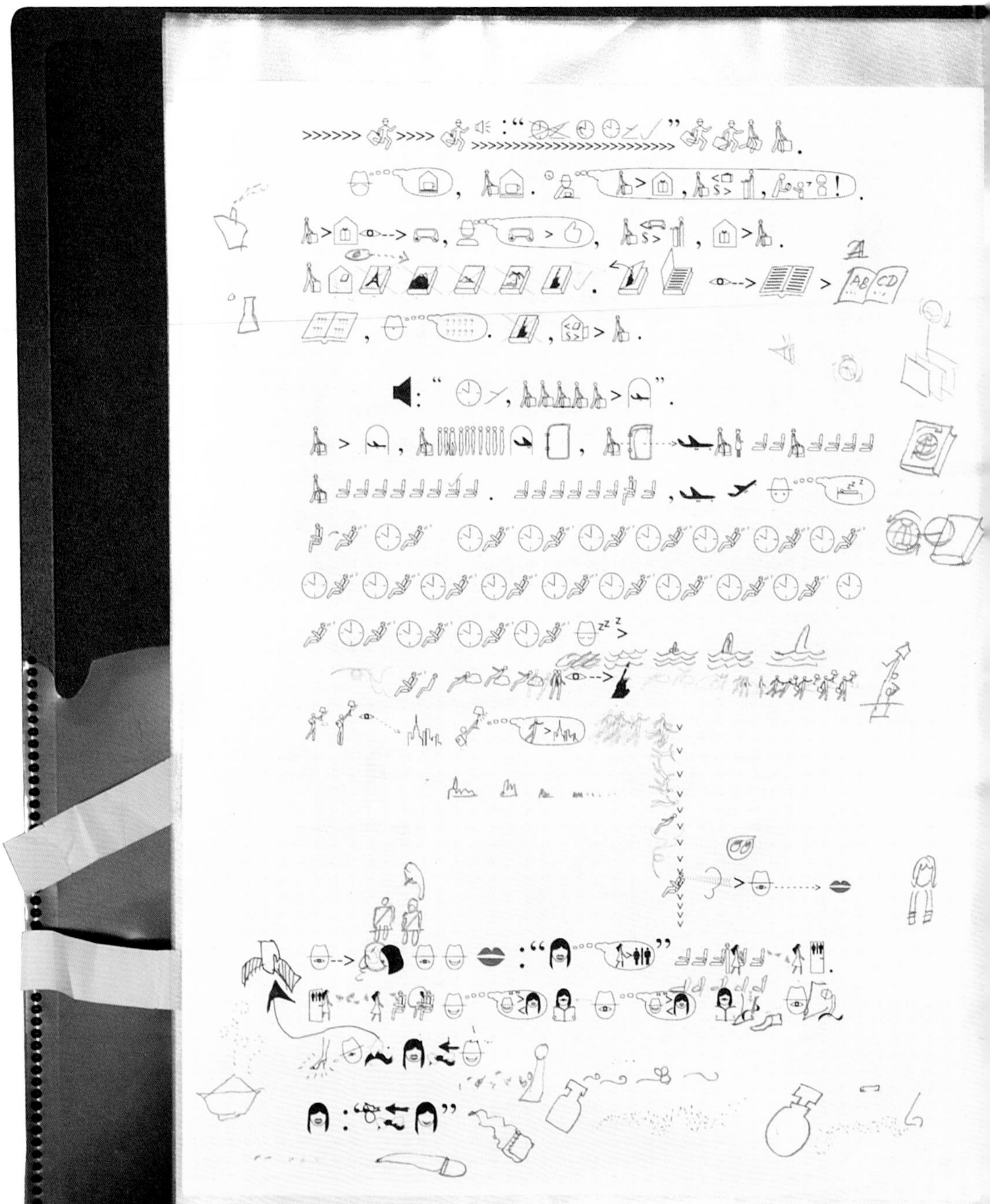

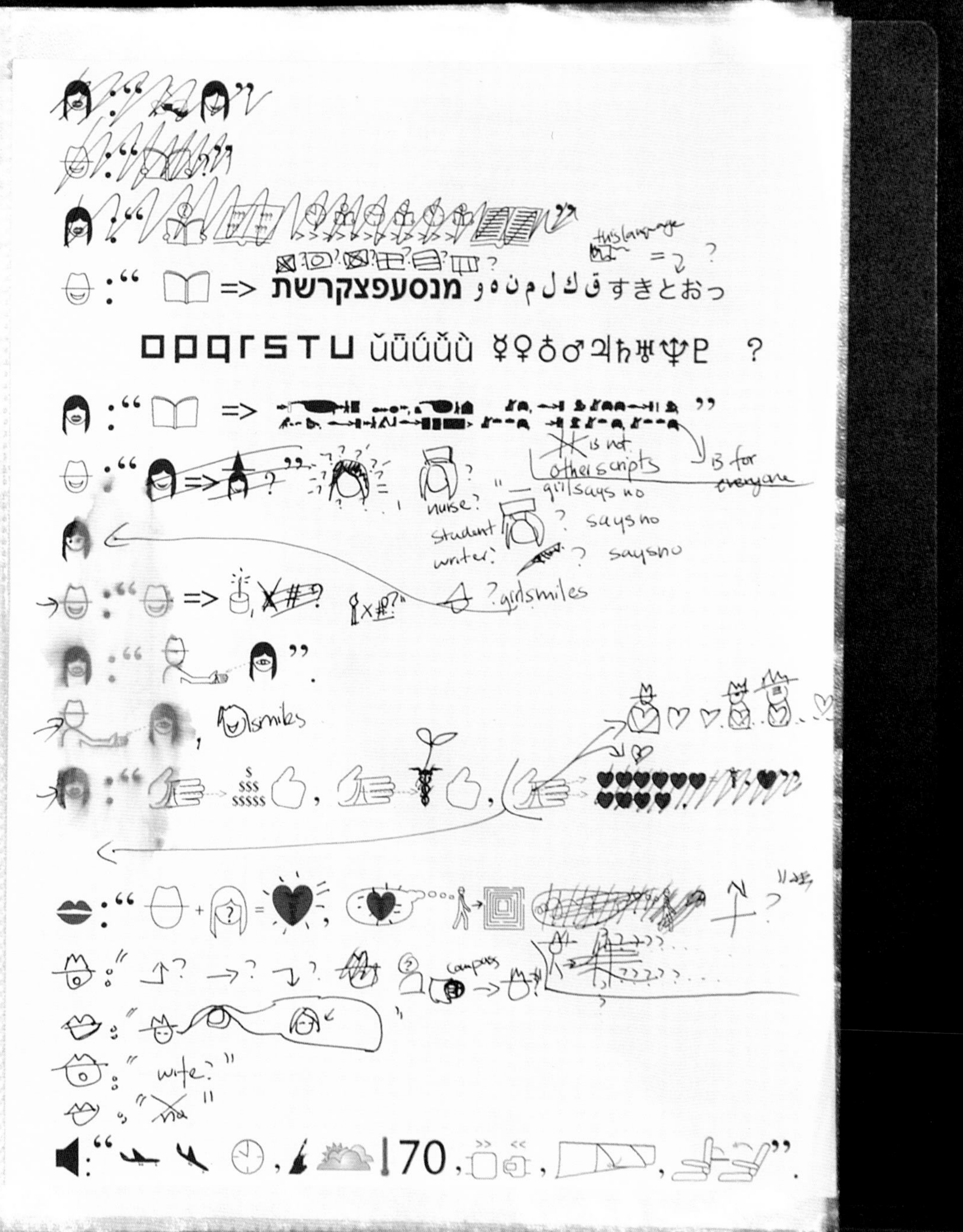

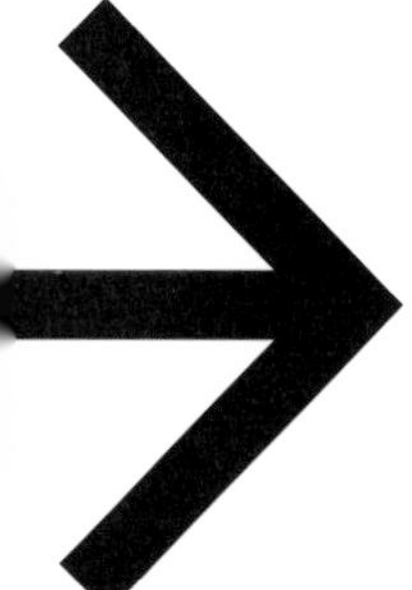

6

7

给电话

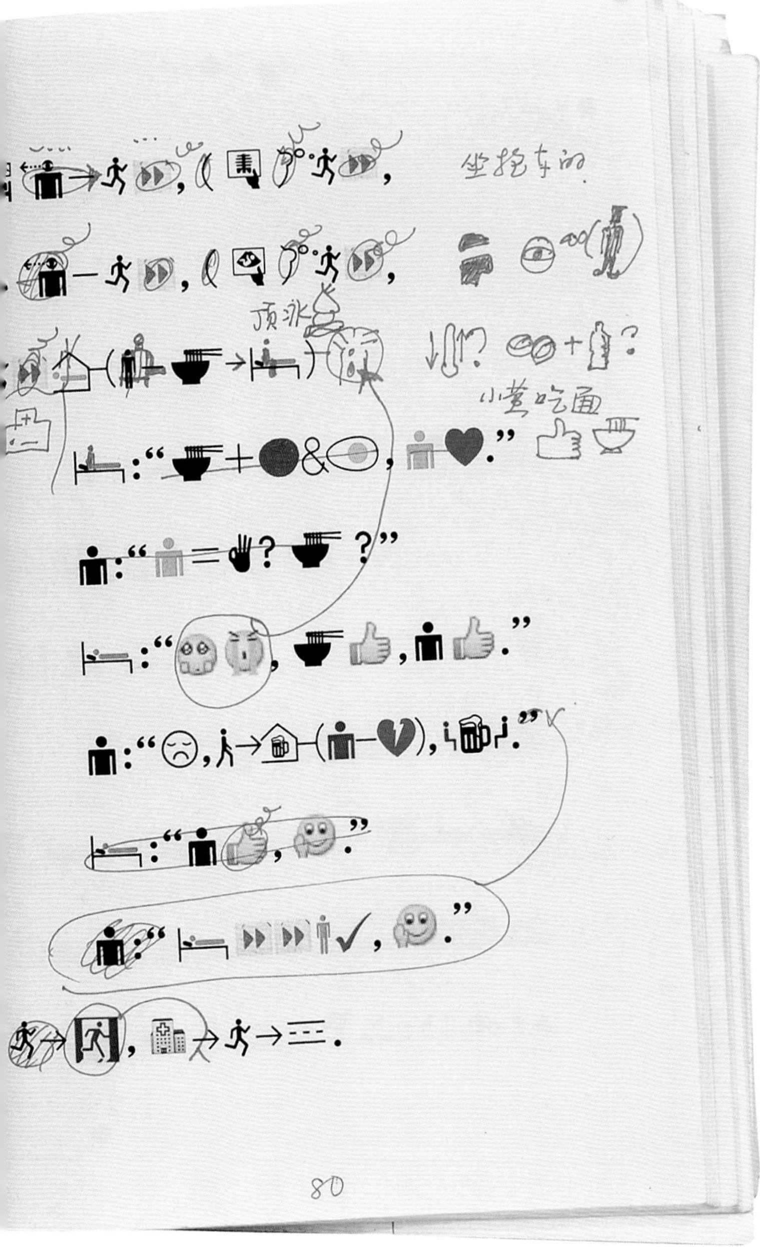

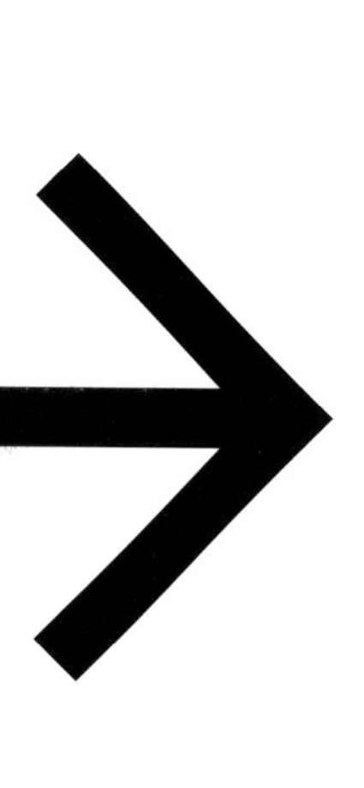

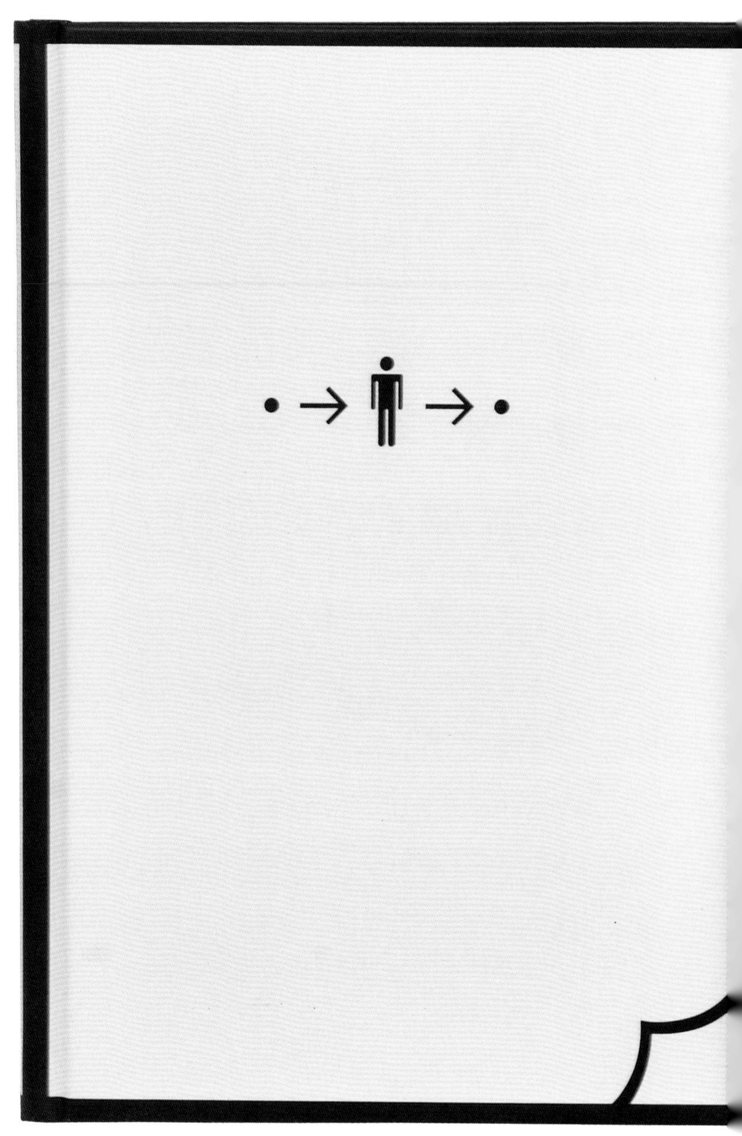

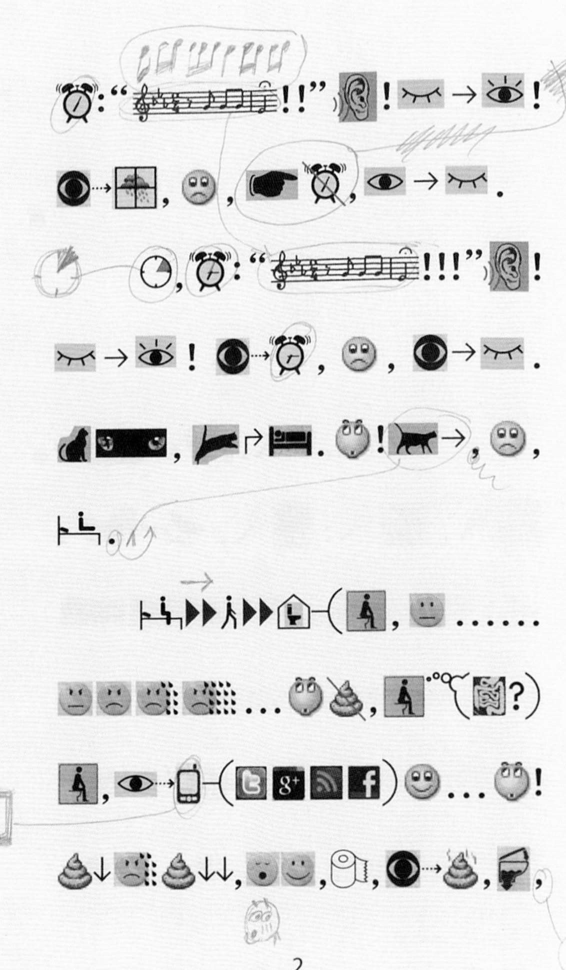

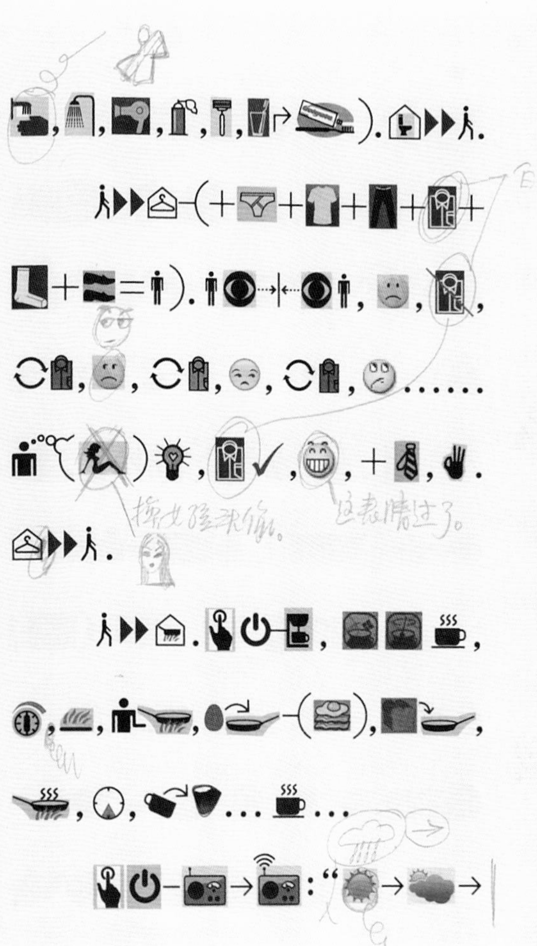

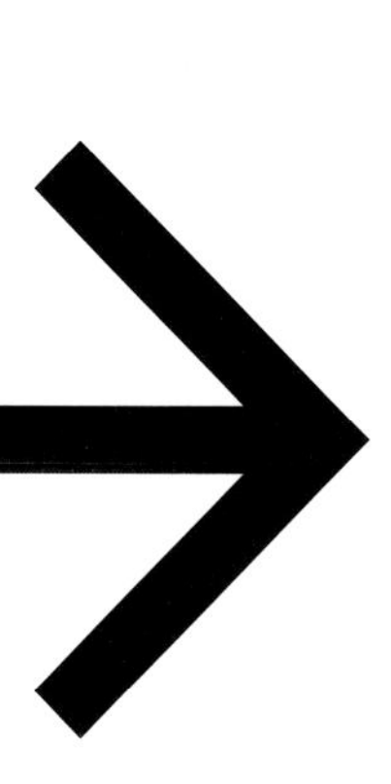

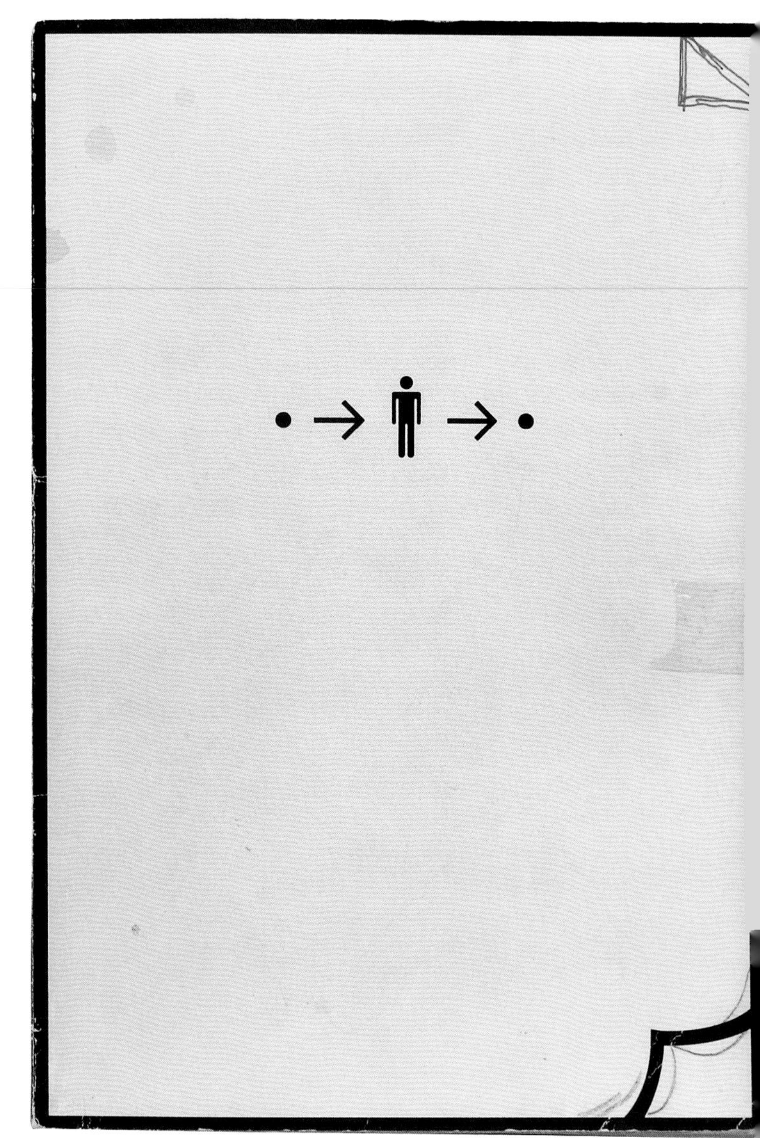

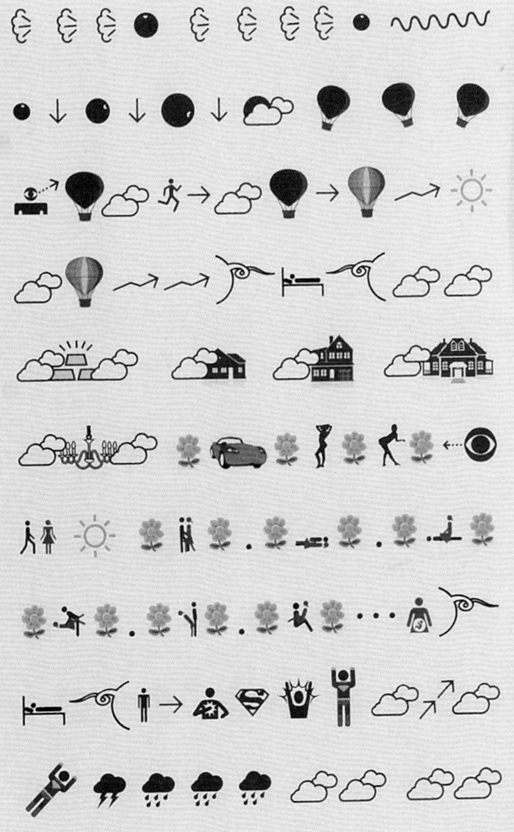

BOOK FROM THE GROUND: CAR CRASH COLLAGE

2006

paper collage on graph paper

280 x 840mm

Car Crash Collage is the first handmade collage that Xu Bing completed entirely with found icons and signs. It depicts the process of a man getting up in the morning and racing to catch a plane. In the middle of his escapade, and the picture's composition, there appears to be a car crash or traffic jam. Xu Bing made this piece in 2006 after collecting and researching the world of symbols around him. The experience he gained through this work helped Xu to further develop the much more complicated narrative found in *From Point to Point*.

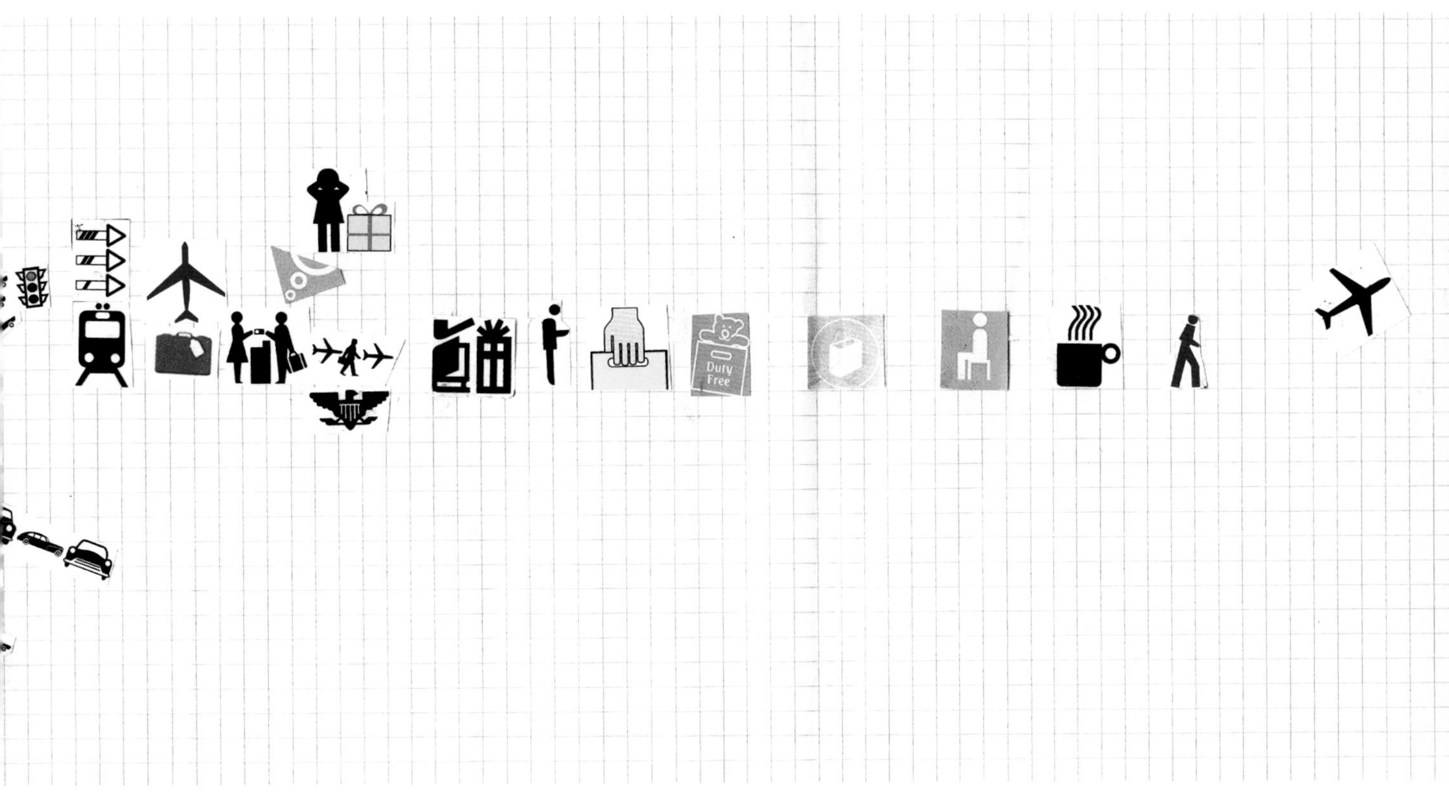
Duty
Free

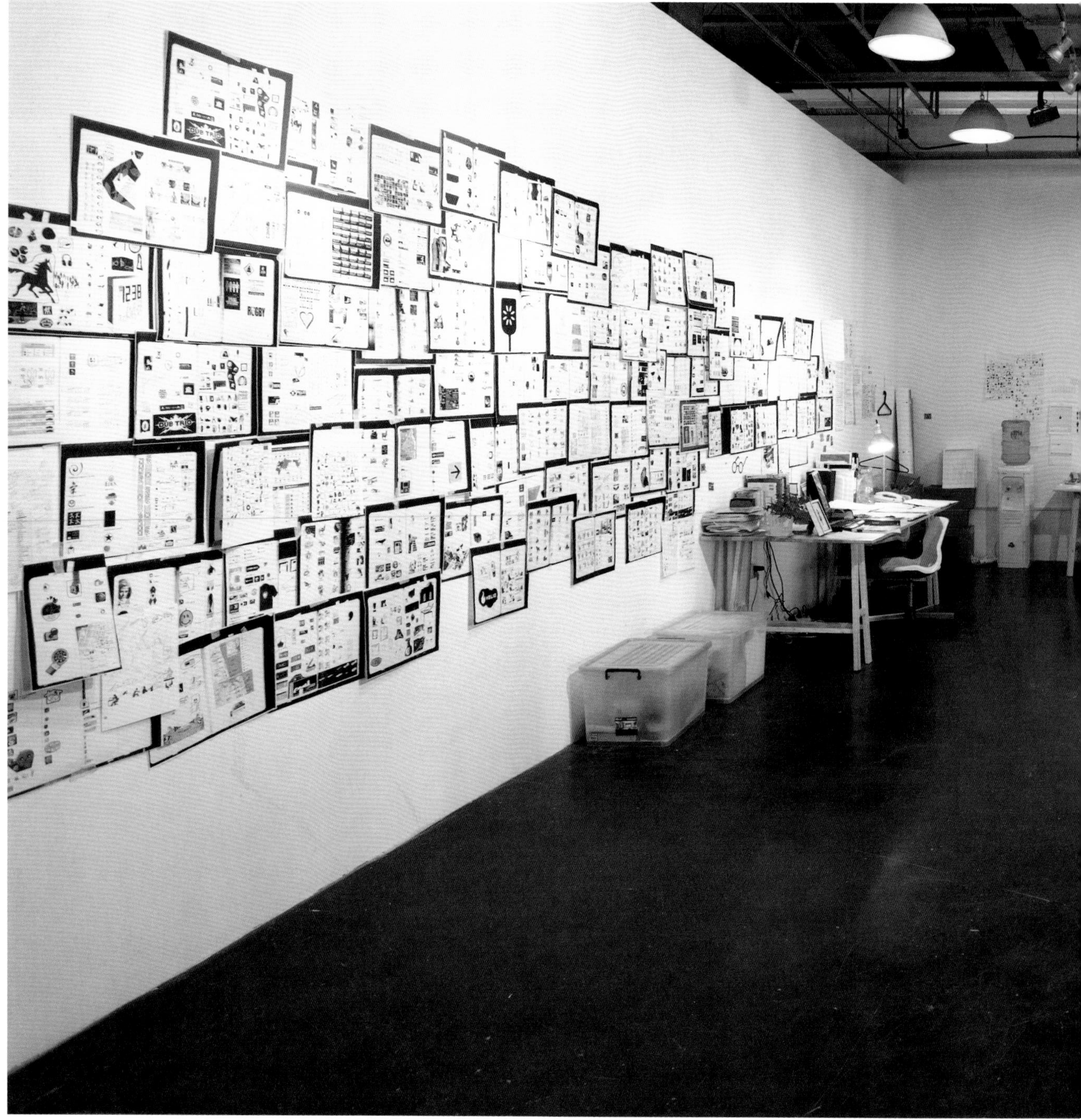

BOOK FROM THE GROUND, SHANGHAI STUDIO

2003–2012

office furniture, original design drafts, computer with *Book From the Ground* icon editing software, notes, photographs, reference books, airport safety manuals, Xeroxes of notebooks, photos, digital material, collage, computers, water dispenser,etc.

dimensions variable

Xu Bing's original studio was re-created in the space of the exhibition to show the intensity and breadth of the artist's research and work. We see original reference materials, notebooks, drawings and snapshots, as well as pilot versions for products that will later fill his "concept store". Here the real, messy, atmosphere of an artist-at-work becomes an interactive space for the audience. However, unlike many artists' studios that are often filled with paints and canvases, this studio looks more like a modern day dot-com start up's office.

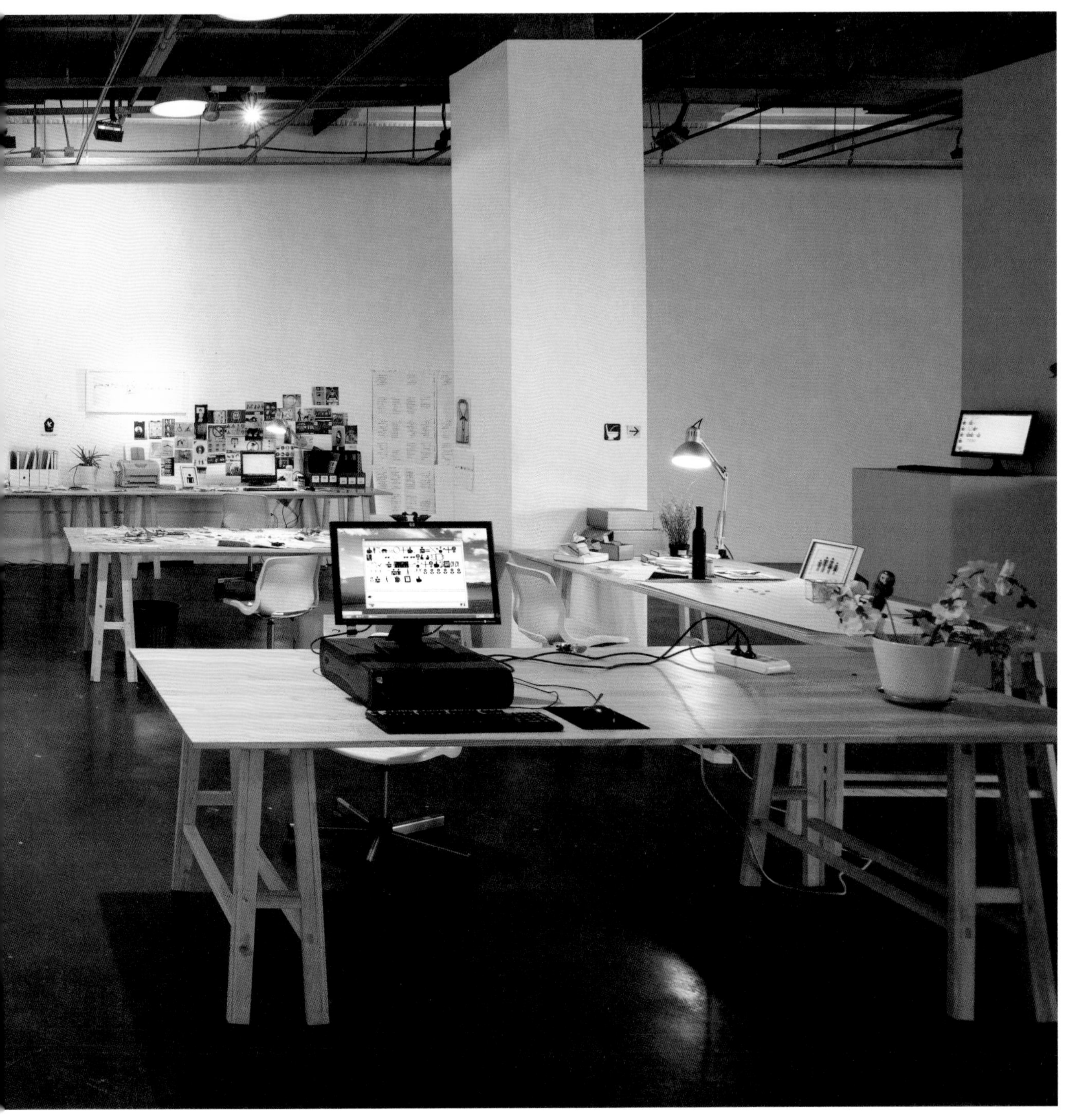

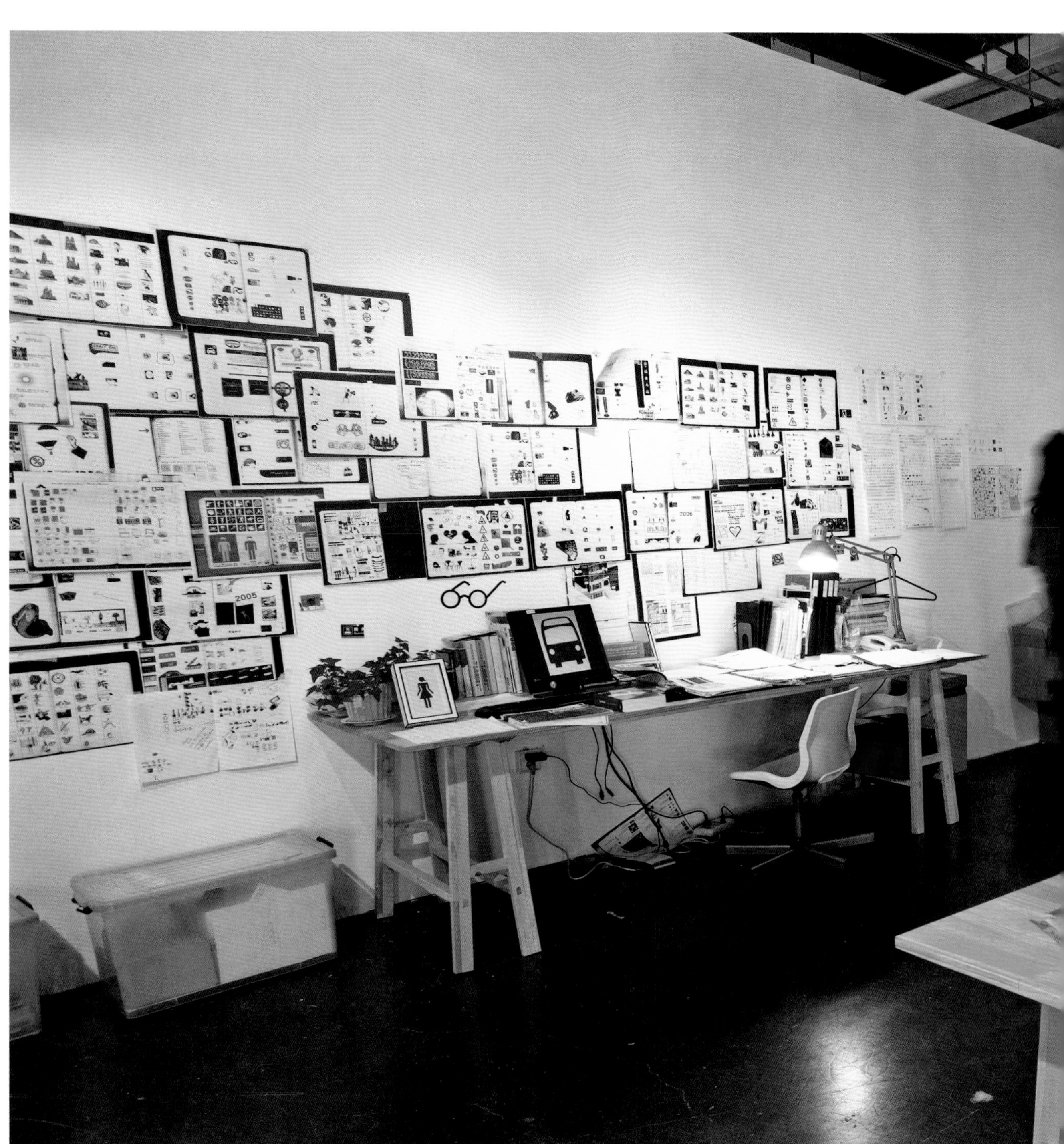
2005
2006

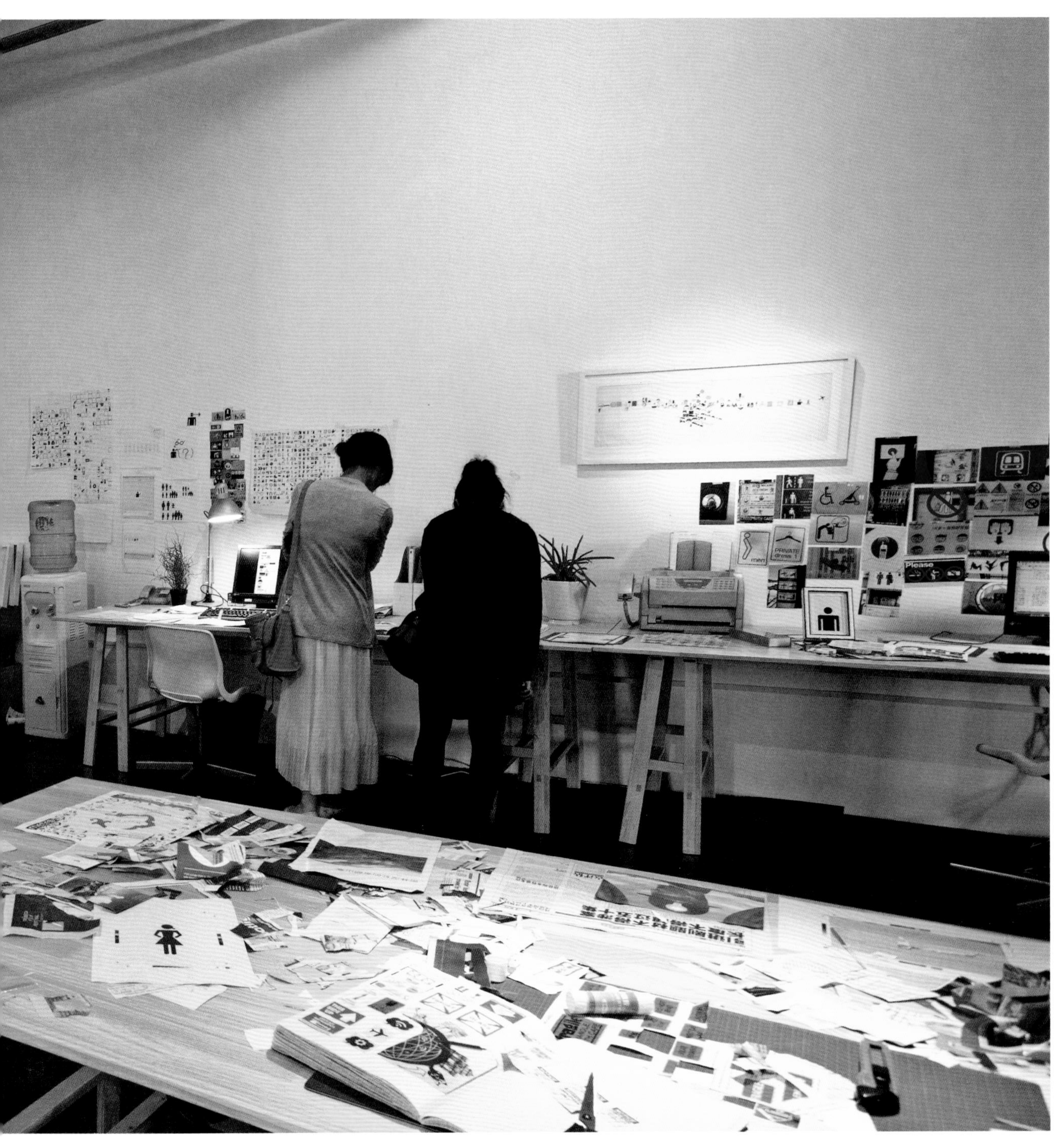

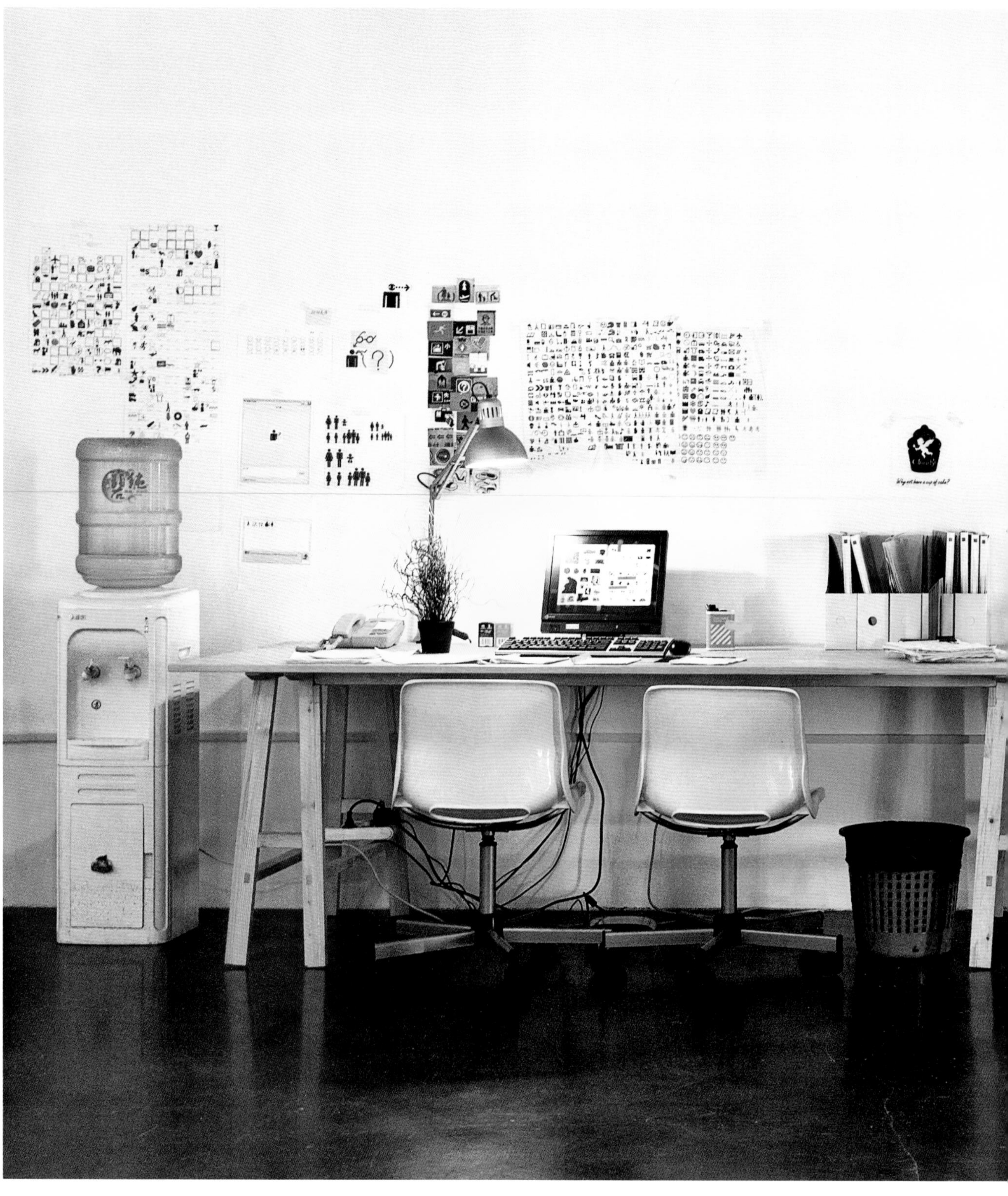

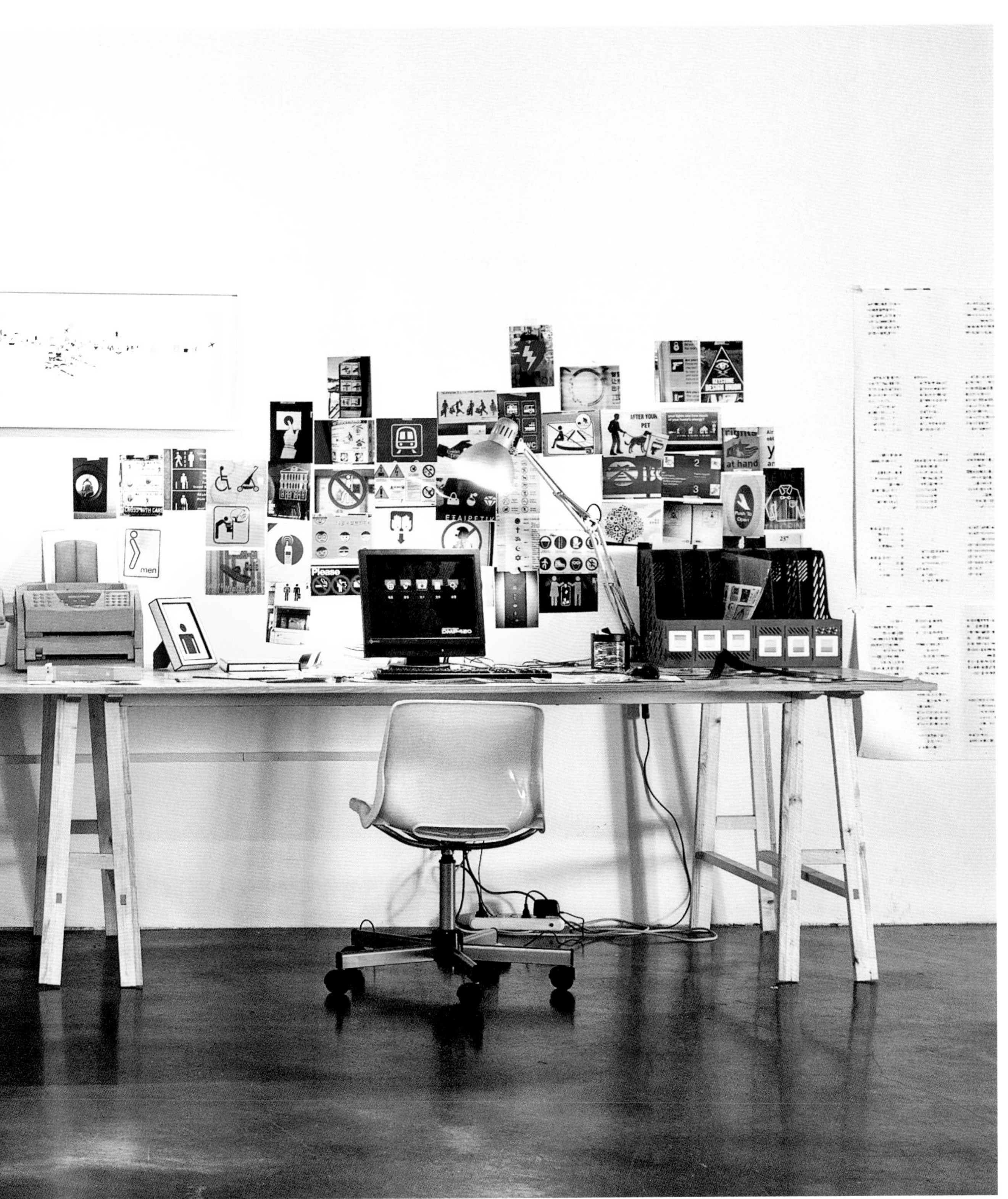

men
Please
AFTER YOUR PET
at hand

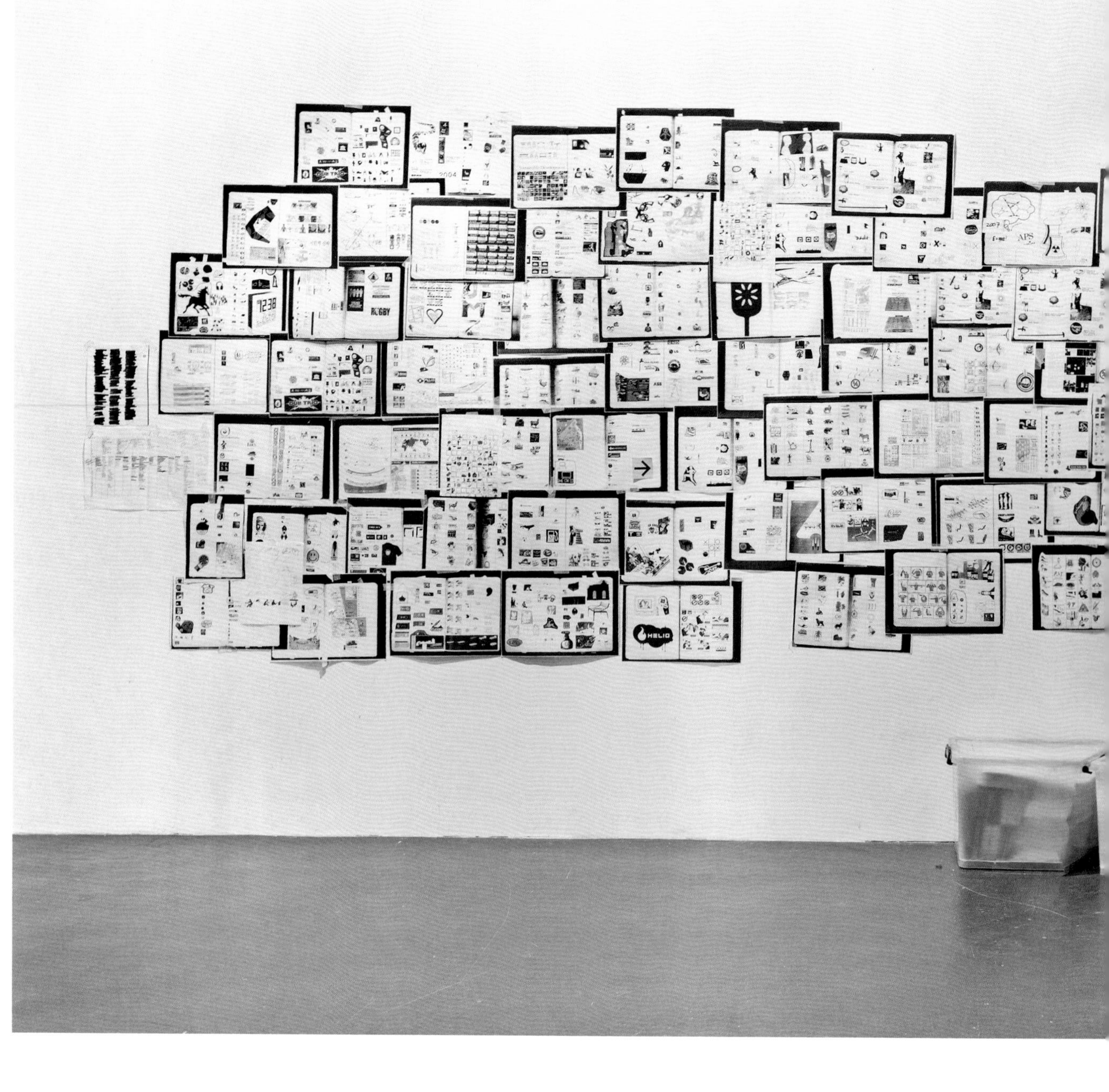

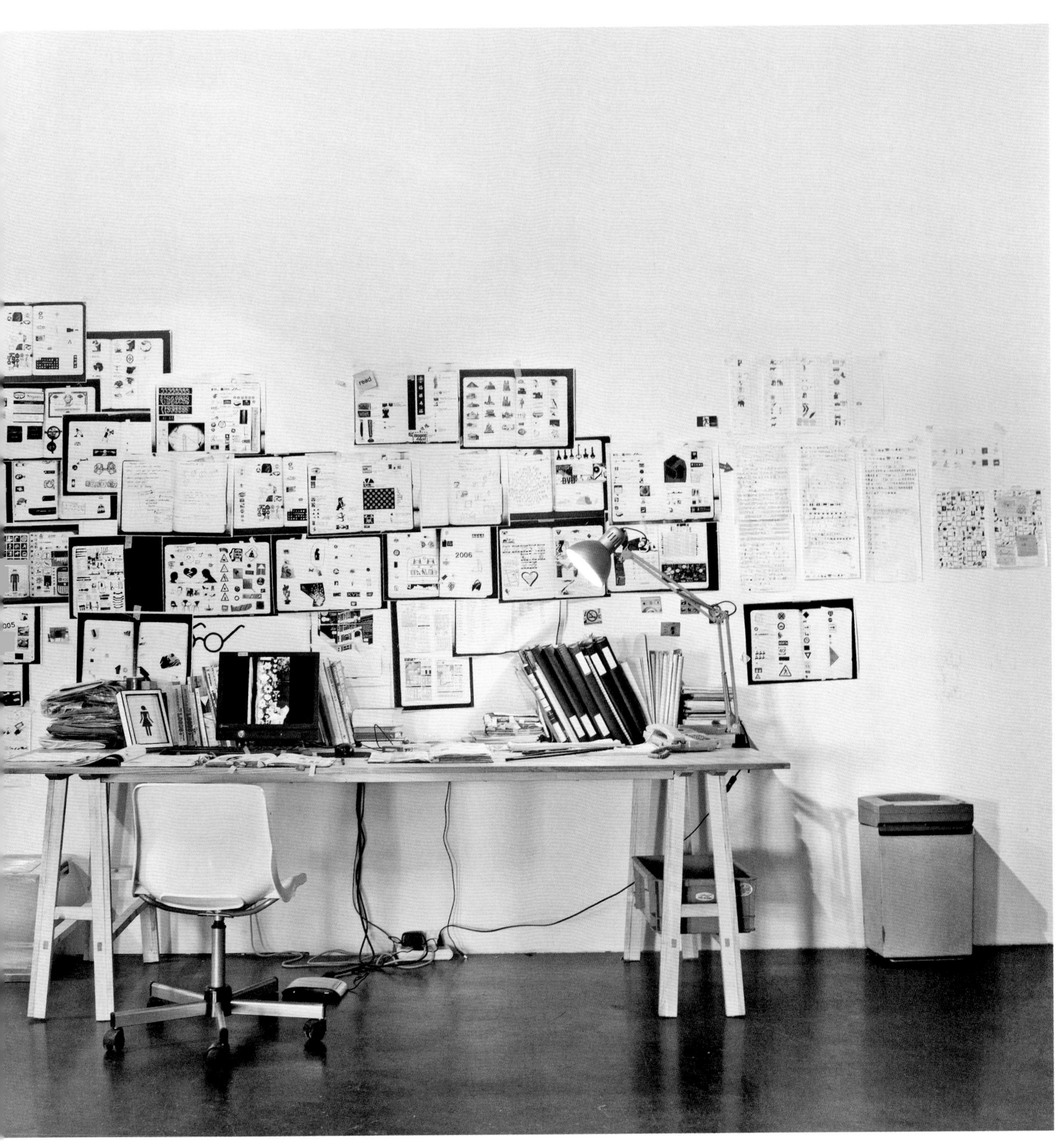
read
2006
DVD

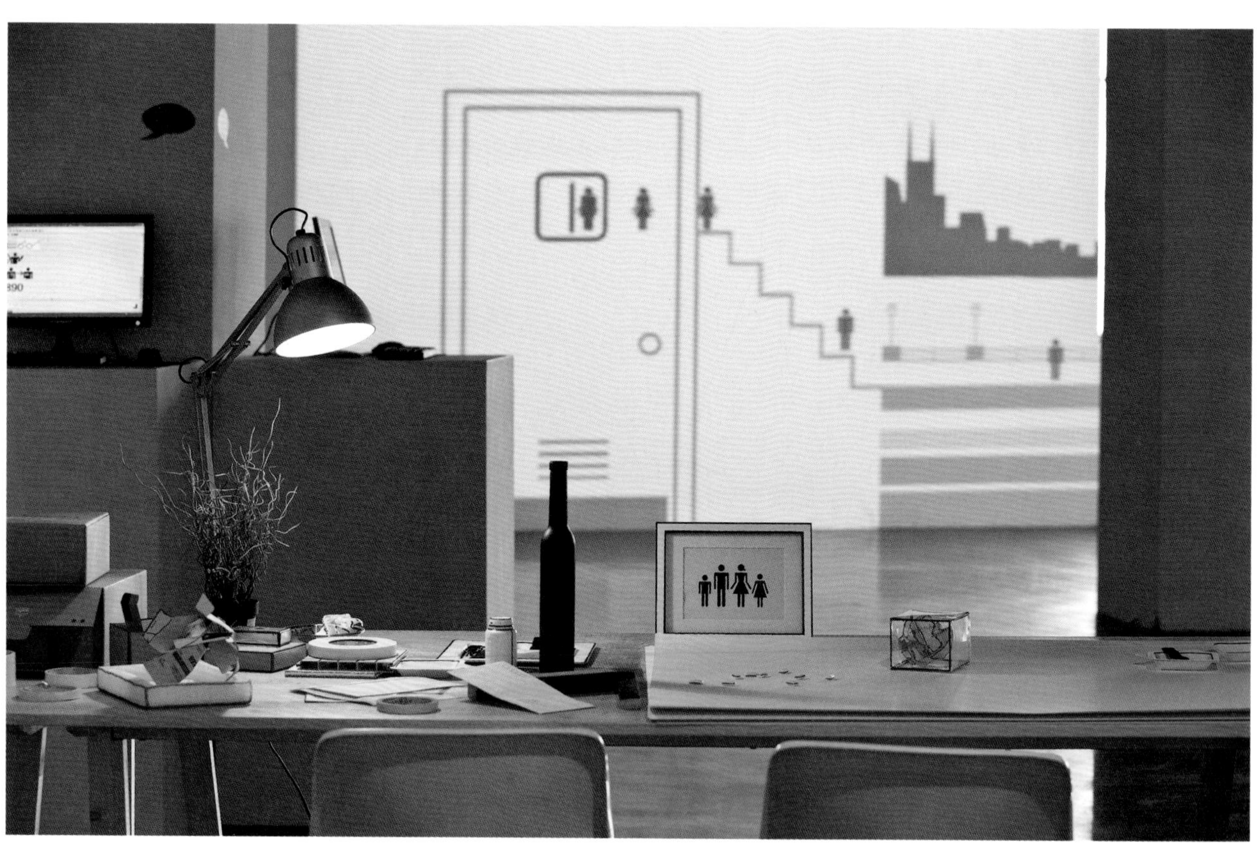

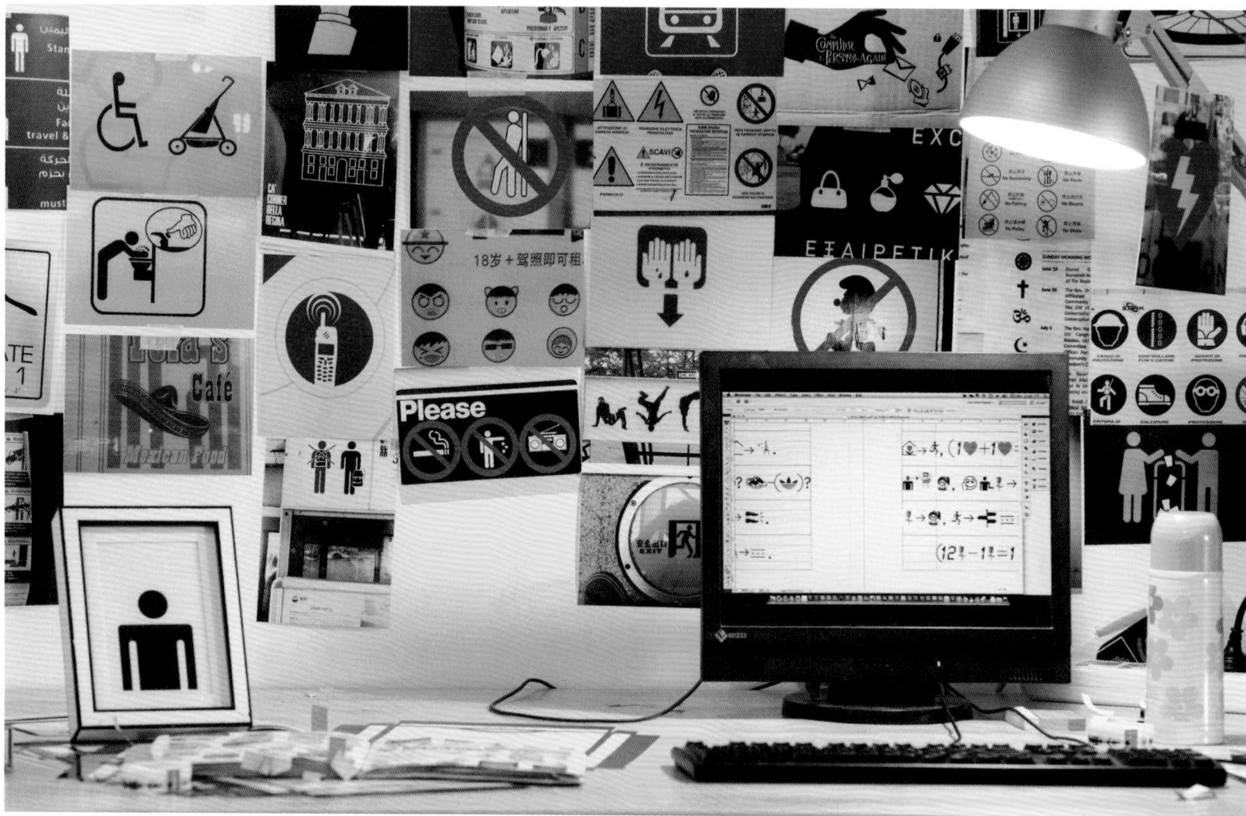
18岁+驾照即可租
Café
Mexican Food
Please

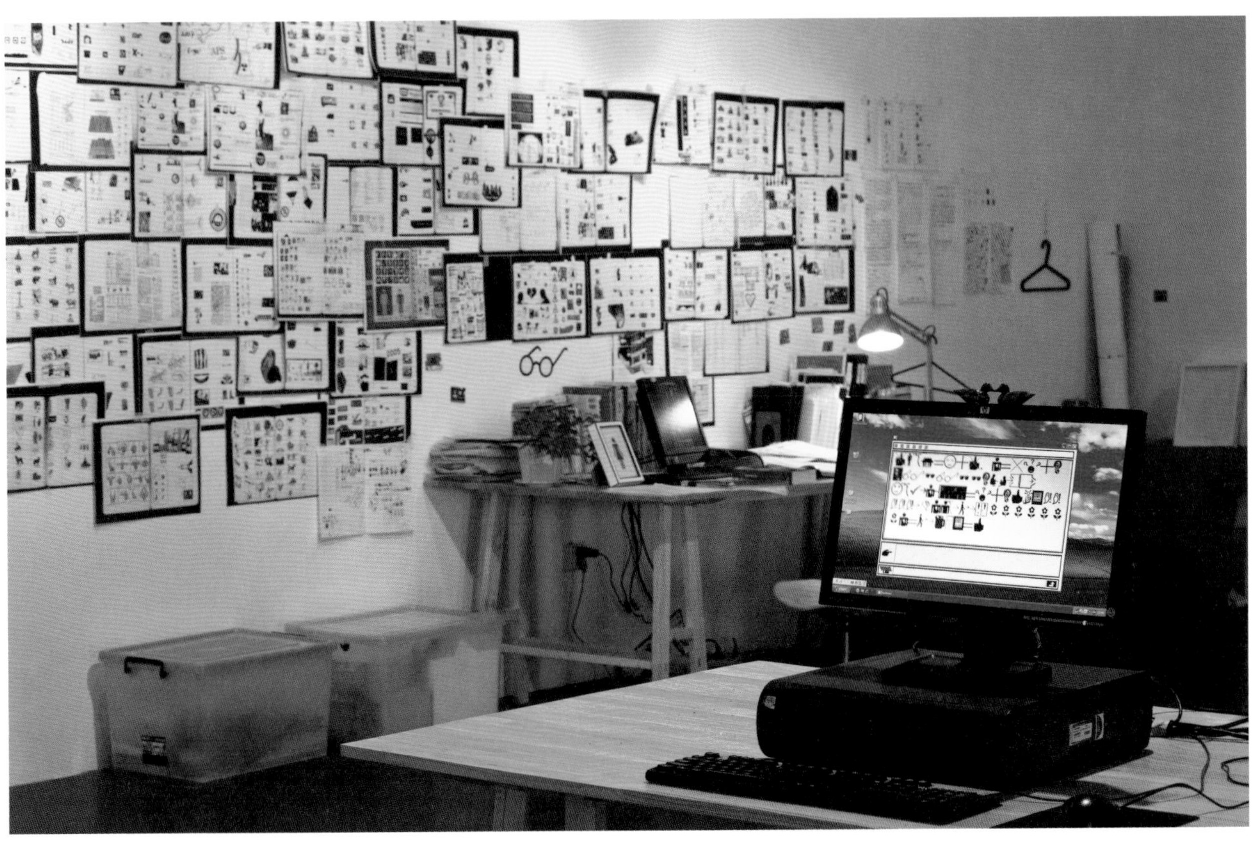

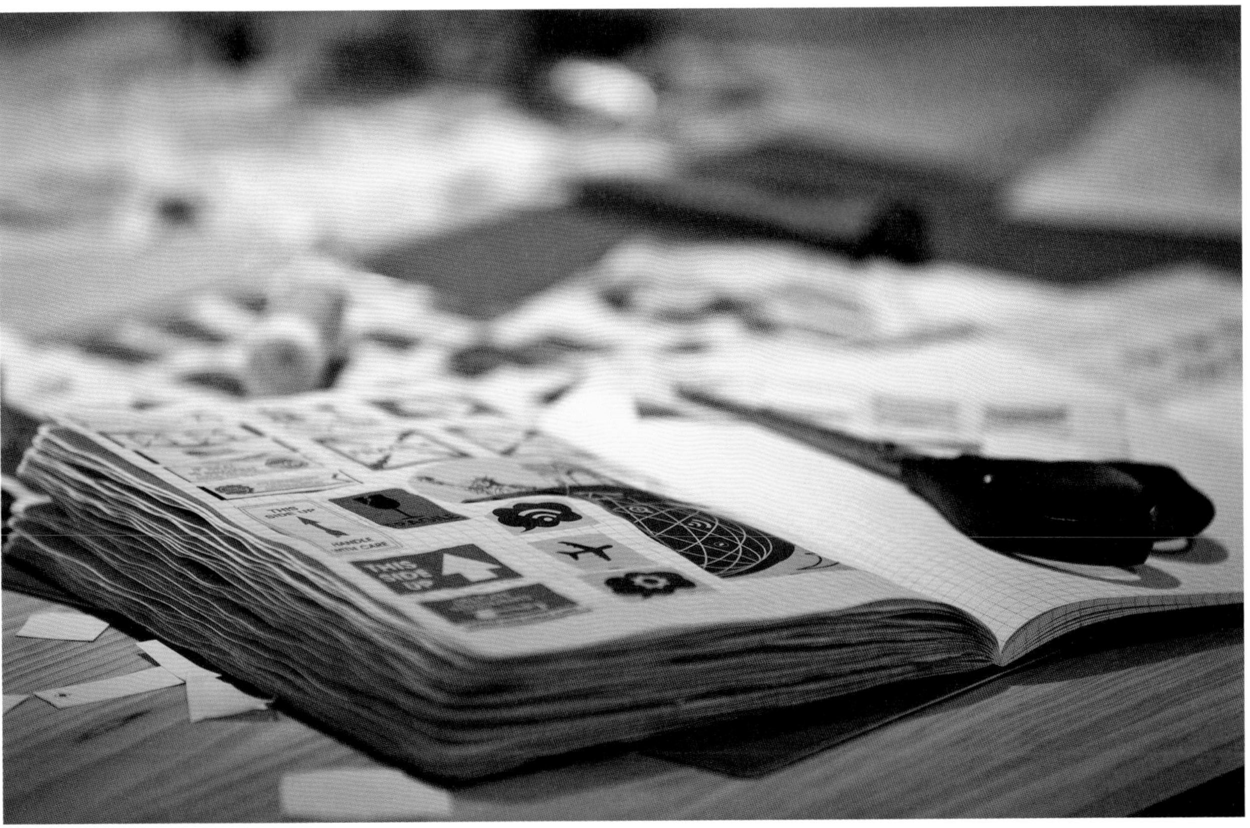
THIS SIDE UP
HANDLE WITH CARE
THIS SIDE UP

BOOK FROM THE GROUND ICON EDITING SOFTWARE
2012
computer software

This editing software developed by Xu Bing is a computational database which allows users to translate Chinese or English text into commonly recognized pictographs, signs, icons, and symbols. This software also allows users to edit the size, sequence, and placement of the icon within the dialogue window frame.

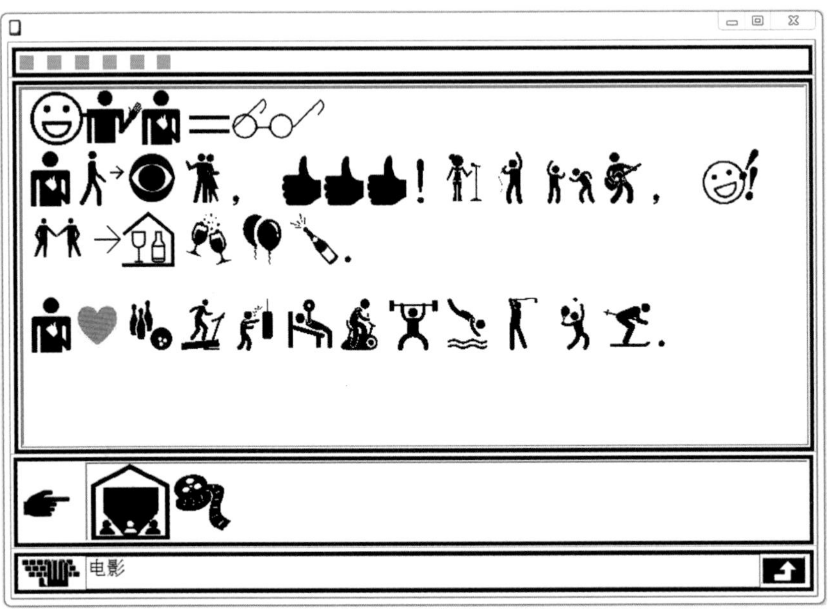

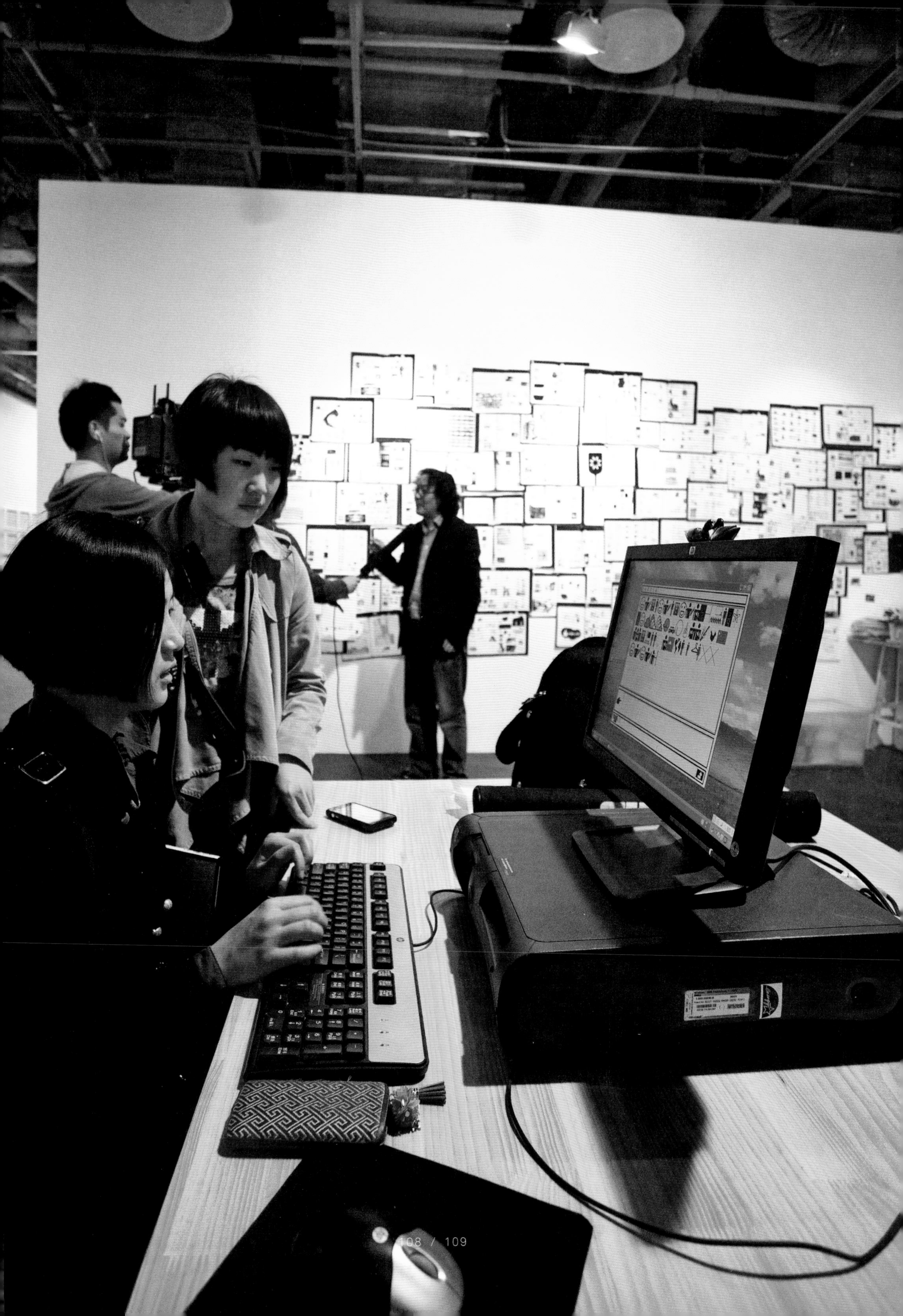

BOOK FROM THE GROUND, ICON CHAT SOFTWARE

2012

computer software, two computer terminals running Windows operating software

The *Icon Chat Software* translates Chinese or English into the language of icons, allowing two people who speak different languages to communicate immediately and directly with this new intermediate language. This work was originally made in 2007 and exhibited at the Museum of Modern Art, New York. Presented here is an updated version of the software.

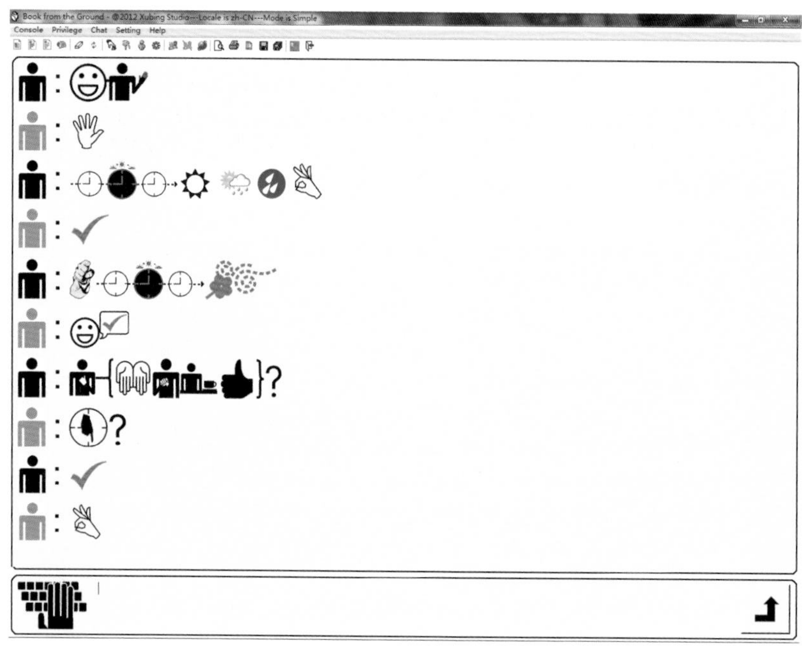

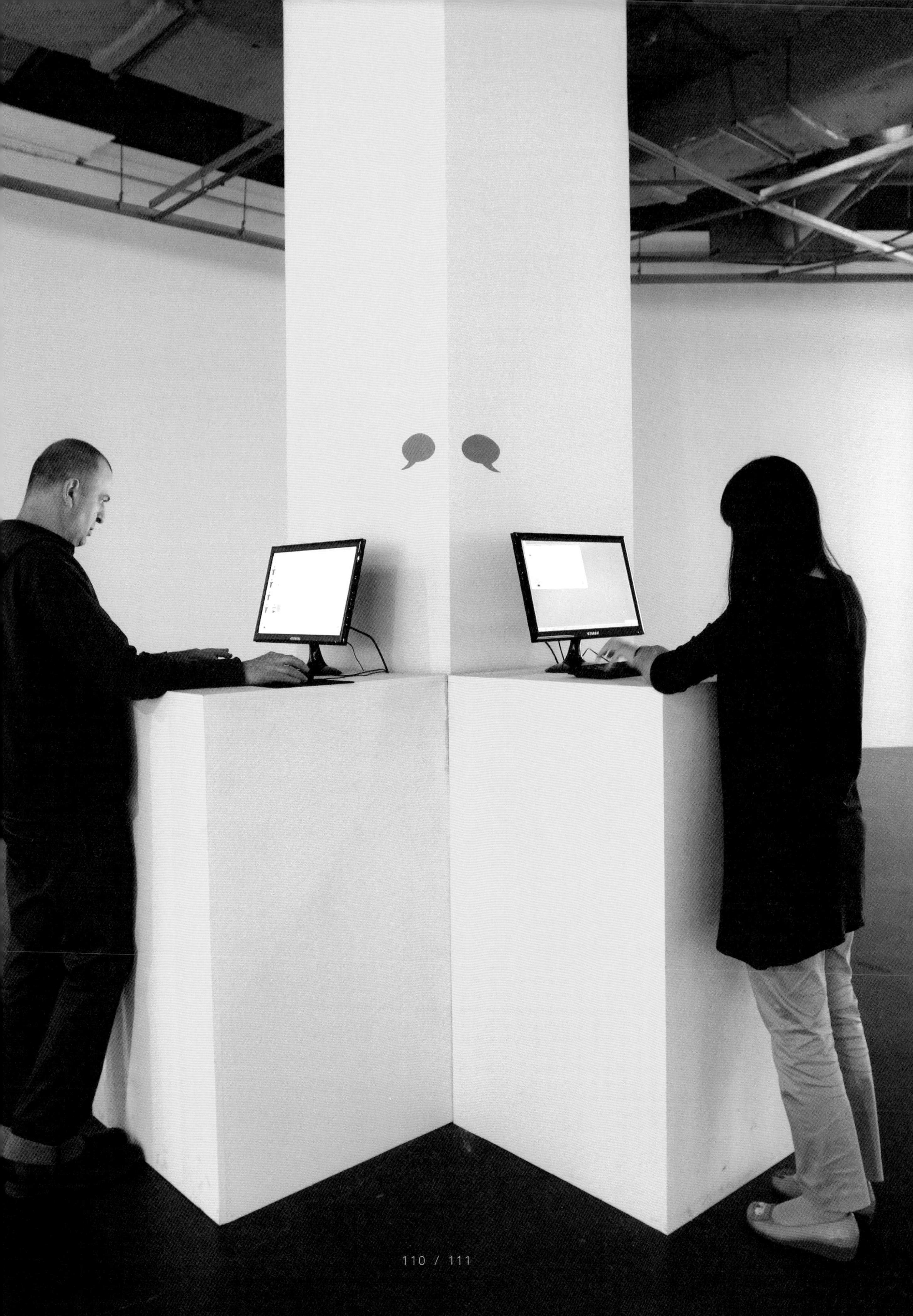

BOOK FROM THE GROUND: LANGUAGE AS PICTURES

2007

Installation at Museum of Modern Art, New York

glass board, polyester film, two computers running Windows, chatting software

This work shows the *Icon Chat Software* when it was first exhibited at the Museum of Modern Art, New York, 2007. For the exhibition *Automatic Update* Barbara London, the curator selected art works that reflected the world after the dot.com boom. Xu Bing exhibited *Book From the Ground: Language as Pictures*, as a comment on pictographic communication in our highly technological society. Two persons sitting on either side of the glass partition can enter English or Chinese text into the computers which is then communicated via the icon language. On the panel separating the two users some example sentences are printed along with their English and Chinese translations.

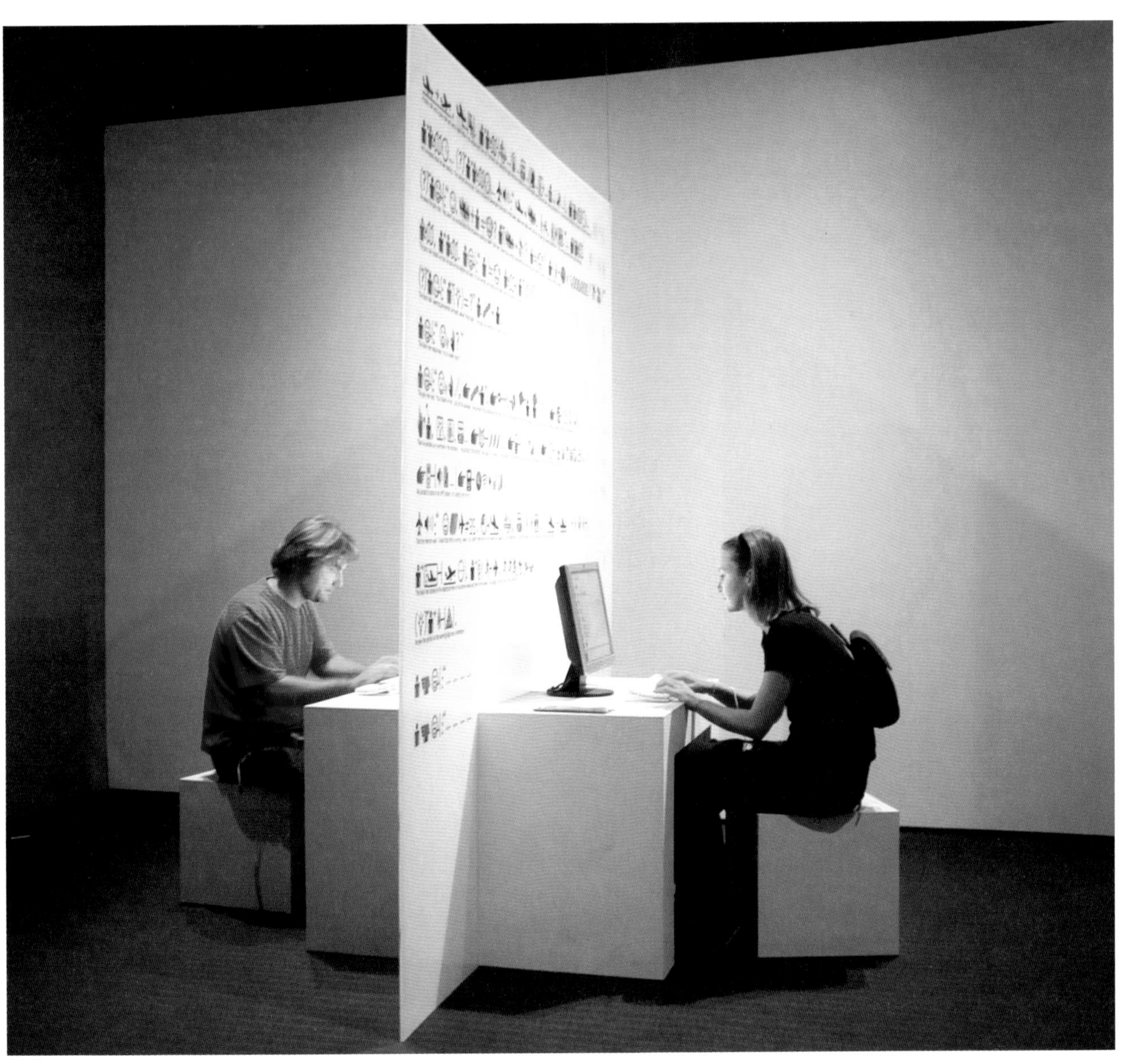

MR. BLACK AND HIS FRIENDS VISIT THE BUND

2012

animated HD video, 4 minutes

This short video made especially for the Shanghai exhibition of *Book From the Ground* depicts Mr. Black and his friends visit to Shanghai. Animated entirely with icons, symbols, and signs, this site-specific video begins with Mr. Black and his friend exiting a public bathroom and meandering along the Bund, one of Shanghai's major tourist destinations and home to the exhibition space. In this extra-wide, three-channel projection we see people daydreaming, while others argue; boats and helicopters pass by; buildings rise up with construction, and traffic accidents occur. The video is projected against the gallery window facing the Bund and shows the very humorous, animated activity in parallel to the actual reality of the promenade outside.

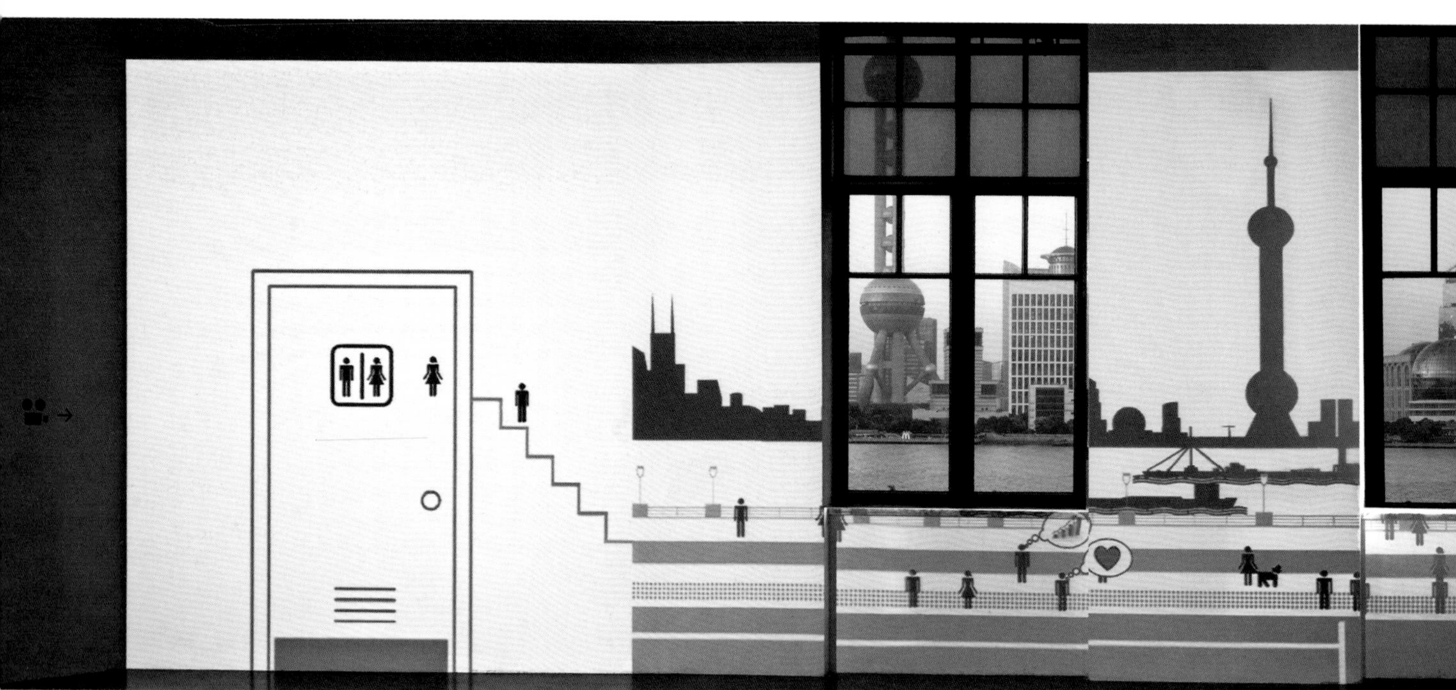

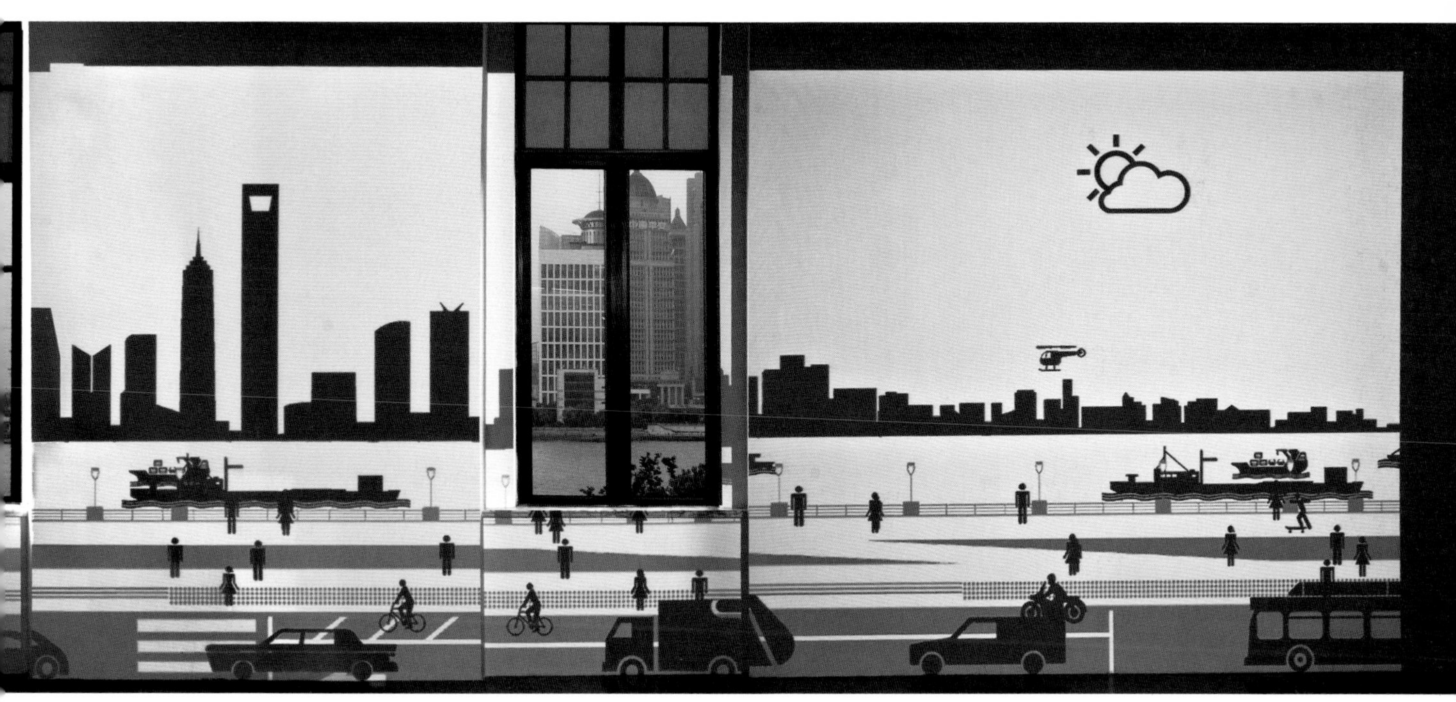

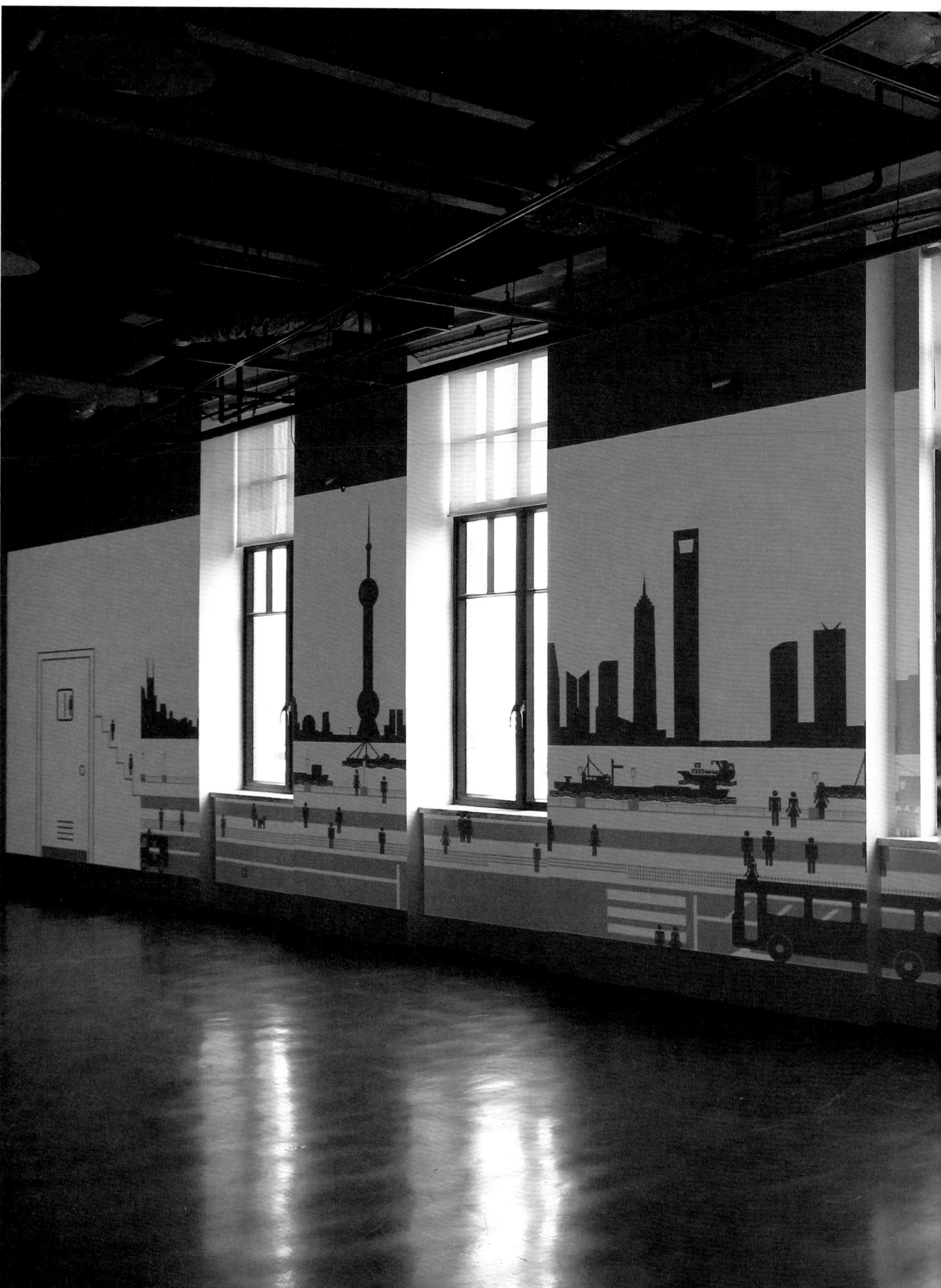

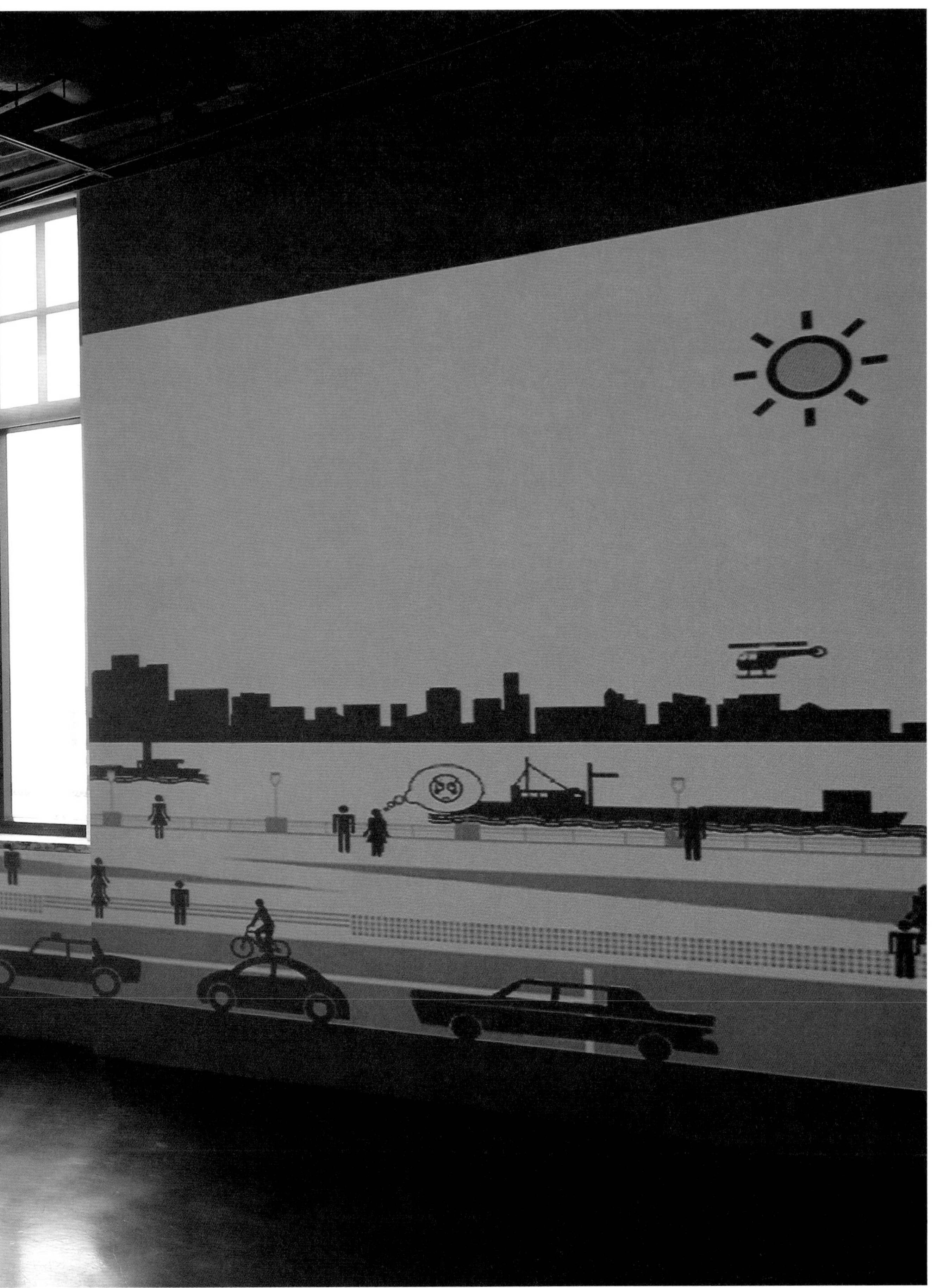

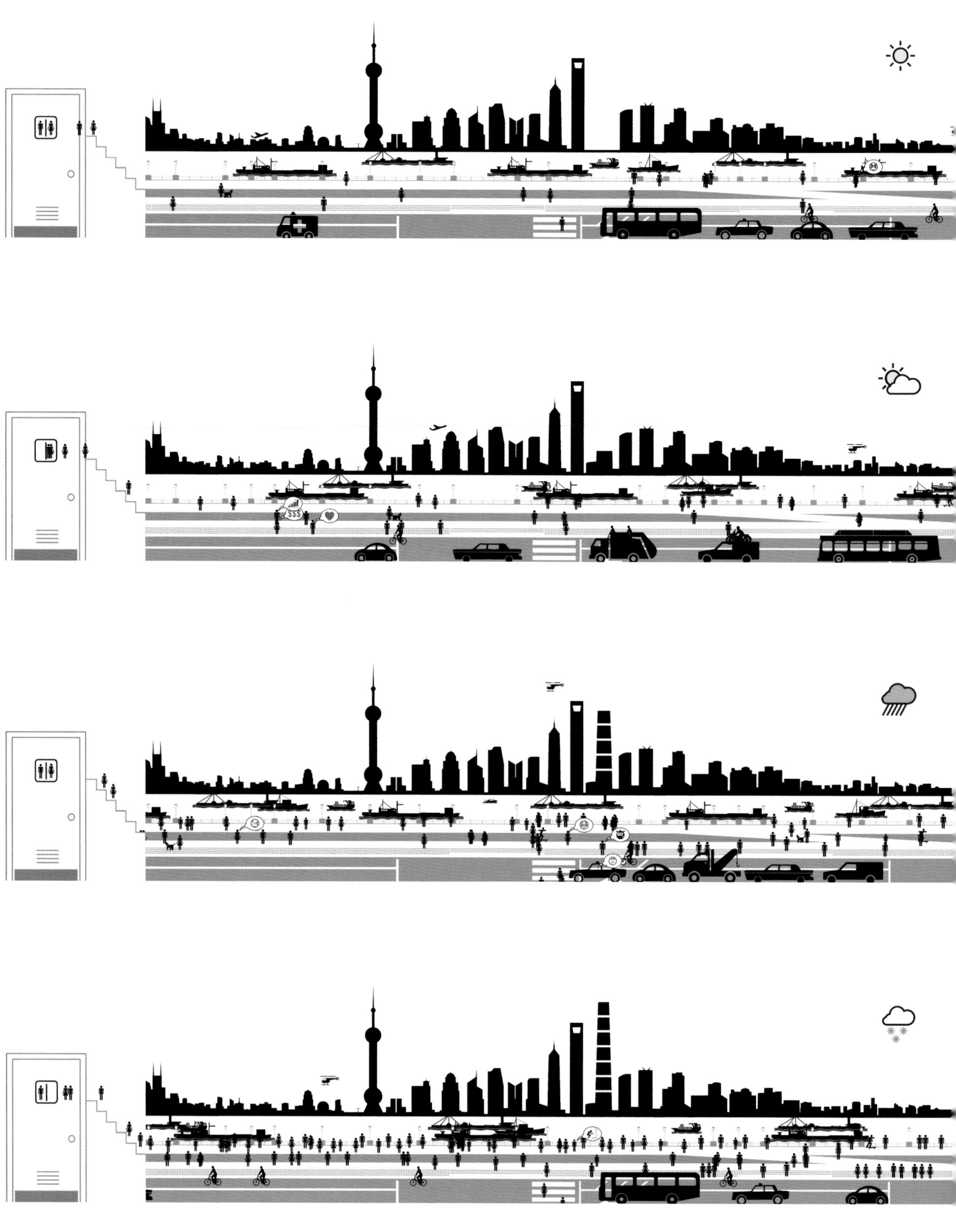

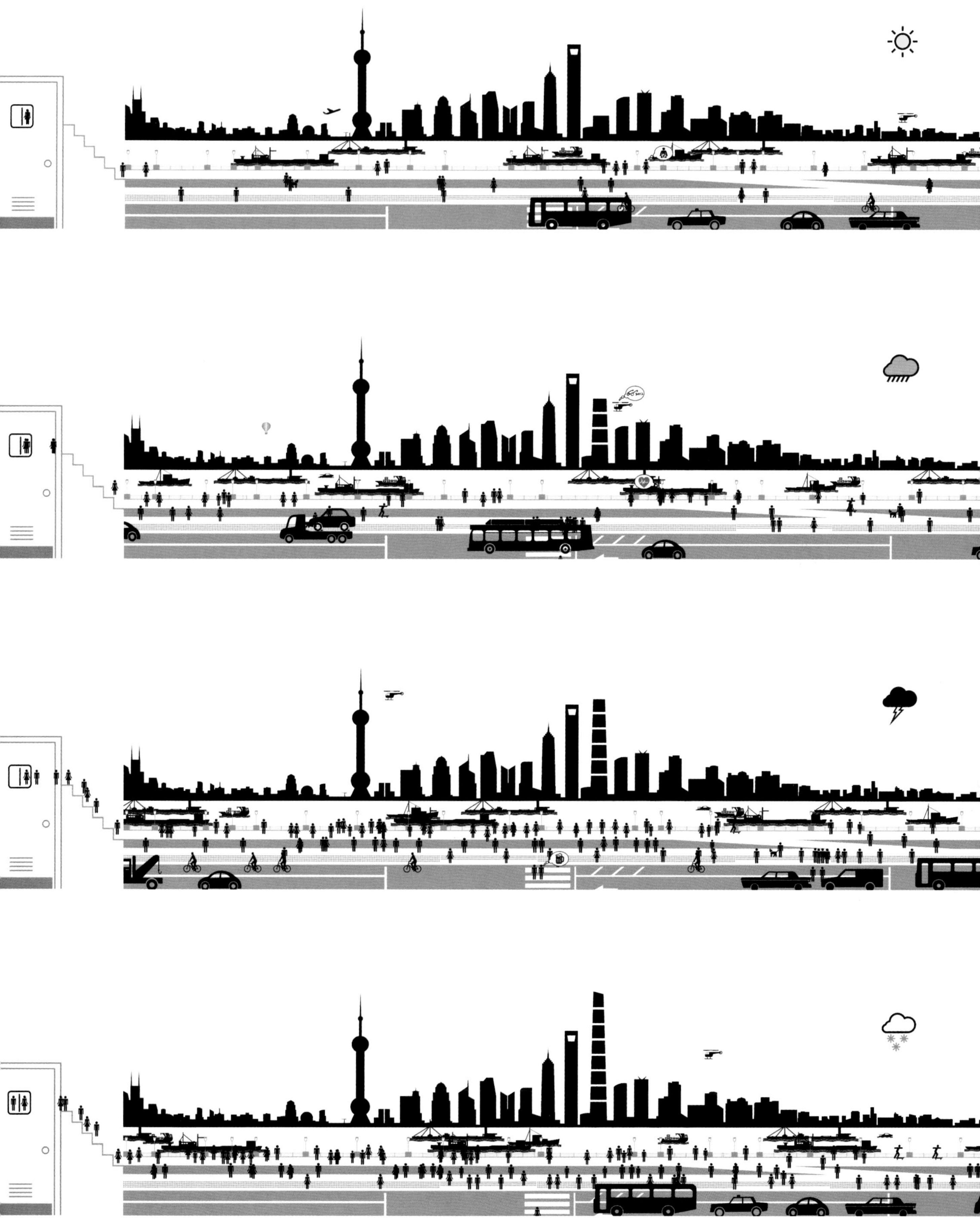

BOOK FROM THE GROUND P2-3
BOOK FROM THE GROUND P54-55
BOOK FROM THE GROUND P100-102
BOOK FROM THE GROUND P106-107
2012
laser-cut woodblock print, color ink
37×54cm

These limited-edition works showing spreads excerpted from *From Point to Point*, have been made with a combination of woodblock and computer-printing techniques.

A/P 3-1 P100-101 2012

A/P 3-1 P106-107 2012

BOOK FROM THE GROUND: SHANGHAI CONCEPT STORE

2012

Installation: clocks, newspaper, t-shirts, umbrellas, books, dining-table placemats, rings, refrigerator-magnet sets, men's shirts, chocolate, furniture, etc.

dimensions variable

In the *Shanghai Concept Store* Xu Bing has turned signs into practical consumer objects. All kinds of daily supplies such as tableware, clothes, umbrellas, clocks, magnetic stickers, and chocolate comprise *Book From the Ground* merchandise. Visitors can shop or browse the consumable "icons" inside a three-dimensional manifestation of the symbol for "store." This interactive consumer experience once again reminds us of the close relationship between signs and our daily life.

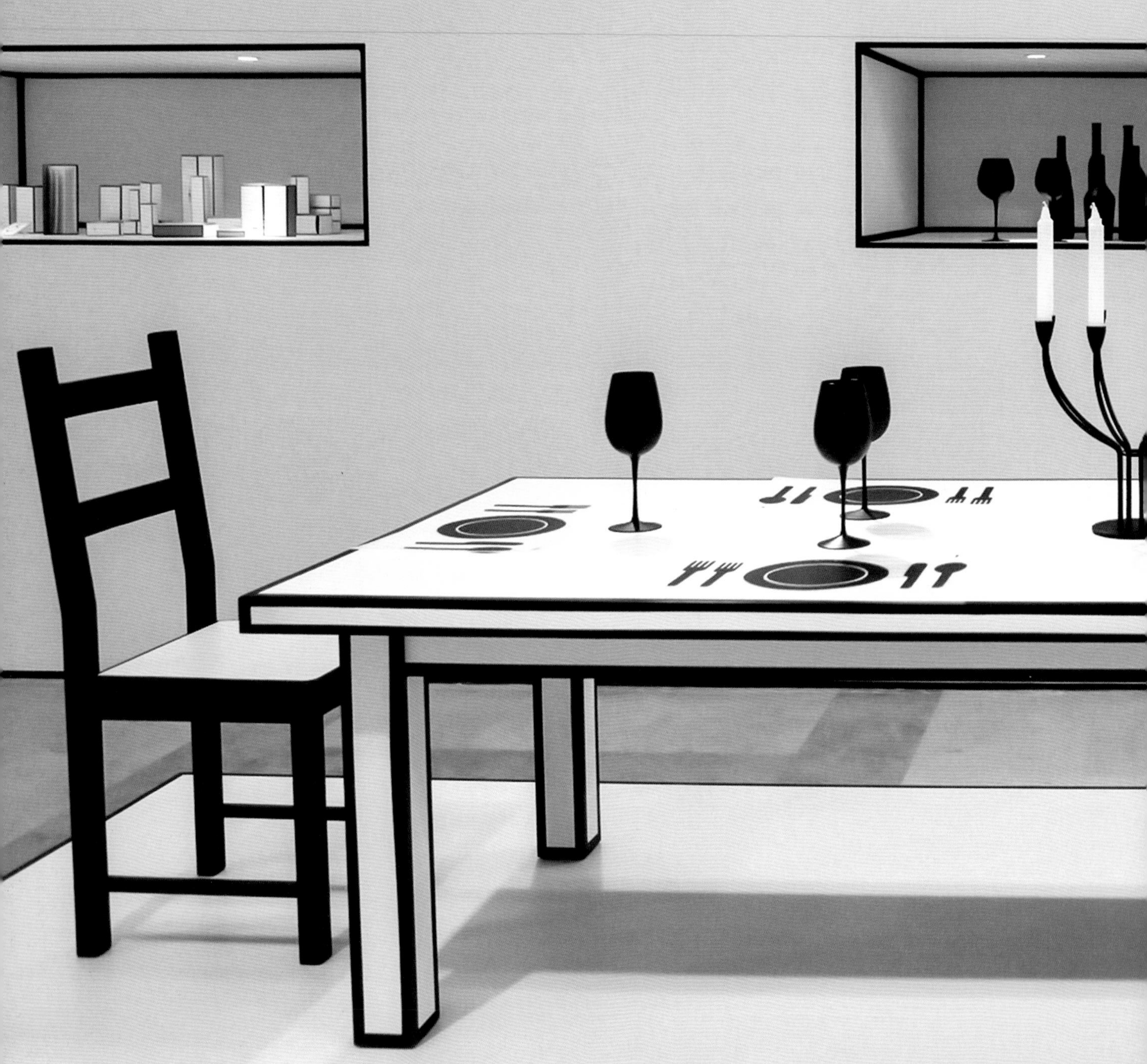

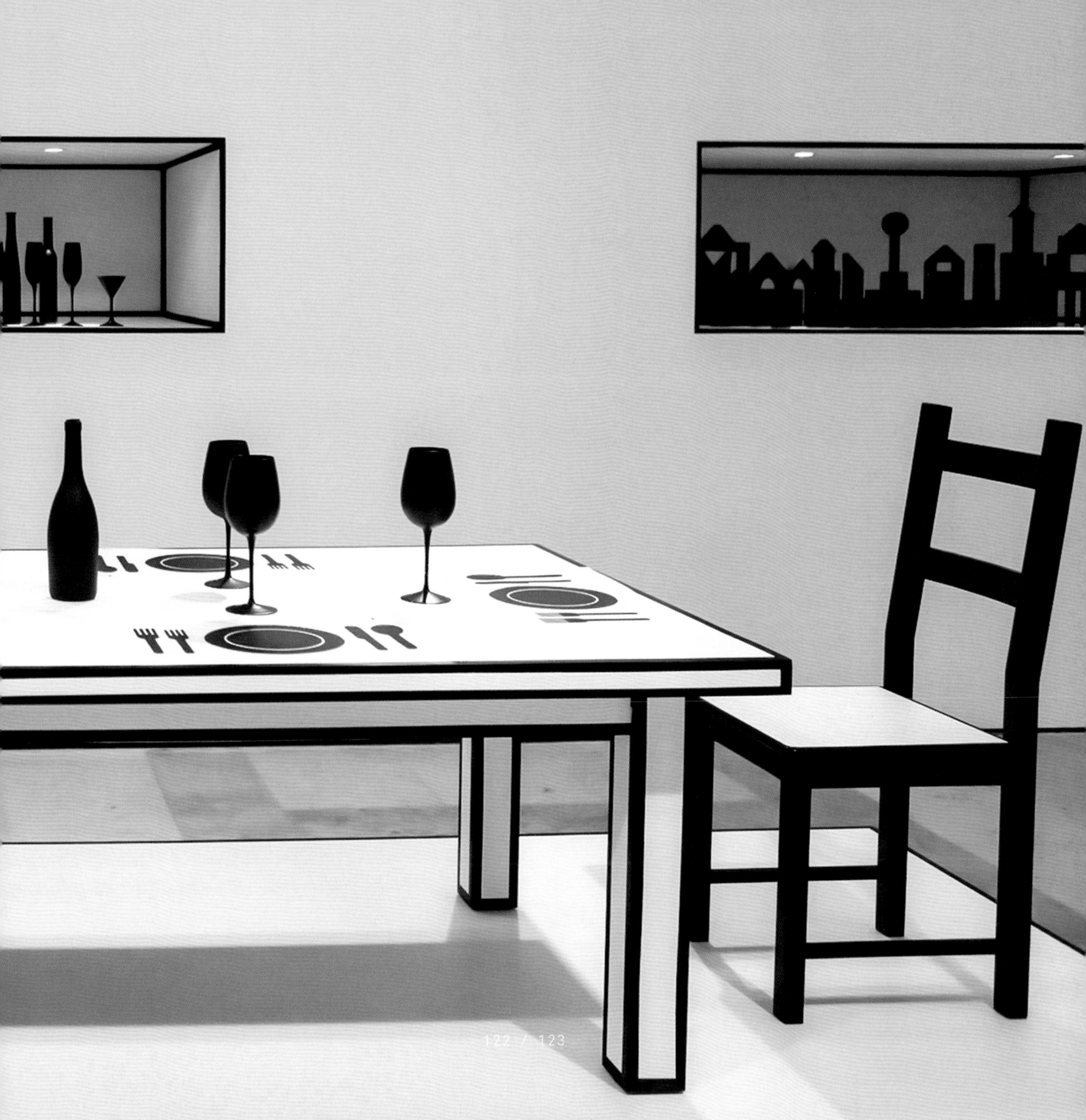

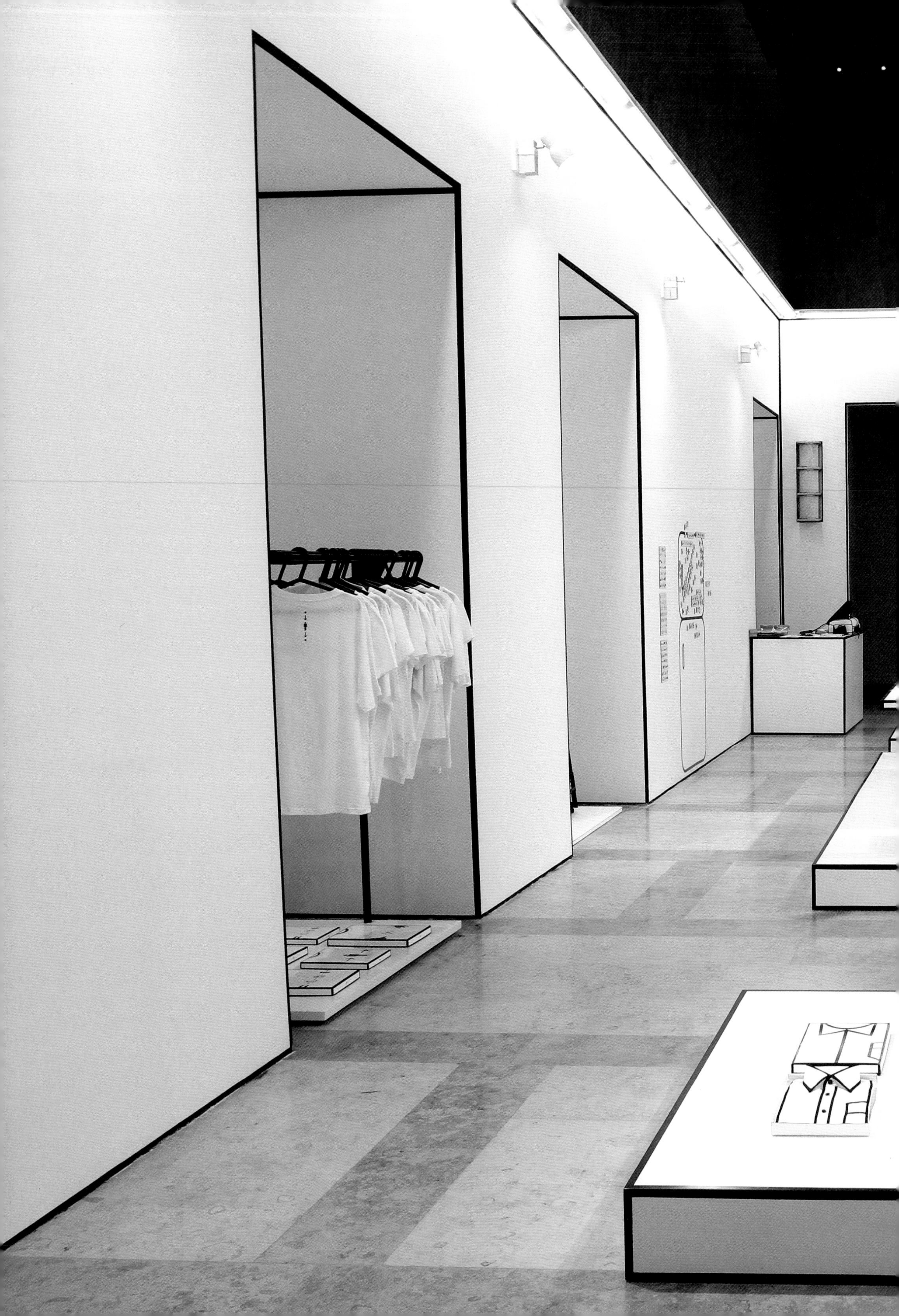

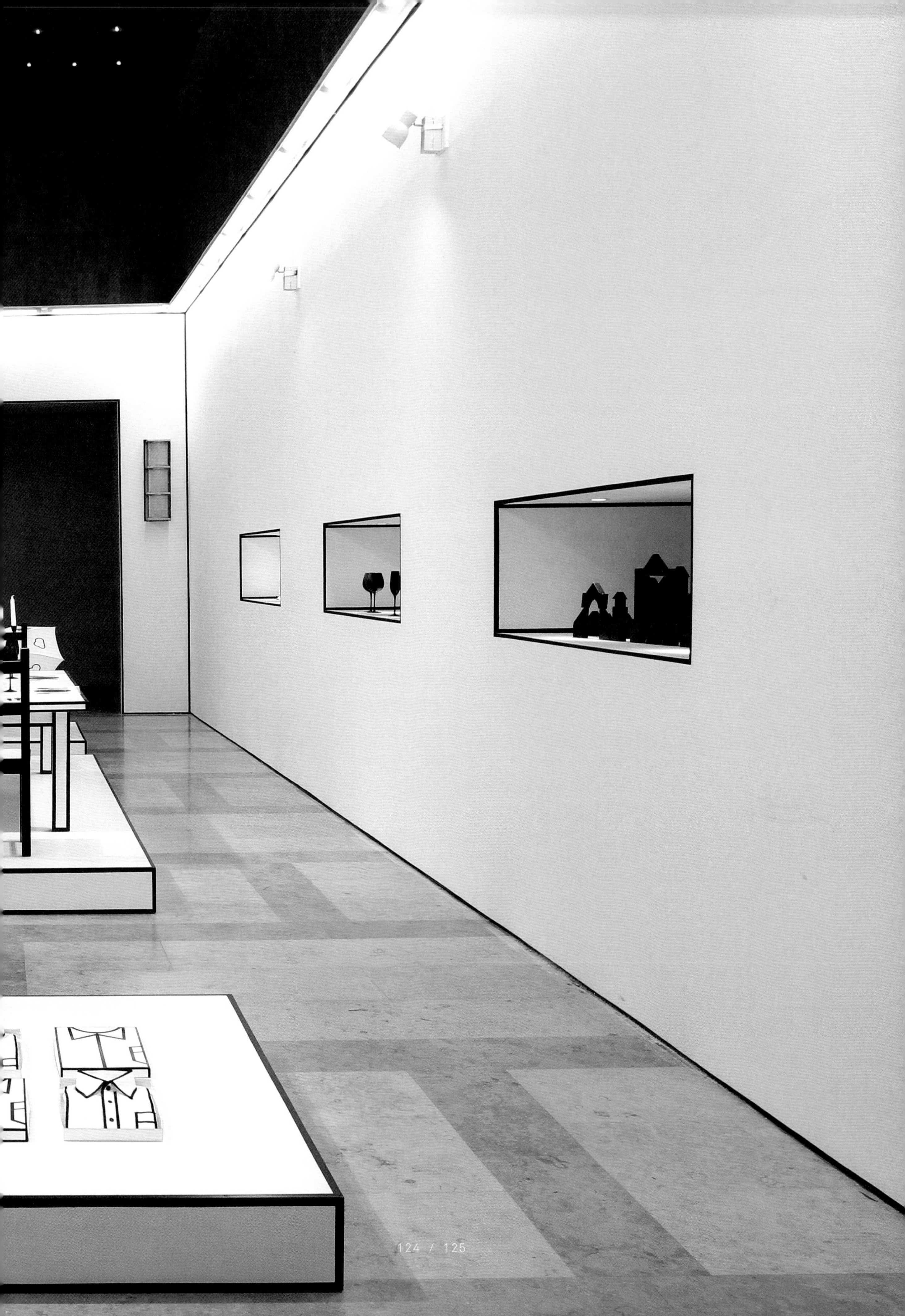

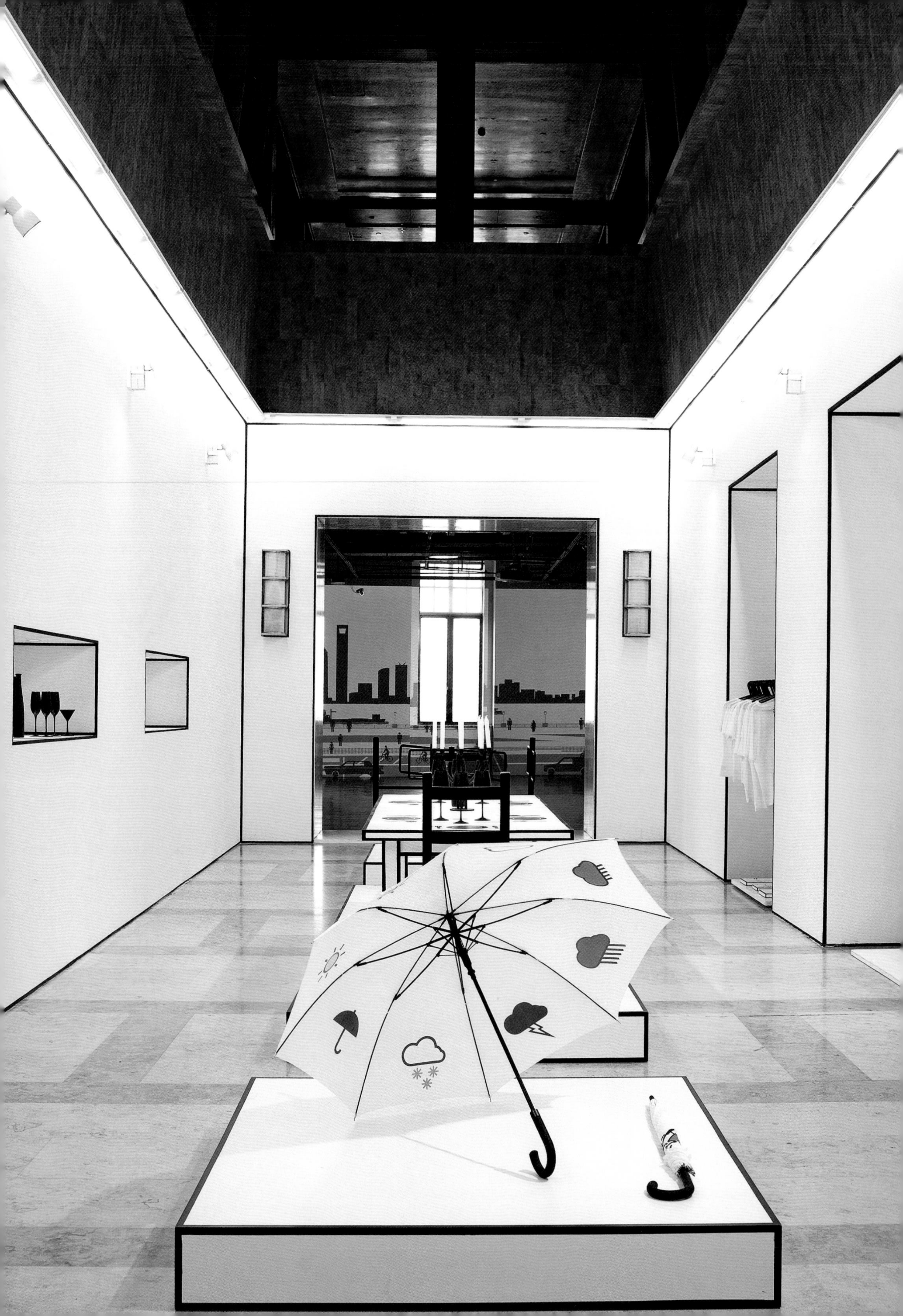

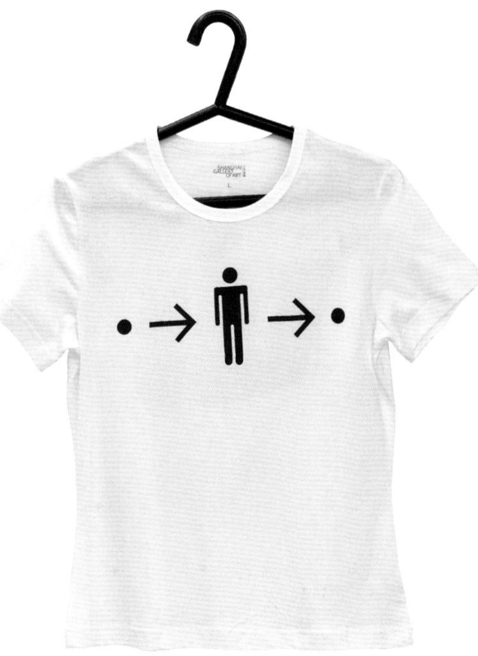

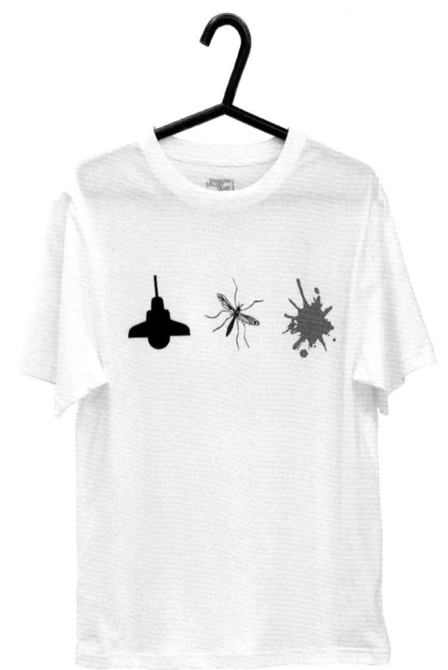

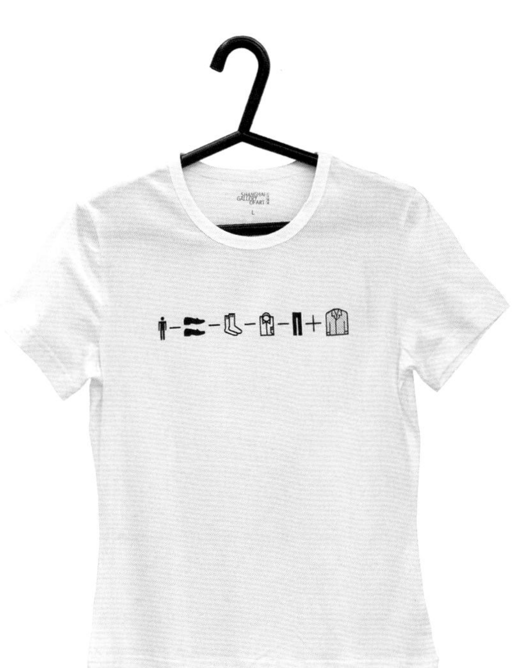

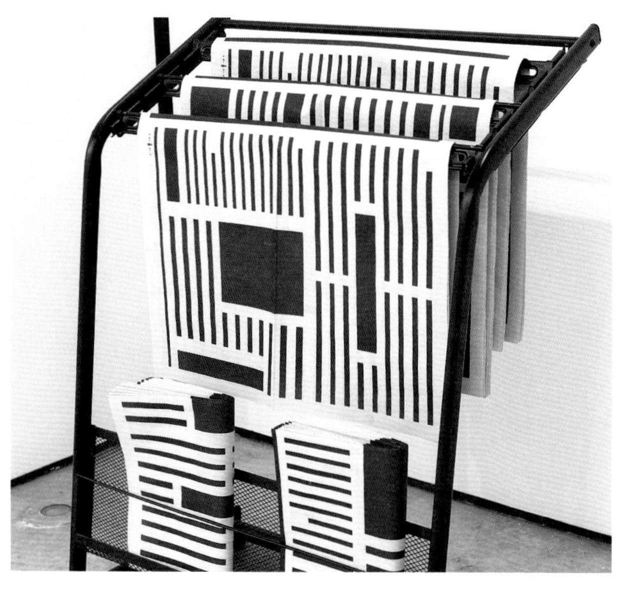

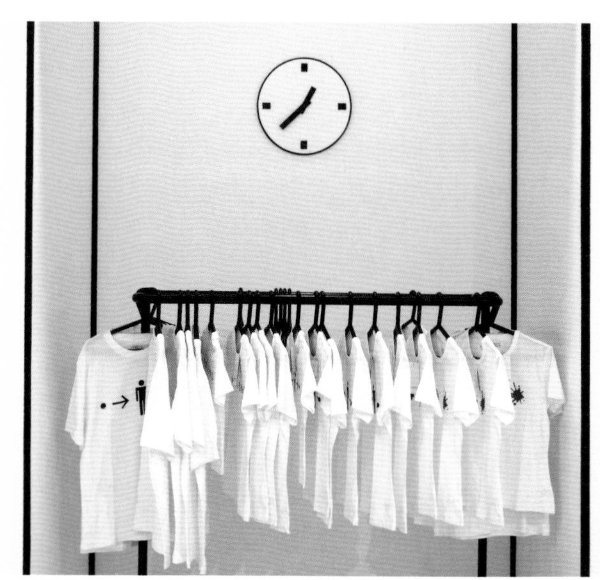

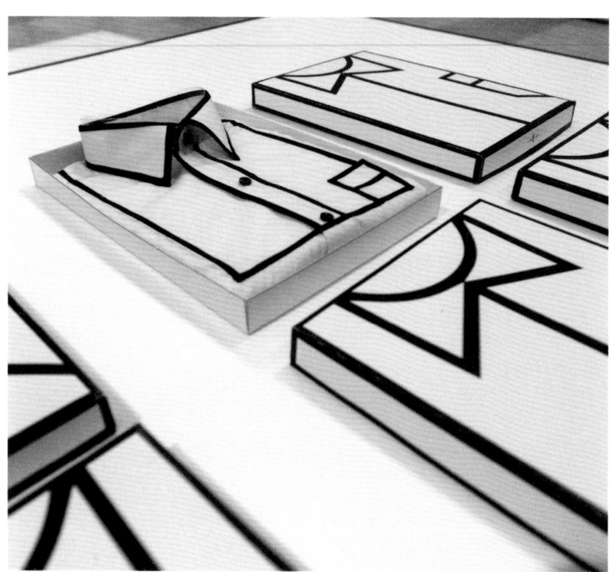

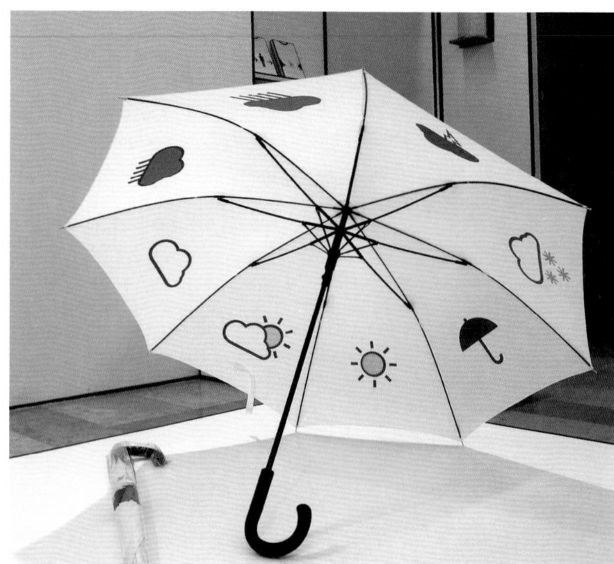

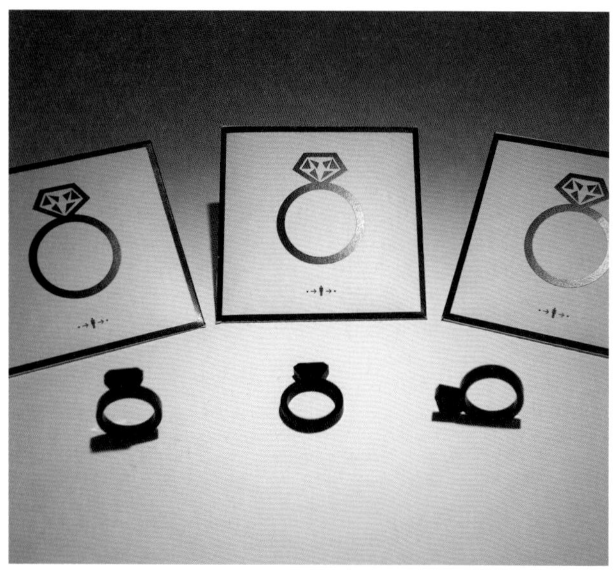

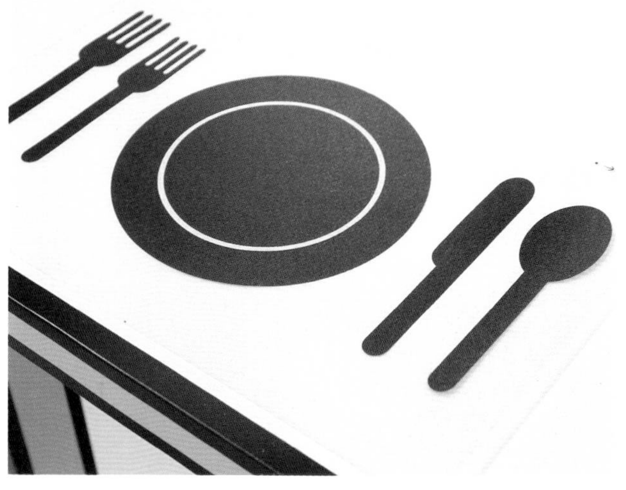

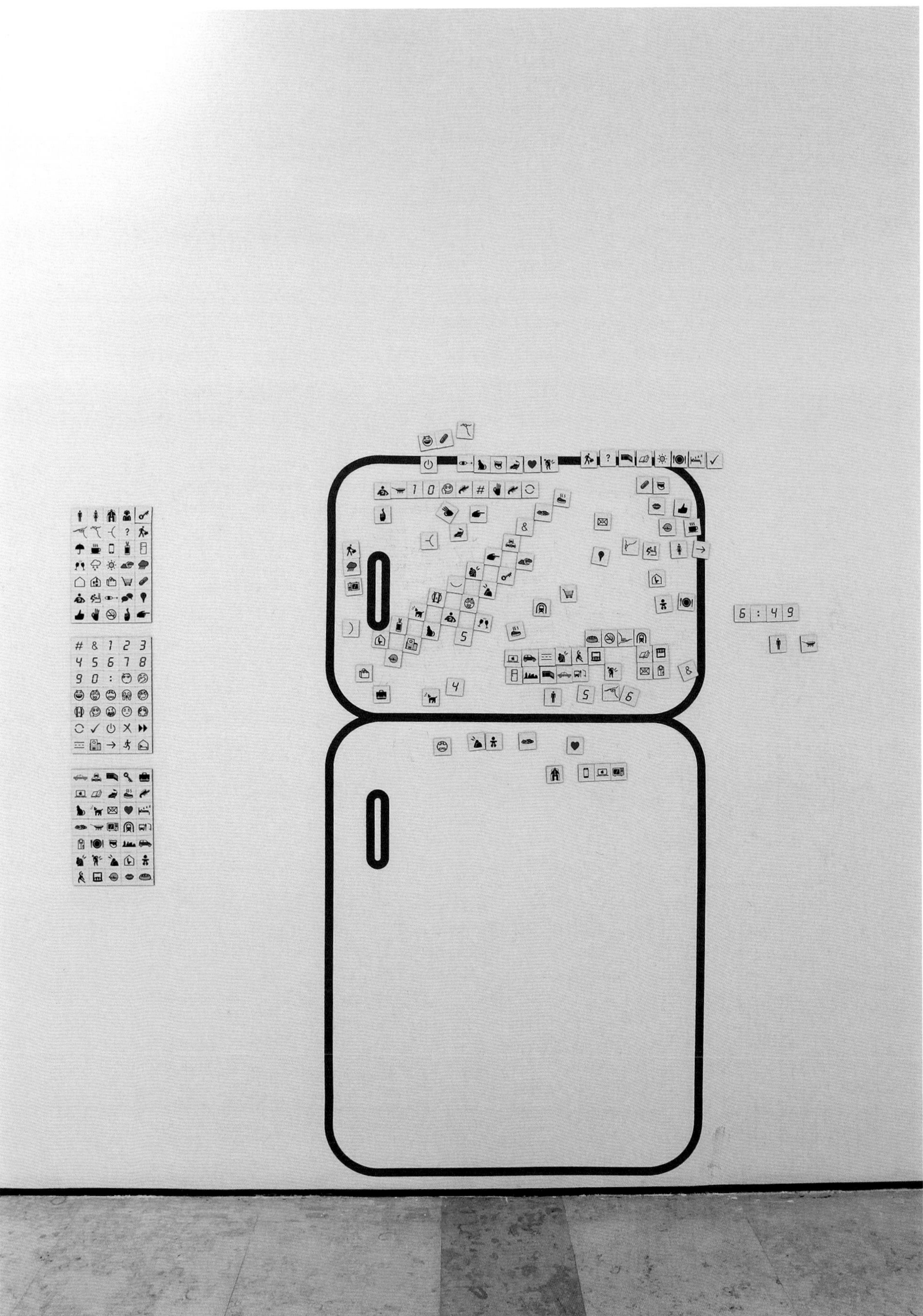

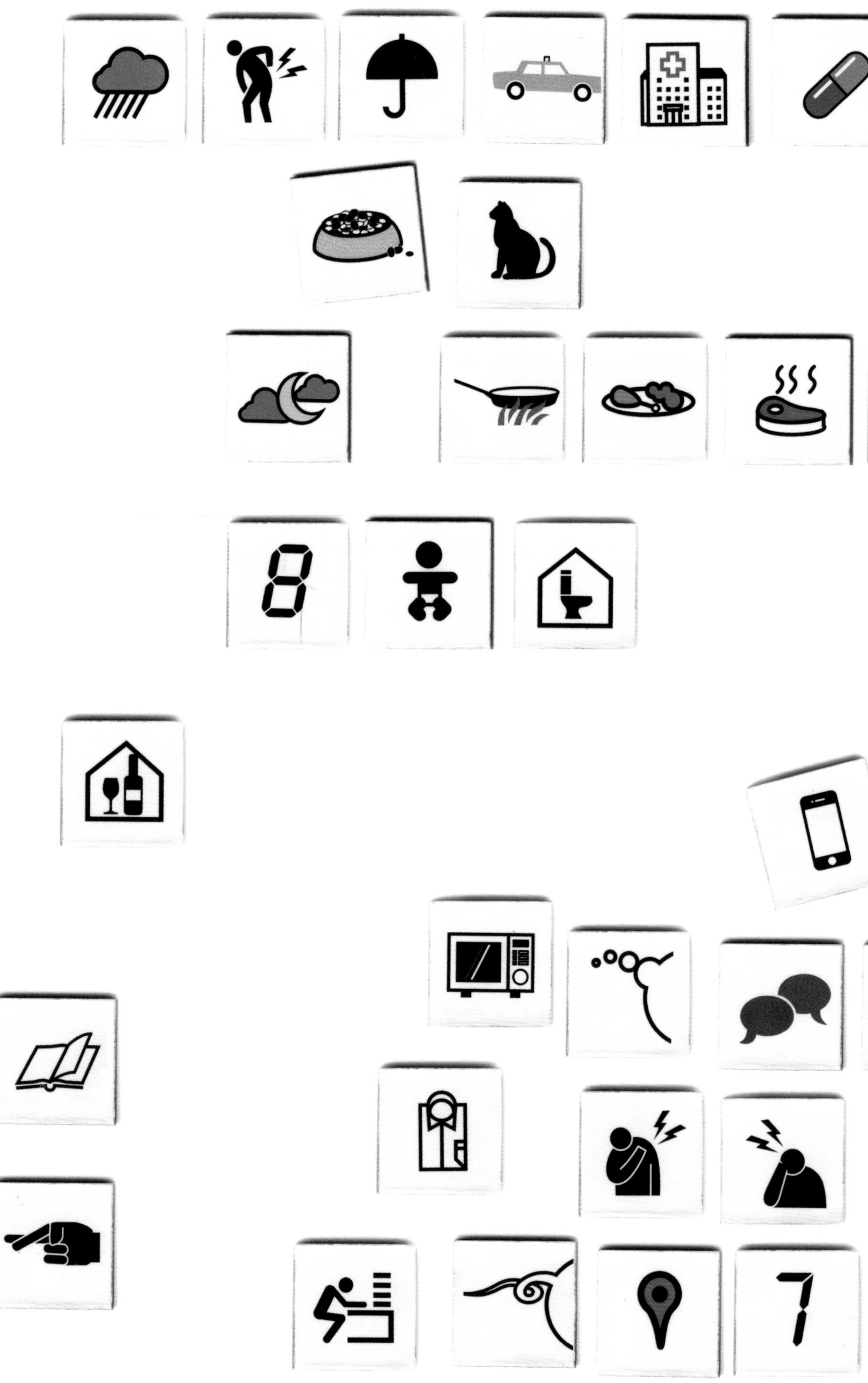

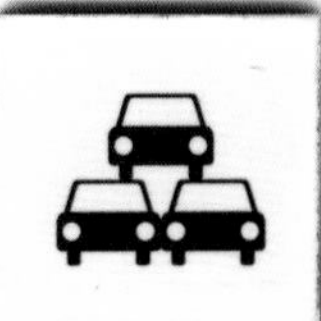

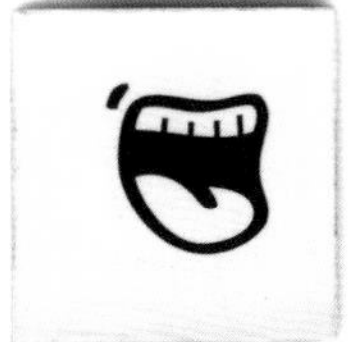

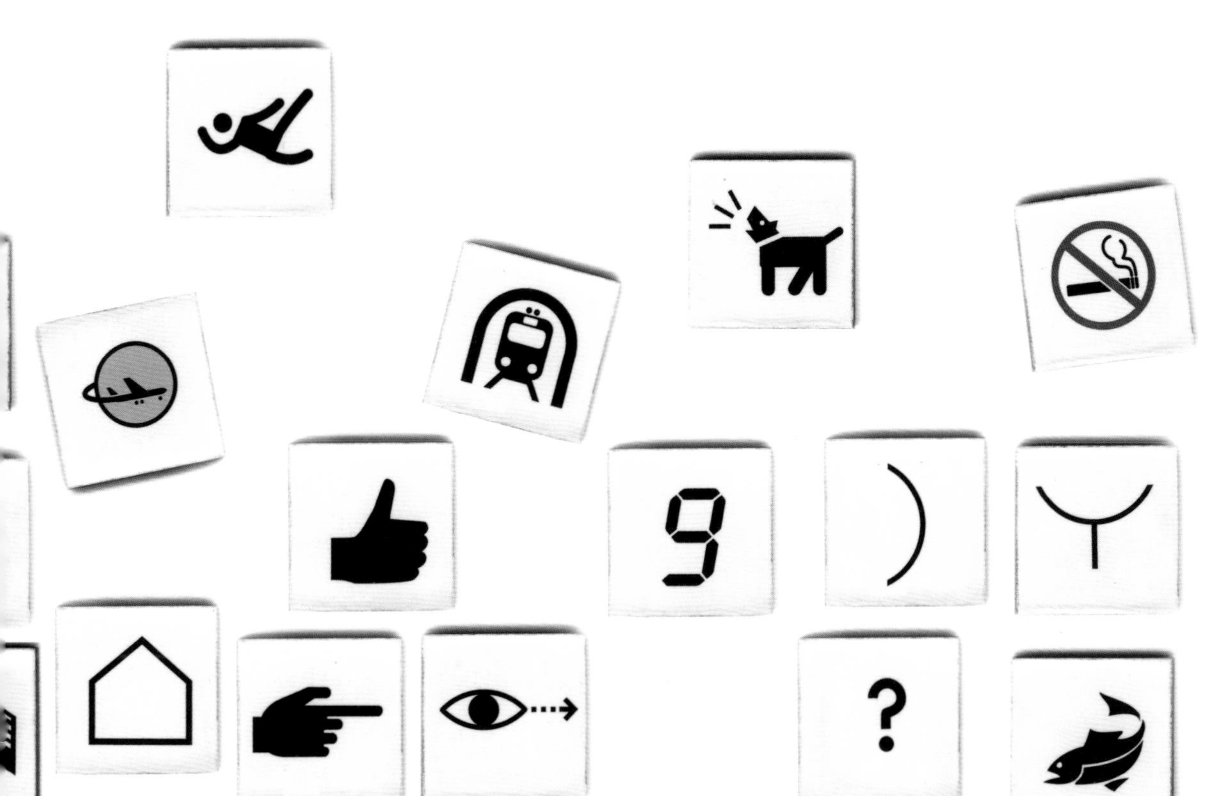
9
?

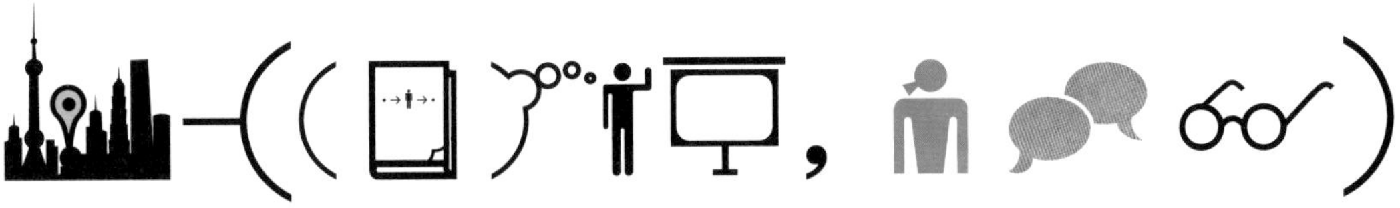

,

By Kaimei Olsson Wang

CONVERSATION GROUND IN SHA & MIAN MIAN

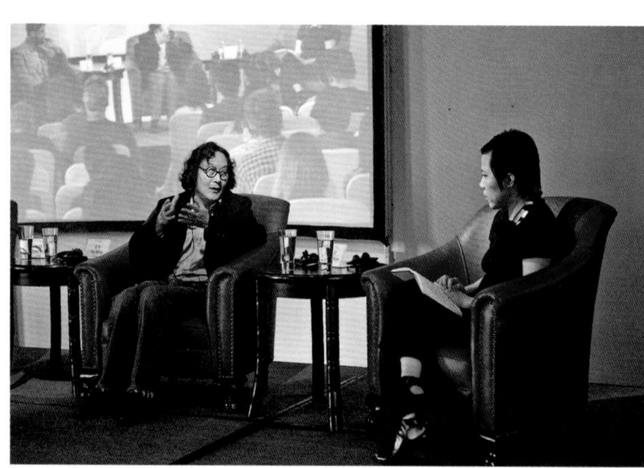

Three Talk at Three on The Bund, Shanghai
Xu Bing, Mian Mian and Mathieu Borysevicz
22, April 2012

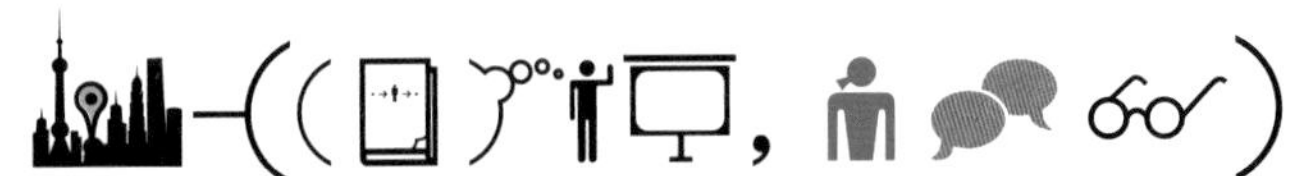

ROM THE NGHAI: XU BING

The first work that viewers encounter in Xu Bing's exhibition *Book From the Ground*, is the *Tower of Babel,* an installation made up of 2,400 copies of *From Point to Point* books stacked together to form a tower. This installation is based on the tale from the Old Testament and illustrates the root of human miscommunication. For Xu Bing, language and communication have always been at the core of his artistic practice. *Book From the Ground* is written solely using signs, symbols, and icons that are common in our daily life. The book describes a day in the life of "Mr Black", from his waking up in the morning, going to the toilet, to his rushing to work, dealing with his demanding boss, drinking with friends, and surfing the internet in search of a girlfriend — in short, it is a typical day of a white-collar city bachelor living and working in our contemporary society. Through the signs, symbols, and icons the story is told in a direct, funny, and vivid way.

Book From the Ground is an experiment whereby Xu Bing raises the language of signs and icons to the height of literature.

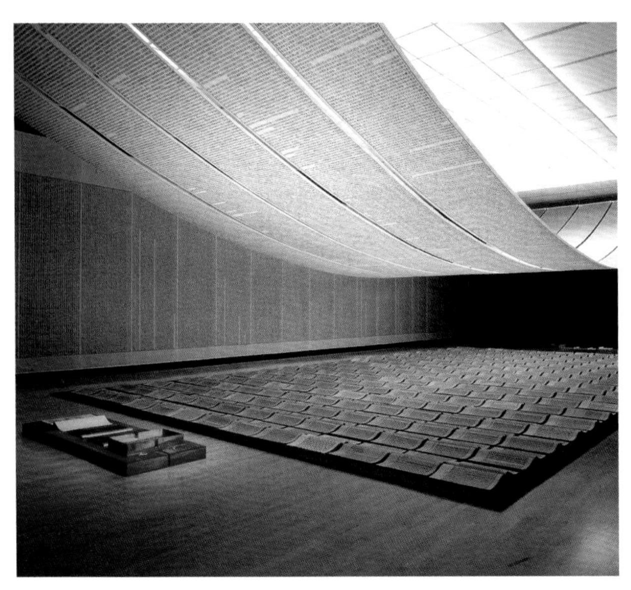

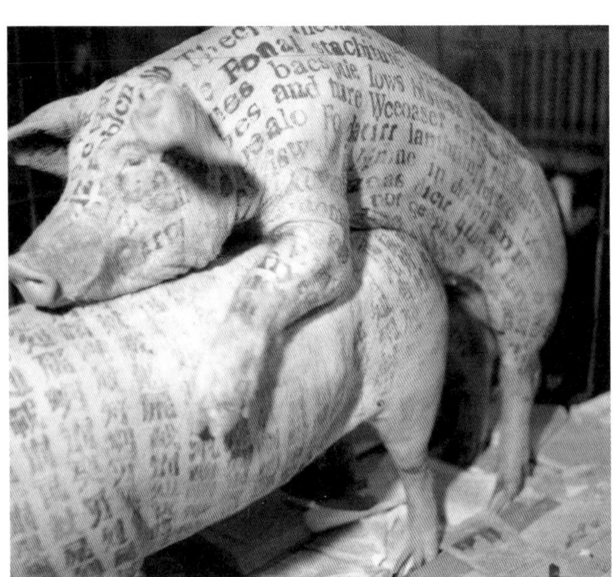

Xu Bing
Book From the Sky
1998

Xu Bing
Details from *Book From the Sky*
1989

Xu Bing
A Case Study of Transference
1993-1994
Performance in Beijing
Photographer: Xu Zhiwei

Xu Bing
New English Calligraphy
2007

Thirty years ago, Xu made *Book From the Sky* by inventing four thousand Chinese characters. Each character in *Book From the Sky* contains sections of actual Chinese text. However, their compound structure is meaningless. In *Book From the Sky,* Xu has created an ambivalent reading experience that challenges readers with its in-betweeness. While Chinese readers are seduced by the beautiful characters and elegant calligraphic presentation, they are also frustrated by these characters' absence of meaning. Western readers, unaware of the illegibility of the work, are simply consumed by the physical experience of the large-scale installation. *Book From the Sky* is in the realm of neither being correct nor incorrect. At the time *Book From the Sky* was created such artistic freedom challenged a system that controlled political power, moral correctness, as well as historical freight[1]. Changing the language would affect the entire ideological system. Xu's gesture of abolishing the previous writing structure was perceived as a threat to the cultural and historical heritage. Such has been the case throughout Chinese history.

While Xu Bing's early works were strongly connected with Chinese cultural issues, his entire artistic trajectory has in fact been the pursuit of a more direct and simple way to convey language. In *A Case Study of Transference* (1993), Xu presented two pigs with their skins covered in letters — one with English letters and the other with Chinese characters. This work was intended to discuss the notion of cultural transference, however, it was viewed as an expression of cultural inequality because the Chinese words were written on the female pig while the male pig donned English words. This experiment made Xu reflect on the complex nature of written languages and their inextricable links to culture and cultural identity.

So, is there a way to communicate beyond language barriers and cultural identities, a way of communicating that is reliable and direct? *Book From the Sky* looks like a classic Chinese manuscript but it is completely unintelligible. *Book From the Ground* may look like coded language but in fact everyone can read and understand it. If signs and icons can replace traditional language, can we anticipate that human communication is entering a new phase? *Book From the Ground* offers some answers to these questions.

On the occassion of the *Book From the Ground* exhibition, a discussion between the curator of the exhibition, Mathieu Borysevicz, writer, Mian Mian, and Xu Bing was organized as a way to, together with a live audience, flush out the possibilities and challenges of this emergent writing form. Mian Mian is a critically acclaimed writer whose novels about young people growing up in today's Shanghai are written in Chinese but have been translated into 15 languages and distributed worldwide. While she uses text as her medium Xu, making a debut as an author, uses icons to compose his novel. The following are excerpts from that discussion:

XU BING: I am pleased to have an opportunity to have a dialogue with Mian Mian. You can see in my work a great amount of text and books. I feel a sort of strange relationship between my generation and today's culture. It is sort of an awkward relationship where you can neither go in nor get out. But I pay respect to the culture and writers. So many works of mine look like books, however unintelligible or barrier-creating they may appear. This is the relationship between writers and me. This kind of disruptive book reflects my respect to the book, the culture, and the writer.

MIAN MIAN: Congratulations on your new book! As a writer myself, I can understand the great effort that you put into it. For me this book is a full-length novel. What is the greatest challenge in using this language to tell a story?

XU BING: The greatest difficulty is that we don't have existing experience about how to use these icons to tell a story. To create a narrative is also not easy. I find that I am not a great storyteller.

MIAN MIAN: Did you write the book in ordinary Chinese first and then translate it into icons?

XU BING: In the beginning, we wrote a draft in Chinese — an amateur novel. We thought about using icons to translate the draft, but it turned out to be impractical. It is hard to convert a fixed Chinese language structure and its components into these symbols and icons. Later, I decided to tell a story about a person's life over the course of 24 hours that became the 24 hours in the life of Mr. Black. This structure turned out to be more suitable for the icon language, so this book was written directly with icons.

MIAN MIAN: Undoubtedly *Book From the Ground* is about contemporary people living in the present moment, from mobile phones, SMS's, Tweets and Internet dating. For most people living in the Internet-connected world today, icons and signs have already become the new language of cyber-communication. In turn, this cyber-language of symbols and signs constantly extends back into our daily reality. If this is the case, what does your icon book tell us?

XU BING: I want to express my understanding of the future of communication through this book. Current phenomena tell us that our traditional language is not suitable to our present lifestyle. Second, I want to express the "icon-ized" life we are living today. There is a special relationship between reality and icons. The description of Mr. Black's daily life may not be so funny and rich, but in essence, it holds a certain depth. In addition, I wanted to do an experiment. I wanted to present a book to the world. This is a book everybody can read and understand without the need of translation. With that I mean this book presents a concept that reverts and subverts our traditional perception of culture. The limitations of this book lie in your life experience, not in your educational level or geographic location. This creates a new standard for culture and reading that never previously existed.

MATHIEU: Everybody can read this icon language. When we talk about "everybody" today, we tend to associate *them* with their cultural background and identity, but with this sign language we don't need to. It unites us as readers. Of course, there are people excluded from this language, people who aren't indoctrinated into the so-called modern world.

Then there is the question of standards. For example, there are many variations for the symbol "cup." There is a cup of water, a coffee cup, a tea mug, many which are culturally specific. Also, this is a book about the quotidian life of Mr. Black. Is it possible to go beyond basic descriptions to express philosophical thoughts and more in-depth ideas with this icon language?

MIAN MIAN: Yes, I have also thought about that. Can such simple icons express the uniqueness of your inner thoughts? As for in-depth ideas, I want to ask Xu Bing - Do you have icons for death, for literature, and for poetry? When you transform language into icons, where did you start and why?

XU BING: What you said is quite interesting. It touches the core of this issue. Do I have icons for death? Of course. In my book I use death icons in three different places. This icon has a skull and two bones underneath it. This symbol doesn't mean "death" exactly but instead, "poison" or "danger." Another time, Mr. Black saw a car accident on his way home and someone had died. This is presented with the contour line of a person lying on the ground. This means death that is related to crime or an accident. And finally when Mr. Black comforts his friend Mr. Green, who had just broke up with his girlfriend, telling him about the car accident saying "he was much luckier than the dead guy." Here we just use a single skull to represent death.

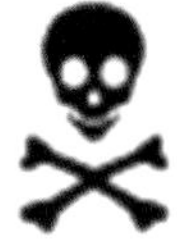

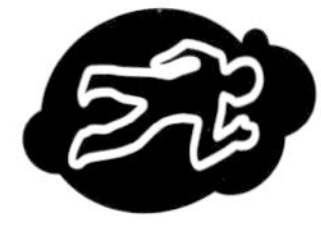

You ask if icons can write poems. I think we have to put literature aside first. When we create an icon language, we are looking for different symbols for one and the same thing. Based on this collective information, we abstract the most precise symbols for this item. What we look for is shared visual or physical experiences and convert them into the icon language. If such experiences can be converted into a symbol, its signifier is recognizable among people of different cultural backgrounds and then this symbol is universal.

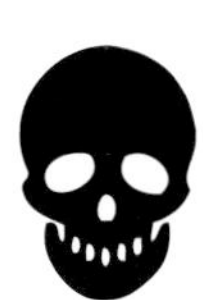

MIAN MIAN: The storyline in your book is simple enough to allow the icon language to fully express itself, but can the icon language also articulate our more abstract thoughts and reflections? In the world today when normal communication is difficult enough even with traditional language, will the icon language build up a bridge for communication or become a barrier?

XU BING: As a matter of fact, my book has a very simple way of expression. This icon language is actually very effective for expressing feeling, action, and imagination. It has some advantages over ordinary languages, for example, when it is used to express speed, inner emotions, and even mood. There are lots of symbols and visual information to choose from that can convey emotions.

MIAN MIAN: I'd love to try to write with icons.

XU BING: Surely you can. For example, when you want to tell your friend something that is difficult to say directly in words, use icons. The icon language helps you soothe the situation.

MIAN MIAN: Human communication is very difficult. Do you think that the icon language will help to build better understanding than traditional language?

XU BING: Actually, both languages have elements that lead to misunderstanding but in different ways. Many people doubt if the language in *Book From the Ground* is able to express delicate issues and human emotions. In fact, all languages are crude. We believe English and Chinese are good at expressing inner emotions and delicate issues but it is because we are used to these languages and the way they express feelings. When we use any given language for a period of time, both readers and writers learn to fill in the gaps between words and characters. For example, the Chinese word 杯子 "cup" are two characters that look like matchsticks. They look very basic, but since we use these two words everyday, they have become imbued with the meaning of "cup".

We think the language in *Book From the Ground* is crude because we have no relevant reading experience. We don't know how to react and fill in the gaps in order to enrich it. It is like sign language. It is hard for you to imagine that the deaf can express something profound, something sophisticated, and something delicate through their sign language. However, when we see deaf people chatting happily and excitedly in the subway, I believe that they do talk about things that are profound. This is the core of the language.

MATHIEU: The grandeur of *Book From the Sky* is that it contains masterly elements of Chinese traditional calligraphic arts. In comparison, *Book From the Ground* looks understated. Many viewers who were awed by *Book From the Sky* felt partially disappointed with *Book From the Ground*'s lack of "Chinese" elements. Are there any Chinese elements in *Book From the Ground*? Do we even need Chinese elements in the icon language? What is the future of the icon language?

XU BING: There is no calligraphy in *Book From the Ground*. I can think of two ways to deal with Chinese culture and calligraphy in my work. I can write oracle script in a beautiful way, like most calligraphers. Oracle script, or ancient Chinese script, will become a piece of artwork itself. This approach may look very Chinese, but I think it's quite meaningless. In fact, the profound connection between my icon language and Chinese culture is far deeper than just beautiful ancient scripts. The art of calligraphy has changed over time, as has the written language itself, from oracle script to seal characters, to cursive writing, and, eventually, to script that is hardly legible, as shown in *Book From the Sky*. I think the development of calligraphy depends on the development of language. It is a hard task for the calligraphers.

In a way, I think my *New English Calligraphy* series is more a work of contemporary calligraphy because it has to do with language itself. Its essential development is linked with the progress and reformation of language.

What represents contemporary calligraphy? I think that it is this sign language. If you look, you will find an internal connection with Chinese culture.

MATHIEU: As a Westerner, I can understand the background of your book, but I also think this book could have only been made by a Chinese person. It is not only directly related to ancient Chinese script but also Chinese ideograms in general, which are based on visual communication as opposed to languages for which a set alphabet is the foundation. From my perspective, it seems that your cultural background has certainly made you more sensitive to the language of signs around us.

AUDIENCE: How did you decide the size of the signs? Apparently, the signs in this book are bigger than an ordinary font. Line spacing is also looser than ordinary books as well. Some signs are simple, some are relatively complicated, but both are the same size. Why not shrink the size of the simple signs a bit? Also, the color of the signs: Why didn't you abstract the sign for hair dryer for instance, directly into black-and-white instead of using a colored sign?

XU BING: Very good questions! What we are doing here is dealing with our visual experience. If we replace the signs with a font, we have to use a very big size as do antique books from the Song dynasty. Why do books from the Song dynasty have such big fonts? It is because we are not familiar with this language. If we look at books today, we find that the fonts are getting smaller and smaller. It can be so small that we don't even see the details of each character but only get a glimps of their outer contour. We are still not familiar with the icon language so we can't depend on the contour of the signs yet. So just as in antique books, we need the icons to be big. We have actually done some adjustments to character sizes. For example, in the book the size of a person is similar to the size of a house. It is not a map. They are icons. The size of characters rest with their needs. Sometimes we decided on the size from an aesthetic perspective.

AUDIENCE: The pair of large eyes is outlined with black. Why?

XU BING: Many of the signs were collected from newspapers and collaged together to form the story. We had kept this format in the beginning because we wanted to reveal the process of collecting icons. As the story progresses the staring eyes become standardized into a black-and-white icon. That's how the idea was formed.

MATHIEU: *Book From the Ground* reverts and subverts our traditional perception of culture. It provides an equal standard for everybody. The limitation of this "everybody" rests only on life experience, not on cultural background or educational level. While Xu Bing's *Book From the Ground* confounds our reading comprehension habits, it offers us another kind of reading-aloud experience.

We now welcome Ella from the audience to read a chapter of *Book From the Ground*. Ella is 12 years old, lives in Shanghai, and speaks English, Swedish, and Chinese. She will read this book in English.

ELLA: Chapter One. Once upon a time, there was a little black dot. Going closer, you will see that is the Earth. Zooming closer to the Earth, you will see a city. In the city, there was a house. Outside the house there was a tree. On the tree, there was a bird singing. Mr. Black was sleeping in his bed. His alarm clock suddenly rang. The bird was singing. After five minutes, the alarm clock still rang, but the bird was not singing any more and flew away. The alarm clock rang again. This time, Mr. Black heard it. He woke up and turned off the alarm clock. He looked outside and it was raining. He felt pretty upset, so he went back to sleep again. After five minutes, the alarm clock rang again. This time, he woke up. He knew that he was late, but he still wanted to sleep. His cat was staring at him and jumped onto his bed. Mr. Black was surprised. So he got up and went to the bathroom. He sat on the toilet and tried to get something done. He couldn't get it done, and he wondered if there was something wrong with his digestive system. So he stayed on the toilet and looked at his cell phone. He looked at Twitter, Google Plus, Wi-Fi, and Facebook. It was coming down, it was coming down! Finally, it all came down! So he wiped his butt and flushed it. Then he took a shower, dried his hair and shaved himself. Then he brushed his teeth. Later he got out of the bathroom and entered the changing room. He put on some underwear, T-shirts, some pants and a shirt, a pair of socks, and shoes. He looked into the mirror and thought he didn't look so good. So he changed his shirt to a green one and then to blue and then to red. He still thought it was bad. He thought about what a woman would think. So he chose a white shirt and a tie. And he thought now he looked perfect.

MATHIEU: We have time for one last question.

AUDIENCE: Thank you for bringing us a new language, Mr. Xu. Yesterday, I took my child to your exhibition. He has already finished reading your book. Today, when I checked his homework, I was shocked to see he was scribbling down characters from *Book From the Ground* in his exercise book. He actually completed his homework with your icon language! It shows your experiment is successful. We adults tend to use existing viewpoints to judge things, but kids are different.

XU BING: We have too many pre-existing cultural perceptions and concepts. (To child) In the eyes of your father, these symbols may not be our culture. The generation of your father is not as sensitive to symbols as yours is. This is the culture! A universal language that surpasses the limitation of the written word has been born!

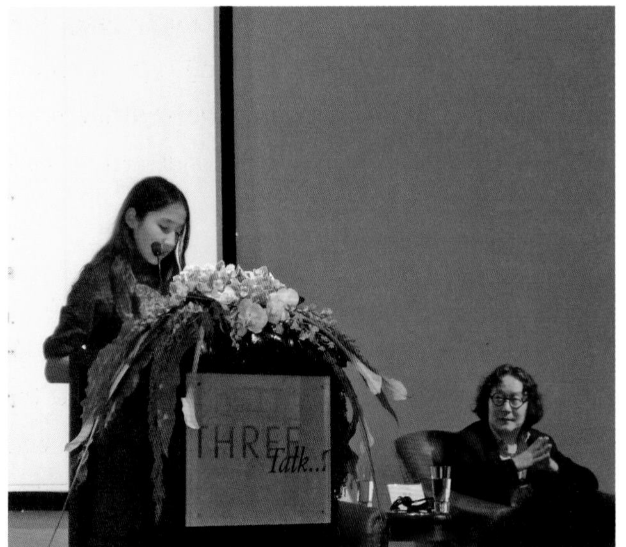

Ella Wang Olsson reads a passage from *From Point to Point*
April 22, 2012

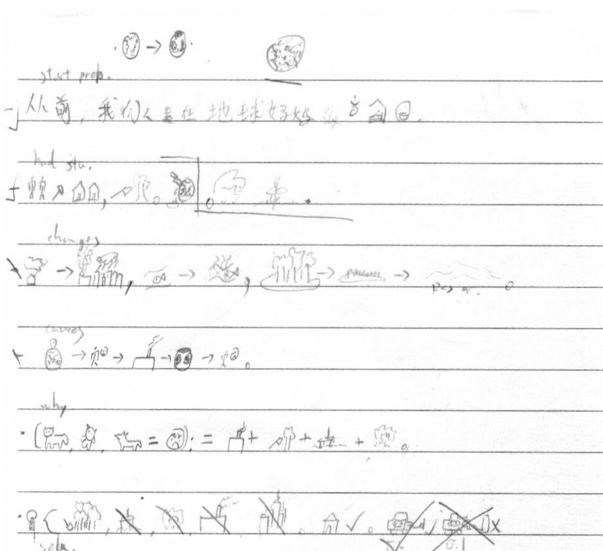

School homework written with Xu Bing's icon language.

1. Link, Perry.'Whose Assumptions Does Xu Bing Upset, and Why? in *Persistence/Transformation*, USA: Princeton University Press, 2006 p.49.

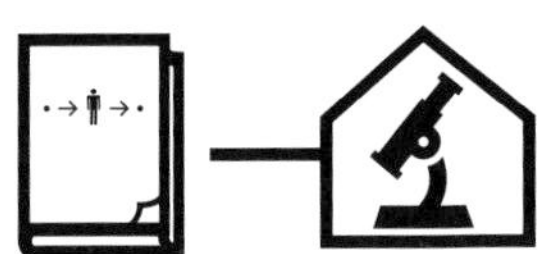

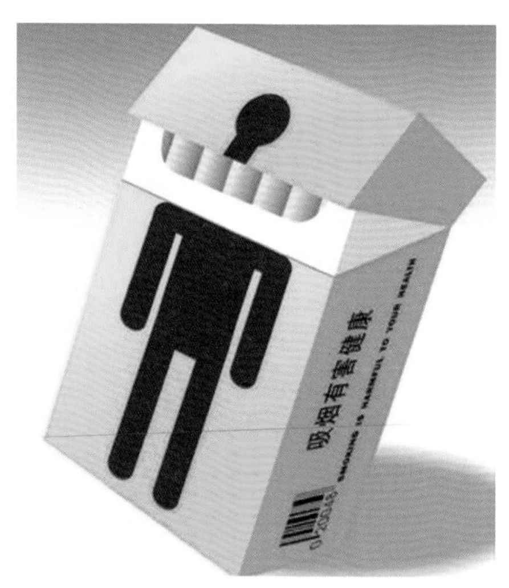
吸烟有害健康
SMOKING IS HARMFUL TO YOUR HEALTH

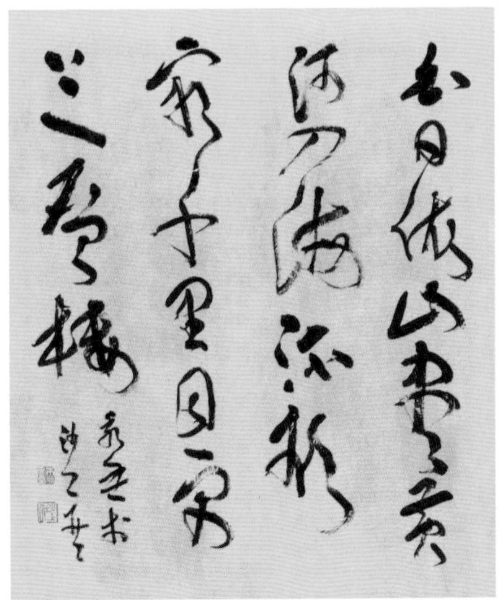

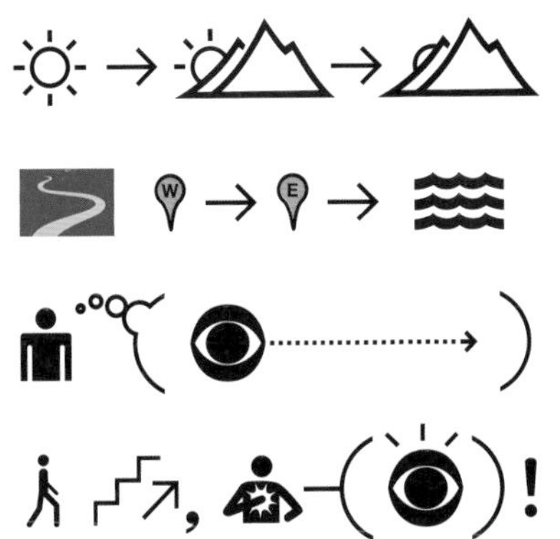

W
E

PERSONAL AD

I AM LOOKING FOR THAT SPECIAL GUY TO BE IN MY LIFE. HE NEEDS TO BE OUTGOING. HE ALSO HAS TO LIKE TO HAVE FUN AND PARTY AND OCCASSIONALLY GO OUT TO THE BARS. HE HAS TO ALSO BE ABLE TO JUST STAY AT HOME ONE NIGHT AND CUDDLE AND WATCH A MOVIE.

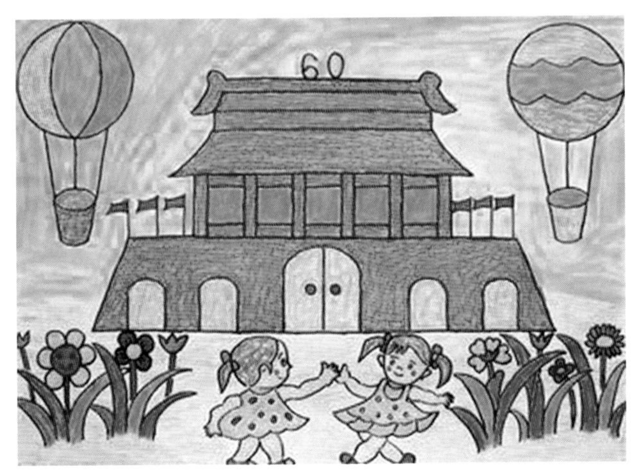
60

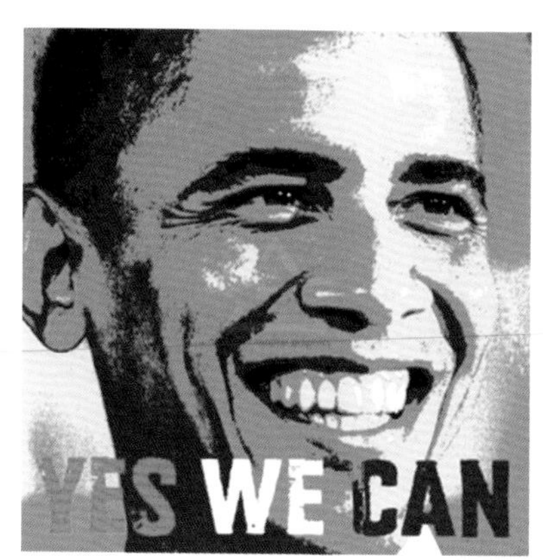
YES WE CAN

✓,

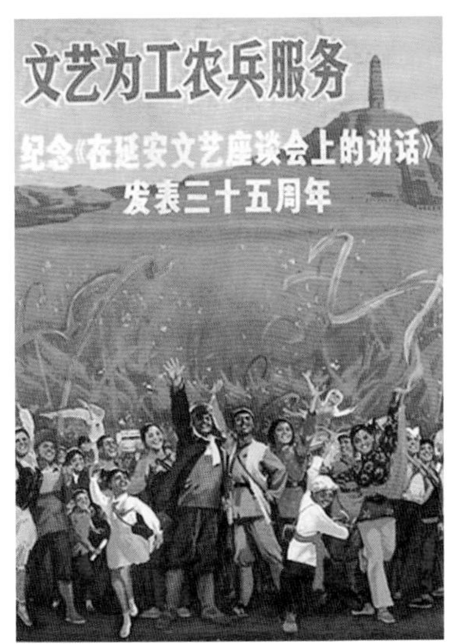
文艺为工农兵服务
纪念《在延安文艺座谈会上的讲话》
发表三十五周年

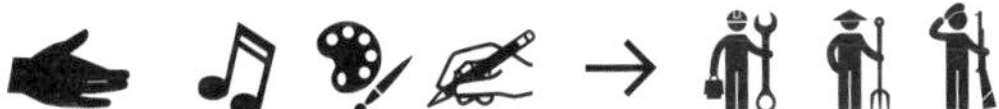

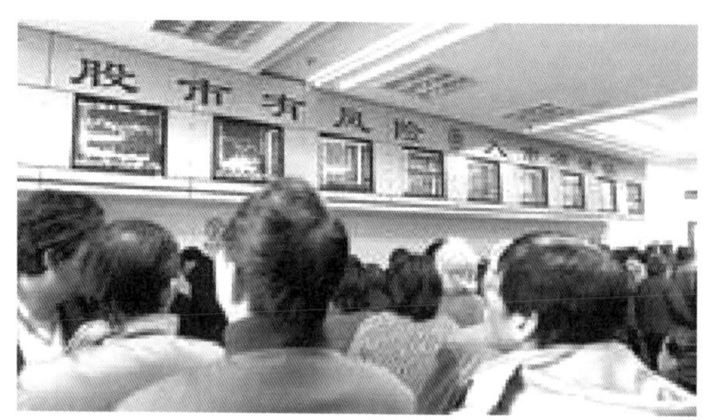
股市有风险

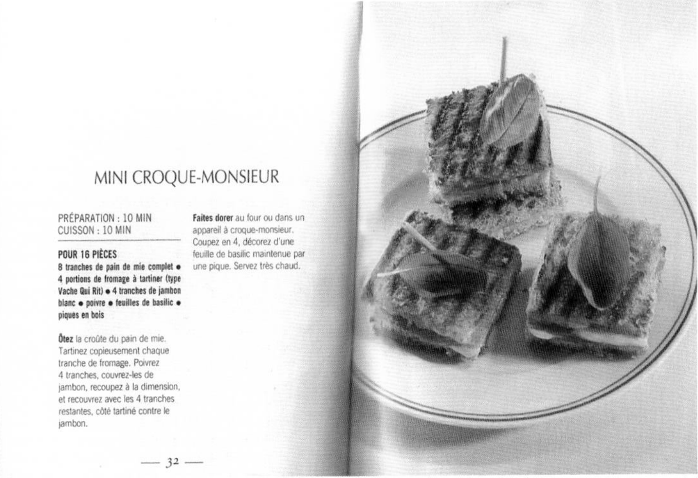

MINI CROQUE-MONSIEUR

PRÉPARATION : 10 MIN
CUISSON : 10 MIN

POUR 16 PIÈCES
8 tranches de pain de mie complet • 4 portions de fromage à tartiner (type Vache Qui Rit) • 4 tranches de jambon blanc • poivre • feuilles de basilic • piques en bois

Ôtez la croûte du pain de mie. Tartinez copieusement chaque tranche de fromage. Poivrez 4 tranches, couvrez-les de jambon, recoupez à la dimension, et recouvrez avec les 4 tranches restantes, côté tartiné contre le jambon.

Faites dorer au four ou dans un appareil à croque-monsieur. Coupez en 4, décorez d'une feuille de basilic maintenue par une pique. Servez très chaud.

— 32 —

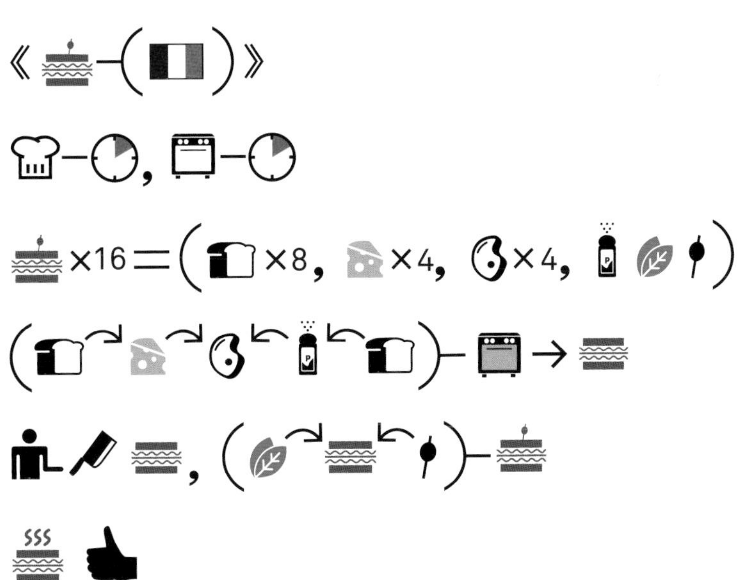

XU BING'S BIO

Xu Bing traces his family roots to Wenling, Zhejiang province. He was born in Chongqing, China in 1955 and grew up in Beijing. In 1977, he entered the printmaking department of the Central Academy of Fine Arts, Beijing, where completed his bachelor's degree in 1981 and stayed on as an instructor, earning his MFA in 1987. In 1990 he visited the United States of America as an invited honored artist and stayed for more than a decade. Xu Bing returned to China in 2007 and currently serves as the Vice President of the Central Academy of Fine Arts. He is also professor, and a tutor for Ph. D. students.

Solo exhibitions of his work have been held at the Arthur M. Sackler Gallery, Washington DC; the New Museum of Contemporary Art, New York; the Joan Miro Foundation, Barcelona, Spain; National Gallery of Prague; and the Spencer Museum of Art, Lawrence, Kansas, among other major institutions. Additionally, Xu Bing has shown at the 45th and 51st Venice Biennales; the Biennale of Sydney; and the Johannesburg Biennale among other international exhibitions.

Over the years, Xu Bing's work has appeared in high-school and college textbooks around the world including Abram's, *Art Past Art Present*; Gardner's *Art Through the Ages*; Greg Clunas's *Chinese Art*, a volume in the *Oxford History of Art* series; Jane Farver's, *Global Conceptualism: Points of Origin 1950s –1980s* and *Art Worlds in Dialogue*. In 2006, the Princeton University Press published *Persistence/Transformation: Text as Image in the Art of Xu Bing* a multidisciplinary study of Xu Bing's landmark work *Book From the Sky*. In 2008, professor Robert Harrist, chair of Chinese Art at Columbia University, New York, began teaching a graduate seminar entitled "The Art of Xu Bing." London bookseller Bernard Quaritch published *Tianshu: Passages in the Making of a Book,* a monographic study of *Book From the Sky*. Research on Xu Bing's works also include *Xu Bing and Chinese Contemporary Art* edited by Cao Xingyuan, (New York University Press), *Tobacco Project* written by John B. Ravenal, etc. (Virginia University Press)

In 1989, Xu Bing was honored with the Huo Yingdong Education Foundation Award from the China National Education Association for his contribution to art education. In 1999, Xu Bing was the recipient of a MacArthur Fellowship in recognition of his "capacity to contribute importantly to society, particularly in printmaking and calligraphy." In 2003 Xu Bing was awarded the Fukuoka Asian Culture Prize; and in 2004 he won the first Wales International Visual Art Prize, Artes Mundi. In 2006, the Southern Graphics Council awarded Xu Bing their lifetime achievement award in recognition of the fact that his "use of text, language, and books has impacted the dialogue of the print and art worlds in significant ways." Xu was awarded Doctor of Humane Letters by Columbia University in 2010.

MATHIEU BORYSEVICZ is an artist, writer, and curator based in Shanghai whose involvement with the contemporary culture of China dates back to 1994. His writings have appeared in *ARTFORUM, Art in America, ArtReview, tema celeste, LEAP*, and other publications. His essays are featured in *Chinese Art at the End of the Millennium*, many monographs, and exhibition catalogs. His book, *Learning from Hangzhou*, a semiotic analysis of urbanization, was chosen by the New York Times as one of the "*Best Architectural Books of 2009*" and was given the prestigious DAM (Deutsches Architekturmuseum) Book Commendation in Frankfurt. He is now the founder and director of MABSOCIETY, a curatorial studio based in Shanghai.

HAYTHAM NAWAR is an artist, designer, and researcher. He currently lives and works in Egypt and Switzerland. He is a Ph.D. Candidate at the Planetary Collegium, Centre for Advanced Inquiry in Integrative Arts, School of Art and Media – Faculty of Arts, University of Plymouth in England.

KAIMEI OLSSON WANG Kaimei Olsson Wang is a former Nordic correspondent for Xinhua News Agency in Sweden. She holds a MA in Contemporary Art from the Sotheby's Institute of Art and is currently an independent art critic and frequent contributor to some of the most influential magazines on Chinese contemporary art such as *Art China, Randian, and ART FORUM*.

MIAN MIAN is a Shanghai based writer and former nightlife promoter. *Candy*, her first novel, officially banned in China, became an underground bestseller. *Candy* was published in 15 languages worldwide. Her second novel *Panda Sex* was published in France, Germany, and Poland. The influence of Mian Mian's authentic, honest portrayal of the new future of Shanghai has made her into a cultural icon for the generation of Chinese youth born in the 1970s and 80s.

FROM POINT TO POINT, PAGES 1-112 ENGLISH TRANSLATION

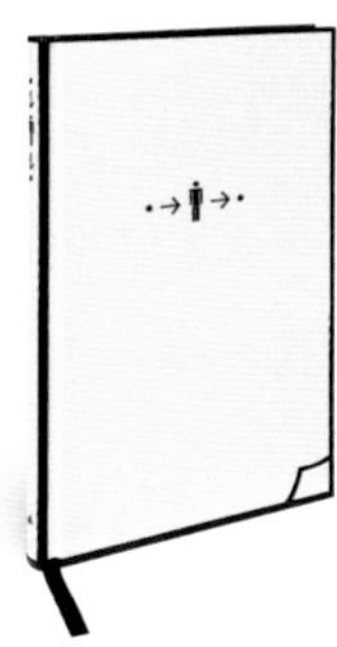

\- 1 -

7:00 AM

A black dot, magnified until we see that it is the planet earth. On planet earth we zoom into a location, a city. In the city is a house with a tree in the front yard. In the tree a little bird is singing: DO-MI-RE-MI. The melody enters the dreams of Mr. Black. It's 7:00 AM and the alarm clock goes off. As the alarm clock rings the little bird sings a duet with it. Five minutes later the alarm is still ringing, but the bird stops singing and flies away.

\- 2 -

Mr. Black finally hears the alarm and opens his eyes. He turns off the alarm and looks out the window to see that it's a rainy day. Depressed, he closes his eyes again and falls back asleep.

The cat has been watching him and jumps on to Mr. Black's bed. Mr. Black unwillingly sits up and the cat scampers off.

Mr. Black gets up, shuffles over to the bathroom and sits on the toilet. He sits on the toilet for a long time. "En...er...ugh...en..." as much as he tries nothing comes out. "What's wrong down there?" He ponders. Still waiting on the toilet, he takes out his smartphone and proceeds to go online. He checks his Twitter, Google, rss, and Facebook. Suddenly, "Ah!" He feels something, he pushes hard and finally, a poop is released. He lets out a long breath of satisfaction! Finishing up with the toilet paper, he has a look at his creation and then flushes. He then proceeds to take a shower, blow-dry his hair, shave, and brush his teeth. Then he walks out of the bathroom.

In his warddrobe, Mr. Black puts on underwear, an undershirt, pants, a shirt,

\- 3 -

socks, and his shoes. He looks in the mirror but isn't satisfied. The white shirt just isn't right, so he changes into a green one. The green doesn't seem to work so he changes into a blue one. Wrong again, so he changes into a pink one, which is even worse. Suddenly he recalls a certain girl and realizes that the white shirt is the best one after all. Very satisfied he puts on a tie and quickly leaves his closet.

Next, he hurriedly enters his kitchen and turns on the coffee maker. It percolates; he adds a sugar cube, stirs; the coffee is ready. Next he turns on the gas range, takes out a frying pan and makes bacon and eggs. While he toasts some bread on the frying pan he drinks his coffee.

Then he turns on the radio and listens to the weather report: "Today's weather: rain turning to scattered clouds and showers, during which the temperature will drop..." "I should bring an umbrella." Mr. Black thinks.

He takes another sip of coffee and hears someone knocking at the door. "Who could it be?", He ponders and heads to the door.

\- 4 -

Opening the door he finds an Amazon deliveryman. The book he ordered has finally arrived. He takes the box, closes the door, and begins to open the package. He takes out the book and starts to read. He reads while he drinks his coffee, getting more and more absorbed.

Suddenly he smells something burning. He sees black smoke coming from the frying pan. "Oh no! the eggs are burning" He ingeniously pours his coffee into the frying pan. Soaked with coffee, his breakfast is impossible to eat. What a shame. He throws the burnt meal in the trash. Mr. Black is so hungry that his stomach growls. He looks for something in the fridge. There's some beer, soda, ketchup... "Ah!" He finally finds a carton of milk, takes it out and drinks it, but he's still hungry. Then he finds a bag of popcorn. He puts the popcorn in the microwave and sets the time and temperature. The sound of popping emanates from the microwave.

\- 5 -

The bag grows until the timer stops. He pours the steaming popcorn into a bowl. It smells tasty! He starts to eat but the popcorn has gotten stuck in his teeth. He rushes to the bathroom, takes out some floss, and begins flossing. Up, down, right, left until the kernel slowly comes out. Then he pops a multi-vitamin and flushes it down with a glass of water.

The cat stares at him longingly. "Oops!" He realizes that he still hasn't fed the cat. Mr. Black fills a bowl with cat food and the cat excitedly rushes over to eat...

Mr. Black puts his wallet and ID into his briefcase.

He remembers that the weather report has called for rain, so he grabs an umbrella, puts a hat in his bag, and then leaves in a hurry.

- 6 -

Wait! Did he bring his keys? He looks all over and finally finds his keys. He leaves the house and locks the front door.

- 7 -

8:00 AM

Mr. Black has to go all the way from the west side of the city to the east side. He ponders whether to take the subway or the bus. Using his smart phone he consults the traffic report, which indicates heavy traffic. It looks like the bus won't work, so he decides to take the subway. He goes down into the passageway and sees that the subway station is packed with people.

He lines up at the ticket vending machine to buy a ticket. The line is very long. He looks at this watch and worries that he is going to be late. He begins to sweat with anxiety. Five minutes pass by. The line slowly moves forward. He worries "If I'm late, I am going get chewed out by the boss again, and there's so much to do today." The line is moving so slowly that Mr. Black starts to go crazy.

- 8 -

Mr. Black anxiously waits in line, moving forward slowly, step by step. Fifteen minutes have already elapsed but there are still people in front of him. He becomes more and more anxious. Finally it's his turn. He prompts the vending machine, inserts his money, and the ticket is ejected. He lets out a deep sigh of relief then runs, swipes himself into the station, and takes the escalator down to the platform. The doors of the subway car are just about to close but Mr. Black manages to slips on in. Lucky! Leaning against the door of the car, he lets out a breath and suddenly sees a sign on the door: "Caution, Do Not Lean on Doors." So he moves into the center of the car and grabs the strap.

He sees that he'll have to switch to the blue line after three stops. The car is crowded and passengers on both sides of Mr. Black are squishing him with their backpacks. The train approaches the next station and Mr. Black sees an empty seat. He moves towards the seat, but a girl moving faster has already taken it.

- 9 -

There's only one stop left before the transfer station when Mr. Black starts to notice the unpleasant smells of body odor and farts. He thinks he should be wearing a gas mask. There should really be a sign prohibiting flatulence. Mr. Black is disgusted. Suddenly somebody steps on his foot with a high-healed shoe. He starts to go mad.

The train arrives at the transfer station. He exits along with a lot of passengers. Entering the the next car, he spots an empty seat and runs over to sit down. He is elated.

But having only sat for a short time, someone taps him on the shoulder and points out that he is sitting in a space reserved for the elderly, disabled, and pregnant. Mr. Black sees a pregnant woman standing in front of him and has no choice but to get up and give his seat to her. The train arrives finally at Mr. Black's station and he quickly exits. He takes the elevator out of the station and quickly runs towards his office.

When he gets to the office entrance it is already 8:45. He pulls out his access card, swipes it, and runs through.

- 10 -

Mr. Black arrives at the elevator and pushes the up button. After five minutes the elevator still hasn't arrived so he impatiently pushes the button over and over again. Finally it arrives. He pours in along with a herd of people. He pushes the eighty-ninth floor button, then the close-door button. The elevator reaches the second floor and stops. Mr. Black is angry. "The second floor! Why not take the stairs!?", He fumes at the lazy passenger. The elevator continues on its way up, past the third floor, but then stops again at the fourth floor, and then at the fifth floor. As it stops at every floor Mr. Black gets progressively angrier but there is nothing he can do. When the elevator arrives at the eighty-seventh floor a fat guy enters and an alarm goes off signaling the elevator's maximum weight has been exceeded. Mr. Black presses the door-close button over and over again, but the elevator announces, "Ten persons maximum, the weight has been exceeded, operation suspended." Mr. Black worries. "Are we in danger?" Looking at the fat man, Mr. Black thinks, "This one guy is as heavy as three normal people. He looks just like the Michelin Man." Mr. Black tries to get the fat man off, but he is not willing to leave. Mr. Black starts to steam with anger.

- 11 -

Another five-minute delay! Mr. Black jumps off the elevator and takes the stairs. Passing the eighty-eighth floor, he finally arrives at the eighty-ninth. He turns a few corners and runs furiously to his office. He is so exhausted that his forehead is covered in sweat. He drinks a few sips at the water-cooler and continues running, swipes his card at the door, enters, and keeps on running. His co-workers call out their greetings. "Hi!" He responds as he runs. Finally he arrives at his office and sits down at his desk. He looks at his watch, nine on-the-dot. He's not late! He let's out a long breath. Even though he is gasping for breath, and his back is covered in sweat, he has victoriously arrived on time.

- 13 -

9:00 AM

Mr. Black hits the power button on his computer, the computer slowly, but finally, starts up. First Windows loads, then the volume control, wifi, Bluetooth, MSN, Skype, Yahoo!, AIM, and Internet Explorer all appear on the screen.

Mr. Black looks around to make sure that his boss didn't see him coming in late. He feels a little deviant. He loads his email and finds 25 new messages! Mr. Black clicks to view his new emails...

- 14 -

First he reads the email from Mr. Red: "Hey, want to meet for coffee? I need to talk to you. Does 10 AM work for you? ... Mr. Red"

Mr. Black replied: "Hey! 10 AM works for me! ... Mr. Black"

Mr. Black then opens an email from Mr. Orange: "I'm sick. A while ago, I caught tuberculosis from Mr. Gray. I am getting the chills. Can you send me a bowl of noodles? I'd be very grateful. I am in the hospital.

\- 15 -

"My dear," Mr. Black reflects, "He's in the hospital!"

Mr. Black: "Unfortunately, I am at work now and there's no way I can leave but I'll bring you a bowl of noodles at 8PM tonight, is that okay? Make sure you drink a lot of fluids! ...Mr. Black"

Mr. Black then reads an email from his friends, Mr. and Mrs. Line: "Hello. We just had a baby! Please look at the attached photos! ... The Line Family"

Mr. Black clicks on the attachment, and is shocked! He thinks the baby resembles an alien! But he kindly keeps his opinion to himself and replies: "He's so cute, congratulations! ... Mr. Black" ... "Suckers", he thinks.

\- 16 -

Mr. Black then opens an email from Mr. Green: "I'm heartbroken, my girlfriend broke up with me. She left me for another man. I cant stop thinking about them kissing and sleeping with one another. It's torturing me! Do you have time tonight around 9PM for a beer? ... Mr. Green"

Mr. Black is angry, "That girl is no good."

Mr. Black replies: "9PM works for me, Don't feel bad! .... Mr. Black"

\- 17 -

Mr. Black then reads the email from Mr. Purple and his girlfriend: "You are invited to our wedding ceremony on the 24th of this month at the Church, Love, ... Soon-to-be Mr. and Mrs. Purple"

Mr. Black updates his calendar with the event.

Mr. Black thinks about how Mr. Purple bought his girlfriend's love with, first a diamond ring, then a new BMW, and finally a house.

Mr. Black reads the next email from Mr. White: "I'm having a party to celebrate my birthday!!! I'm turning 30, so excited!! ... Mr. White"

Mr. Black wonders, "I need to get him a present, but what?"

\- 18 -

Mr. Brown's email: "What's up, I am moving to a new apartment building. The new building doesn't allow dogs so I was thinking of giving my dog to you. He's really terrific. Do you like dogs? ...Mr. Brown and his dog"

Mr. Black replies: "Hi, I already have a cat, which would most definitely fight with the dog. I remember that Miss Pink likes dogs; I will forward her your email. Fingers Crossed! ... Mr. Black"

Mr. Black then reads an email from Mr. Blue: "Hey, do you want to go hiking in the mountains with me?

\- 19 -

C'mon! .... Mr. Blue"

Mr. Black replies: "Hey man, I like hiking, but not on crazy, mountainous slopes. Let's go fishing instead! I have all the fishing equipment plus we can eat the fish! ... Mr. Black"

Mr. Black reads an email from the blood bank: "We hope that you can participate in our annual blood drive, each drop of blood is equivalent to a drop of love!"

Mr. Black thinks about the scary prospect of giving blood — the needles and pain, and then shamefully deletes the email.

\- 20 -

Mr. Black reads an email from Amazon: "Books at 30% off! Click to purchase"

"I hate junk mail," he thinks, as he deletes the advertisement.

It's 9:30AM, "Time to look at the news" Mr. Black reminds himself. He signs on to the CNN website and views the news:

Volcano erupts in Central Asia killing 30; 100 houses on fire. (Sad)

Earthquake in the Middle East! 2000 deaths. (Disillusioned)

A Flood in Mexico! Houses destroyed! Cars swept away! More than 200 deaths!

Tsunami in Japan caused by an earthquake destroys a nuclear plant leading to nuclear leakage!!! (Oh No!)

\- 21 -

A Tornado in Texas! Overturned cars! Tumbling houses! 13 deaths. (Bewildered)

America and Israel sign an agreement.

A regional war in Northern Africa leaves 3000 dead.

City News: Drinking while driving cases lead to 8 more arrests as the trend rises in recent weeks! (Surprised)

Economic News: Stock prices turn the bull into a bear market, which means it is time to save as oil prices soar and housing prices decline. (Angry)

Medical Alert: Keep vigil as the number of Bird Flu infections has increased sharply. (Worried)

Movie Schedule: The Silence of the Lambs: (9:00PM, 11:00PM, 11:50PM)

Saw: (10:00PM, 10:30PM)

\- 22 -

Movie Schedule (cont'd): Transformers: (3:00PM, 4:30PM, 9:20PM, 10:30PM, 11:50PM)

Avatar: (1:50PM, 2:30PM, 3:50PM, 10:00PM, 10:30PM)

\- 23 -

10:00 AM

Mr. Black glances at the clock, it's 10 AM, and he doesn't feel much like working. It's time for a coffee break. He puts the computer on sleep mode and goes downstairs to the Starbucks where he meets Mr. Red.

Mr. Red and Mr. Black start discussing the weather: "It was raining, then it looked like it was going to clear up, but it started raining again." Both sigh disappointedly.

Mr. Black orders: "A cup of coffee & a croissant."

Mr. Red orders: "A cup of green tea & an apple."

\- 24 -

Mr. Red and Mr. Black strike up a conversation over their refreshments.

Mr. Red: "I loved that World Cup match between Brazil and Portugal."

Mr. Black: "Yeah, did you see that play by Portugal! They played so well."

Mr. Red: "Hey, you know I'm looking for a house."

Mr. Black: "I saw online that housing prices are falling. But I also saw that gas prices are rising!"

Mr. Red: "Yeah it just keeps on going up." Mr. Red thinks about how much money it costs to drive his little Toyota and gets angry.

Mr. Black: "The market is always changing."

Mr. Red: "Yeah, the US dollar is going up against the Euro."

- 25 -

Mr. Red and Mr. Black eventually run out of conversation and part ways. Mr. Red goes downstairs, while Mr. Black goes up.

10:45AM, Mr. Black goes back up the stairs but first makes a detour to the restroom because he needs to pee. He sees the urinal, unzips his pants, and pees...

Mr. Black leaves the bathroom whistling. He spots a woman coming towards him. He stops to take a closer look. "What a sexy babe", he thinks.

10:55AM, Mr. Black steps on a wet piece of gum that sticks to his shoe! "Damn", He thinks, "Gum is supposed to be disposed of in the wrapping paper!" He uses some paper to remove the gum and throws it in the trash. He then proceeds to his desk, and sits down.

- 27 -

11:00 AM

Mr. Black looks around and doesn't see his boss anywhere. He chuckles to himself and logs onto an online dating website.

He browses through many different women's photos...

He finally settles on a profile: She's 26 years old, "Perfect", he thinks.

A Doctor with blue eyes, brown hair, "She's smart too", he thinks approvingly.

Hobbies: Shopping (especially for luxurious items) "Whoa", He's overwhelmed.

- 28 -

He looks at another profile: 26 years old. (Happy)

She's a School Teacher with Blue Eyes and Black Hair. (Curious)

She's a Scorpio. (Oh No...)

Hobbies: Taking care of children. (Not exactly what I'm looking for)

He looks at another profile: 26 years old. (Happy)

A P.h.D. Student. (Alright!)

She has blue eyes and orange hair. (Perfect!)

But her hobby is to write novels. (No Thanks)

- 29 -

He looks at yet another profile: She is 26 years old. (Happy)

A Hairdresser. (Skeptical)

Brown Eyes and Red Hair. (Yes, Love that!)

Hobbies: Roller skating, ice skating, biking, swimming, theater, photography... (Yes, Jackpot. He has found his match!)

Mr. Black's heart skips a beat. He thinks of all the activities she likes. His heart is pounding.

He clicks on the attachments to view more photos of her. Pretty!, He gets more and more excited.

He then looks at her height, measurements, and her blood type, all of which are perfect!

He then clicks on to a live chat with the girl.

- 30 -

Mr. Black: "Hi There!"

Miss Blue: "Hi, Who's that?"

Mr. Black: "I'm Mr. Black. I'm 28 years old, my blood type is A, I'm tall, and a Libra". He's ashamed that he's only an office employee, so he says: "I'm the big boss of the office!" And even though Mr. Black doesn't have a car or make a lot of money he says: "I'm rolling in the dough! I saw the hobbies you mentioned in your profile, do you also like fishing by any chance?"

Miss Blue: "Huh, fishing? No, not really!"

Mr. Black: "I love to go camping and fish, then cook the fish over the camp fire."

Miss Blue: "I find baiting fish hooks disgusting, but I love eating fish, especially sushi."

- 31 -

Mr. Black: "So, you like eating fish and what else?"

Miss Blue: "I love music!"

Mr. Black: "Awesome! I love music, especially classical music!"

Miss Blue: "Oh, I'm not into classical music. I like Rock n' Roll."

Mr. Black's heart weakens thinking that Miss Blue is a crazy party lady.

But then he remembers that Michael Jackson and John Lennon are alright, which helps to rekindle his attraction to Miss Blue.

Mr. Black: "I like Rock 'N' Roll too! Would you like to go somewhere where we could have a few drinks and listen to music?"

Miss Blue: "Sure, how about tonight at 7?"

- 32 -

Mr. Black's heart is thumping "Tonight at 7 is super! Can I have your cell number?"

Miss Blue: Sure

Mr. Black: "My mobile phone number is 123-456-7890, and my home phone number is 765-4321"

Miss Blue: "My mobile phone number is 098-765-4321."

Mr. Black: "My AIM number is 89429 and my MSN number is ..."

Miss Blue: "Okay, enough."

Mr. Black: "Hahaha, I will call you!"

Miss Blue: "Okay, bye."

Mister Black: "Great, Yeah!"

- 33 -

12:00 PM

"It's lunchtime", Mr. Black thinks, then telephones Mr. Gray.

Mr. Black: "Hey! Want to go out for lunch?"

Mr. Gray: "Sorry, I have so much work, I can't leave my desk."

Mr. Gray hangs up then Mr. Black calls Mr. Blue.

Mr. Black: "Hey Mr. Blue, want to get lunch?"

Mr. Blue: "Sure, How about Domino's? or KFC? Or McDonald's?

- 34 -

Or we could get some noodles? Some sushi? Or how about a steak?"

Mr. Black: "I'm leaning towards either McDonald's or a bowl of noodles?"

Mr. Blue: "McDonald's it is, let's meet in the elevator in 15 minutes?"

"Sounds good", says Mr. Black as he hangs up.

Fifteen minutes later, Mr. Black and Mr. Blue meet in the elevator and go out to McDonald's.

At McDonalds they ponder over the menu:

Hamburger, Big Mac, Quarter Pounder, Beef, Chicken, Fish, a Vegetarian option.

Large, Medium, and Small Fries; Coke, Sprite, orange, and grape juice.

\- 35 -

As they stride over to the counter Mr. Black wonders, "Should I get a Hamburger or a Big Mac? ... or a Cheese Burger?".

Mr. Black: "I'd like a Big Mac, with a large fries, and a large coke."

Mr. Blue: "I'd like a fish burger, with a small orange juice, no fries."

Mr. Black is shocked, "Isn't fish toxic because of all the nuclear waste! You should be careful!!! Fish isn't such a good idea!"

"But I love all kinds of seafood. It's okay, beef is injected with hormones anyway so it's equally unhealthy!" responds Mr. Blue.

Mr. Blue and Mr. Black examine the menu's ingredients for levels of hormones and additives in the beef, fish, chicken, the vegetarian option, and drinks.

\- 36 -

"The vegetarian option is probably the best!" concludes Mr. Blue. Mr. Black agrees "I will also get the vegetarian option instead of the Big Mac."

The cashier asks, "Is that all? That'll be 2 dollars for the Vegetarian Sandwich with fries and drink and 1 dollar for the Fish Burger and orange juice."

Mr. Black and Mr. Blue pay the cashier, and he places their order.

They proceed to an empty table and start a conversation while waiting for their food.

\- 37 -

Once their food arrives Mr. Blue inquires, "How's the vegetarian option?"

"I don't like fast food anymore! Or fish, I only like home cooked meals and hotpot!" replies Mr. Black

Mr. Blue: "Spicy hotpot is so good, I really like spicy food! I love hotpot with all kinds of seafood and vegetables."

I like my hotpot with all kinds of meat, snail, rabbit, eel and even raccoon." Mr. Black retorts.

\- 38 -

Mr. Black wants to have a smoke but he sees that McDonalds doesn't allow smoking. So he says "I'm going out for a smoke."

Everywhere he turns, Mr. Black sees non-smoking signs, which makes him feel embarrassed but more anxious for that cigarette.

He goes downstairs... but finds the same no smoking signs as upstairs. He becomes so frustrated that he can't smoke anywhere indoors that he decides to go on the street. He goes outside, looks around and lights up a cigarette. He can feel the relief of smoke in his lungs, but then it starts to rain!

He grows worried that the rain will put out his cigarette, so he hurries back into McDonald's again.

\- 39 -

Mr. Black returns and tells Mr. Blue about his adventure "There were no smoking signs everywhere so I went out onto the street until it started raining..."

"And all that for blackened lungs," laughed Mr. Blue

After lunch the two part and Mr. Black remembers that he has to buy a gift for his friend and doubles back.

Meanwhile the weather has cleared and the sun begins to shine.

\- 41 -

1:00 PM

Back on the street, Mr. Black pauses to think about what he should give Mr. White for his 30th birthday as well as a wedding gift for Mr. and Mrs. Purple.

Mr. Black sees a Chanel store, but thinks it's too pricey, so he keeps walking until he sees a bookstore. "A book is always a good present" he thinks to himself.

He walks into the bookstore and looks around. He flips through a romance novel but it's too tragic so he picks up an action packed detective story.

\- 42 -

The violent book excites him but he finally settles on a travel guide, which he thinks will help with a newly wed couple's honeymoon travel plans. He gives Mr. and Mrs. Purple a call and asks "Where are you guys planning on travelling for your honeymoon?" "I'm thinking of going to New York, but Mrs. Purple wants to go to Paris", replies Mr. Purple.

After hanging up, Mr. Black browses through several travel guides. He finds guides for Australia, Japan, India, Canada, Egypt,... and finally the USA.

The guidebook covers Capitol Hill, Disney, Pop Culture, Hollywood, the Statue of Liberty, and the Twin Towers. "Yikes!" Mr. Black immediately recalls the events of 9/11!

In the travel guide, Mr. Black finds information on airports, light rail, flight information, a New York City subway map,

\- 43 -

and hotel recommendations with respective ratings, and available utilities; plus a guide for New York's museums; a map of Central Park; Theatre Reviews, and shopping information.

"This is a great guidebook" thinks Mr. Black and proceeds to the checkout counter. He suddenly stops "Oops what about Mrs. Purple, she wants to go to Paris!" So he goes back and picks up a Paris guidebook as well and then proceeds back to the counter.

\- 44 -

He hands his MasterCard to the sales associate and asks, "Can you wrap these two guidebooks—they're a gift." "Sure" The cashier says as he swipes his card. He then wraps the two guidebooks, places them into a gift bag, and hands it over to Mr. Black, who is quite content with his choice until another book stops him in his tracks! *From Point To Point* "A very strange and surprising book indeed" Mr. Black ponders and puts down the book. As he leaves the store he continues to marvel about this puzzling book.

Mr. Black begins to consider a birthday gift for Mr. White and proceeds to Carrefour for a look around...

He spots a camera, tablet, smartphone, and skateboard. While these would all make good gifts they are just too expensive. Finally, he finds a video game that is priced just right.

- 45 -

Mr. Black imagines that Mr. White would be quite content with the video game and so proceeds to the checkout counter to purchase it. He swipes his MasterCard and the cashier hands him the videogame. As Mr. Black leaves Carrefour he notices that it is already 1:50PM, so he hurries back to the office.

Upon entering the building he swipes his ID card, skips past a few couriers, and slips into the service elevator. It stops at the 89th floor and he exits in the service hallway. He then walks around to the office door, swipes his ID again, and sits down at his desk.

- 47 -

2:00 PM

Mr. Black hits the power button on his computer, waits for it to load, then keys in his password.

He checks his inbox to find an email from his boss waiting for him! "Oh No", he thinks as he opens the mail: "Mr. Black please prepare a presentation for the Three O'clock meeting!"

...Your Boss

- 48 -

Whenever Mr. Black thinks of his boss it's as though he's been struck by lightning. He glances at this watch—there's only 50 minutes left!

Mr. Black thinks about what to do... suddenly, an idea occurs to him.

He starts searching the database. If we take this report, add that client, and calculate his balance, what do we have? ...

Mr. Black takes another look at his watch and realizes there's only 45 minutes left! He continues working but the phone starts ringing!

Mr. Black answers: "Hello! Would you like to remortgage your home..."

Frustrated by the telemarketing call, Mr. Black yells at the caller and hangs up! He continues working, before the phone starts ringing again!

Mr. Black picks up: "Hello there! Are you looking for a way increase your savings?"

Mr. Black yells at the caller and hangs up again! He continues to work but the telephone rings again! Frustrated to his limits, Mr. Black picks up the phone and curses the caller!

But this time it's Mr. Black's mother on the line, not a telemarketer. She's appalled: "Who do you think you're talking to! What the hell is wrong with you!?"

- 49 -

Mr. Black bites his tongue and tries to explain, but it's no use.

Mr. Black: "I screwed up because I'm too overwhelmed by work!"

Mr. Black's Mother: "Work, work, work! Do you want to work yourself to death?"

Mr. Black: "I'm not working myself to death, I have to work to in order to eat."

Mr. Black's mother: "Have you found a girlfriend yet? You're already 30 years old, an old man! You better find a wife soon!"

Mr. Black doesn't see how a having a wife will help to feed him.

Mr. Black's mother: "Did you hear what I said!?"

Mr. Black: " ... I heard! I heard! I'm only 28 by the way."

Mr. Black's mother: "28! Well, you might as well be 30..."

- 50 -

Mr. Black: "Okay! Okay! I will try my best to find a suitable girl!"

Mr. Black's mother: "Thank you dear, By the way have you eaten yet?"

Mr. Black: "Yes, I have! Mom, I really have to get back to work now." 30 minutes remaining!

Mr. Black's mother: "Have you been getting enough sleep these days?"

Mr. Black: "Yes, yes, yes! All is well with me!!! Mom, I'm really busy and have to get back to work!" Only 25 minutes left!

Mr. Black's mother: "Okay then, I'll let you get back to your work. Love you!"

Mr. Black: "I Love you too Mom!"

Mr. Black's mother: "Goodbye now! Bye!..." Mr. Black grows increasingly anxious and hangs up.

Mr. Black resumes working with only 20 minutes before the big meeting, he gets more and more anxious as the clock ticks away...

- 51 -

Mr. Black finally finishes his work with 10 minutes to spare. His shoulder and back are aching...

He's got to use the toilet, so he saves the file, and then copies it to a USB drive, which takes longer than he anticipated. He glances at the time, 5 minutes still left! Mr. Black takes the USB drive and heads upstairs to the meeting.

- 53 -

3:00 PM

As Mr. Black goes upstairs to the meeting, he remembers that he still needs to pee. Everyone has already arrived at the meeting. There are quite a lot of people. Mr. Black gets nervous, and his heart begins pounding. He plugs in his USB drive to the computer, and turns on the video projector.

The projector slowly starts up.

Mr. Black greets everyone, and slowly steps in front of the screen to begin his presentation.

Mr. Black is still thinking of the restroom as he starts his presentation. "Ahem" He speaks into the microphone: "Hi!"

- 54 -

"Hello Everyone" No sound, again he speaks, "Hello". The microphone doesn't seem to be working. He tries again, still nothing. "What's wrong with the microphone", Mr. Black begins to get frustrated and embarrassed as he catches a glimpse of his colleagues and boss, who hands him a bullhorn to use. Mr. Black begins his presentation on environmentally friendly electric cards explaining that 5 electric cars consume less fuel than one ordinary car, but has more mechanical properties than two ordinary cars combined. "Electric cars also come in a variety of colors as well."

Mr. Black continues while the need to use the bathroom gets more urgent. He summarizes, "This can generate a large profit for the company!"

The people at the meeting start mumbling amongst themselves. There is some controversy...

Mr. Black can't stop thinking about the toilet as he eyes the people in the meeting.

He looks at his boss and feels a little uncomfortable. His heart starts pounding faster.

- 55 -

The boss' stern face slowly starts break into a smile and the people in the boardroom begin applauding. Mr. Black is relieved. The boss commends Mr. Black: "Good job lad, you outdid yourself!" He hands Mr. Black a bottle of water at which point Mr. Black's need to pee grows so intense that he finally runs out, leaving the boss perplexed. "Why did he run when I gave him the bottle?"

Mr. Black runs as fast as he can to the restroom but he slips and falls. He's angry because he didn't see that the floor was freshly washed. He gets up and continues running until he finally reaches the restroom...

But there's a long line for both the women and men's toilet. As he gets in line his mind starts wandering. He thinks of his bladder and the damage that he's doing to it, his boss's bottle of water, genital problems, squatter toilets, intestinal problems,...

- 56 -

...the smell of feces, needles, Ah! Now there's only one more person on line in front of him. He excitedly waits as another five, ten, then fifteen minutes pass by. "He's probably taking a dump" Mr. Black worries. Finally the man exits and Mr. Black rushes in, spots the urinal, and relieves himself... "Ahhh!"

- 57 -

4:00 PM

Mr. Black heads back downstairs thinking of the applause he received in the meeting.

Using his smartphone he shares his success at the meeting on Twitter and Facebook.

Mr. Green tweets him back: "Good job! Pop the champagne!

Mr. Purple responds to his Facebook post: So happy for you!

Miss Red sends an Instant Message: Good job! Cheers, kisses!

- 58 -

Mr. Black replies to Miss Red: Sure thing.

He then returns back to his desk and resumes work. He begins to feel his back and shoulder aching and decides to do some stretches, which makes him feel much better.

Mr. Black continues working at his desk, he checks the time—it's 4:30PM. He thinks about his date that evening with Mrs. Violet. He decides to give her a call to confirm. The phone rings.

Mrs. Violet: "Hello?"

Mr. Black: "Hey, remember me, I'm the guy that loves fishing? Are we still on for tonight?"

Mrs. Violet: "Sure, does 7PM work?"

Mr. Black: "7PM is great!"

- 59 -

Mrs. Violet: "Okay, Looking forward."

- 61 -

5:00 PM

Mr. Black's work is quite intense! He makes phone calls, goes over many documents, calculations, and writes reports. Suddenly everything starts going blurry. He covers his right eye but he keeps seeing double. He then covers his left eye and it's also still blurry. Mr. Black thinks he's going to die. His aching back starts him thinking about relaxing, taking a hot bath, and having a massage.

He starts to worry that his boss is going to make him overtime.

- 62 -

Mr. Black's boss insists that he works from 9:00AM to 5:30PM. He says: "You can leave once your job is done."

Mr. Black's exhaustion from work changes into excitement as he begins to think of the evening ahead with Miss Violet. He hurries around the corridors towards the elevator. He then rushes out of the building and onto the street where he hails a cab, thinking that the subway will be too crowded. He tells the cab driver his address.

The cab driver stops at the house and Mr. Black runs in.

- 63 -

6:00 PM

Mr. Black thinks of Miss Violet as he enters his home. He turns the AC up to full power and then proceeds get some Cokes from the fridge, which brings him great relief. He then takes a shower, decides what to wear, and checks himself out in the mirror.

At the same time, Miss Violet is thinking of Mr. Black as she turns on the stereo and proceeds to the bathroom for a shower. Afterwards she enters her wardrobe.

- 64 -

Miss Violet puts on her panties, a bra, a dress, stockings, and heals, and then checks herself out in the mirror with an approving eye.

Mr. Black returns to his bathroom and, after looking in the mirror, combs his hair.

Mrs. Violet applies some blush and spritzes a little perfume, and then contemplates which color of lipstick to apply: violet, red, or pink? She finally decides on the red, applies it and tosses the stick in her handbag. She then adds some mascara, polishes her nails, and then blow-dries her fingertips. Miss Violet remembers Mr. Black's musical tastes as she turns off the stereo. She sprays on a little more perfume and then leaves her house.

Meanwhile Mr. Black is still contemplating what shoes to wear. His Nike, Adidas, or Lacoste? He finally decides on the more formal Lacoste shoes and gives them a quick polish.

Miss Violet smells as sweet as a butterfly as she hits the road.

\- 65 -

Mr. Black grabs the AC remote control thinking that it's his phone, and runs out of the house...

He thinks to call Miss Violet and realizes that he mistakenly brought the AC remote control instead of the phone! Angrily he runs back to his house and looks everywhere for his phone but cannot find it. He decides to call himself and finally locates it, grabs it, then runs out the door again.

He goes into a flower shop and asks, "Can I get a dozen roses please". After leaving the shop he reckons that eleven roses (one one) better represents the love between two people. At that point he spots his friend, and hands one of the roses to him who, feeling awkward, hands it the girl he's with. Mr. Black hits the road again...

Mr. Black reassures himself that giving away one rose and keeping eleven is the perfect number to give to Mrs. Violet.

\- 66 -

Mr. Black is a little lost so he asks an old man for directions: "Hello sir, do you know where I can find this bar?" The old man replies: "What, sorry, I can't hear you." The old man then points to a police officer and gestures that he should ask him . The police officer is a bit combative but points in the direction of the bar. Mr. Black thanks the officer.

He then runs into the bar only to find pole dancers and nude girls! He realizes that he is at a strip club, not the bar he's looking for!!

That police officer is a piece of shit, he reflects.

\- 67 -

7:00 PM

Running into another bar with his heart pounding, Mr. Black looks around and spots Mrs. Gray. "Hi, Here are some flowers."

Mrs. Gray has no clue who Mr. Black is, and, at first shocked, she is also flattered. Then Mr. Gray walks out of the restroom and sees Mr. Black giving the flowers to his wife.

He is furious: "Hey, what do you think you're doing?! This is my wife! Are you trying to come between us?!"

\- 68 -

Mr. Black is mortified.

Mr. Gray continues yelling: "I'm going to kick your ass!"

Mr. Black starts sweating.

Then Mr. Gray takes a punch at Mr. Black and kicks him to the ground.

A police officer appears and says: "No fighting."

Mr. Gray responds angrily: "I will fight him all I want!!! That woman is my wife! He was trying to hit on my wife!!"

The police officer sternly maintains that no fighting is allowed.

Mr. Gray responds: "Who do you think you are?! Fuck you! I am going to kick you ass!"

Mr. Gray knocks out the police officer, who suffers a concussion and is taken away in an ambulance to the hospital...

A bunch of other police officers arrive at the scene and arrest Mr. Gray.

\- 69 -

The police officers then look over at Mr. Black who, afraid of also being arrested, begins to explain: that he mistook Mrs. Gray for Miss Violet and that Mr. Gray jumped to conclusions. The police officer then tells him "Beat it, Mister."

A relieved Mr. Black still needs to find Miss Violet. After looking around he finally spots her. He double checks that it's the same woman from the website then walks up to her and says "Hi!" Miss Violet emphatically returns his greeting and then Mr. Black hands her the roses, causing her to blush.

The two order some drinks.

Mr. Black: "So, you're a hairstylist? What kind of hair do you normally do: men's, women's, perms?"

Miss Violet: "A lot of perms, normally older women's." Mr. Black is instantly reminded of his mom, who also has a perm.

\- 70 -

Miss Violet: "So, you said you're a boss?"

An embarrassed Mr. Black tries to change the subject: "Well, I'm a white collar worker, own a hybrid car, and have investments in stocks. I also travel a lot to make presentations. I actually love to travel, what do you like?"

Miss Violet: "I love travelling and taking photographs."

Mr. Black: "I love color digital photography."

Miss Violet: "I prefer old school black and white film. Digital photography is for the birds."

Mr. Black is at a loss for words then suddenly has an idea.

He starts talking about Horoscopes, "Hey, I'm an Aquarius, what about you?"

\- 71 -

Miss Violet: "You should guess try to guess".

Mr. Black: "An Aries?"

Miss Violet: "No".

Mr. Black: "Cancer?"

Miss Violet: "No"

Mr. Black: "Hmm, you said that you love biking and swimming... that must mean you're a Scorpio!?"

Miss Violet: "Yes".

Mr. Black: "Let me read your palm."

Mr. Black takes Miss Violet's hand and she blushes.

\- 72 -

Mr. Black: "This line means that you will have a long and prosperous life, and this line means you will have lots of money, while this lines says that you will fall in love... your fortune is pretty good! It looks like you are going to get married soon and have five children"

Miss Violet: "Oh dear, that's almost as many children as a mother pig would have!"

Mr. Black: "Pigs are the best, I love them, like in the movie *Babe*."

Miss Violet: " That movie is complete rubbish! I prefer action movies, *Star Wars, Batman...*"

Mr. Black: "*Batman*'s the best! I love that movie."

Miss Violet: "Didn't *Batman* get an Oscar Award?"

\- 73 -

Mr. Black: "No, that was *Star Wars*"

Miss Violet: "Hey, Do you want to go to the movies?"

Mr. Black: "That's a great idea, let's go!"

As Mr. Black and Miss Violet leave the bar, Mr. Black thinks about sitting in the theatre next to Miss Violet.

As they leave the bar, the police officer keeps a watchful eye on them ...

- 75 -

8:00 PM

As they walk and talk the two seem to be kindling their love for each other. All of a sudden, Mr. Black's phone starts vibrating. Not knowing who might be calling, Mr. Black turns it off.

Miss Violet: "You should probably answer the phone."

Mr. Black takes a look at this phone and realizes Mr. Red is calling. He remembers that he's in the hospital! Mr. Black tells Miss Violet how Mr. Red is sick in the hospital and waiting for him to bring some noodles.

Mr. Black awkwardly explains: "I should probably head on to the hospital. I had a great time tonight talking with you,

- 76 -

Can I call you sometime?"

Miss Violet: "I had a great time too, of course you can call me!" A bashful Mr. Black and Miss Violet said goodbye to each other and leave in opposite directions.

Mr. Black sees that it's 8:15PM! He rushes into the noodle shop orders ramen with tomato and eggs, and sits down to wait. The chef packs the ramen into a takeout box and hands it to Mr. Black, who rushes out of the restaurant.

Mr. Black hurries into the hospital and looks around for Mr. Red's room. He passes the injection room, the CT scanning room, the emergency room, the X-Ray room, until he finally sees the concussion center, which reminds him of the police officer that was knocked out earlier. He keeps going and passes the delivery room until he finally finds Mr. Red's room. The nurse hands Mr. Black a surgical mask before entering and Mr Black puts it on.

Mr. Black sees Mr. Red sick in bed burning up with fever...

- 77 -

Mr. Black asks: "How's your temperature? Are you taking medicine?"

Mr. Red is in pain but gets up to eat the ramen: "These noodles are great." He says

Mr. Black recalls his appointment to meet Mr. Green for beers to talk about his recent heartbreak.

Mr. Black tells Mr. Red: "Hope you feel better, take care." Then rushes out of the hospital.

- 79 -

9:00 PM

Mr. Black hails a cab, but no cabs seem to be stopping. He begins to worry that he's keeping Mr. Green and then a cab stops!

Mr. Black tells the driver where to go. They keep hitting red lights, delays caused by construction, and lots of traffic. They hit another red light and more and more congestion.

- 80 -

Stuck in traffic Mr. Black sees emergency tape and wonders what's going on? He sees traffic cones, a helicopter, then a tow truck, an ambulance, and police car rush by. Then he sees a man knocked out on the road! "That man must've been hit by a car!" he shirks. The traffic continues unabated.

The traffic moves ever so slowly until finally the cab stops at its destination, and Mr. Black rushes out.

He runs into the bar and sits down with Mr. Green for a beer...

He notices that Mr. Green is already quite drunk.

Mr. Green: "I can't believe Miss Green left me for another man, screw her!"

- 81 -

Mr. Black: "I never really liked her! You know, while I was in the cab coming here, I saw a man lying unconscious on the pavement, I think he was hit by a car! The ambulance took him away to a hospital, so your heartbreak is nothing in comparison to losing your life. Death far outweighs heartbreak! You'll be okay, which is more than I can say for the man who was run over back there."

Mr. Green has another few beers and gets more intoxicated.

He starts to reminisce about the night he met Miss Green: "That night I was working late and was about to leave the office to catch the bus but realized it was raining pretty hard. I noticed Miss Green didn't have an umbrella."

- 82 -

Mr. Green: "You don't have an umbrella, do you? Are you going to the bus station?"

Miss Green: "Yes, I'm taking the bus, but I'll just wait until it clears up."

But I was convinced that the weather was only getting worse.

"I'm going to the bus station as well, want to share my umbrella?" asked Mr. Green

"OK" replied Mrs. Green

We then walked together under my umbrella to the bus station. When we arrived we waited separately for the bus. But as time elapsed, we began moving closer and closer to each other until we finally we kissed..."

Mr. Green had grown incredibly drunk and Mr. Black took notice.

- 83 -

He began to worry just how Mr. Green would get back home safely.

- 85 -

10:00 PM

A few more beers later...

Mr. Green very drunkenly recounts: "After I kissed Mrs. Green, I thought of how this rain had brought us together. A while later, it started thundering and lightning and I professed my love for her. Then I proposed to her with a diamond ring. I was so nervous to hear her response...

She rejected me, saying that she was in love with someone else.

She broke my heart..." sobbed Mr. Green.

- 86 -

"Two more beers!" Mr. Green shouted. Mr. Black noticed how drunken Mr. Green had gotten, and grew nervous,

Mr. Green ordered again: "Two more beers!!" then suddenly fell over into a drunken sleep, as the waiter arrived with the two beers.

"We don't need the beers anymore!" said Mr. Black

"Well, who is going to pay for these then?" asked the waiter.

"You friend ordered seven beers and several other drinks"

Mr. Black handed over a small fortune to the waiter.

"How am I going to get Mr. Green back home like this?" thought Mr. Black. Then someone helped him carry Mr. Green into a cab.

Mr. Green was laid down in the back while Mr. Black sat in the front and told the taxi driver Mr. Green's address.

- 87 -

The cab arrives at Mr. Green's house and Mr. Black drags him into the elevator and up to his apartment. He then searches for Mr. Green's apartment key in his pocket but pulls out a lighter, wallet, and his smartphone with a cover photo of Mrs. Green. Mr. Black laughs at the photo and feels around in the pocket again this time pulling out the key! A relieved Mr. Black slowly begins to unlock the door, when all of a sudden a dog begins barking, making him very nervous!

Mr. Black looks at Mr. Green who is sound asleep. He starts yelling at him to wake up, and then nudges him, but he doesn't budge. The dog starts barking again, frightening Mr. Black. He decides to splash water on Mr. Green, which finally wakes him up. Mr. Black lets Mr. Green unlock the door and once the dog sees Mr. Green, he stops barking and wags his tail.

Then Mr. Green passes out again.

- 88 -

An exhausted Mr. Black then drags Mr. Green to his bed. The dog lies down at the foot of the bed, sniffing the alcohol.

With Mr. Green finally asleep in his bed, Mr. Black leaves, looking up at the night sky to see the Big Dipper.

- 89 -

11:00 PM

It's late and Mr. Black wanders on the street until he finds a cab. He gives the cab driver directions to go home and, feeling tired, Mr. Black shuts his eyes...

But a sudden stop at a red light causes the cab to collide with the car in front waking Mr. Black up. Shocked, he watches as the cab driver and the woman from the other car quarrel.

The woman driver: "What's the matter with you! Didn't you see the red light?!"

- 90 -

The cab driver: "What about yourself! You shouldn't have stopped so quickly!"

They curse each other until the police arrive...

The policeman stops them from fighting and asks each of them for their license and registration...

Mr. Black manages to avoid the entire conflict, until the policeman sees Mr. Black.

Policeman: "You, where is your license and registration?"

Mr. Black nervously hands it over and the policeman starts to take note of his ID and cellphone number. Suddenly, the policeman smells alcohol!

Policeman: "Mr. Black, have you been drinking!?" Mr. Black begins to perspire and the policeman asks Mr. Black to take a Breathalyzer test.

Mr. Black: "I wasn't the one driving though, I was only a passenger in the cab."

- 91 -

Policeman: "Oh okay, you can leave then."

The policeman then changes his focus to the cab driver: "Where's your license and registration?"......

- 93 -

0:00 AM

Mr. Black can't find another cab. He notices it's midnight. It's unlikely that he'll find a cab at this hour and starts to walk all the way westward across the city back to his home.

He walks and walks, past several bus stops, and a lonely cat. He sits down to take a rest at the next bus stop and thinks of Mrs. Violet. He then looks up again at the Big Dipper in the sky.

- 94 -

After a long walk Mr. Black finally arrives at his house.

- 95 -

1:00 AM

At home, his cat is waiting. When Mr. Black enters, the cat greets him. He pats the cat and then offers it some milk, which he drinks before curling up to sleep again.

Mr. Black walks into his bedroom and sits on the bed. He turns on the television, lies down and watches a war film on ABC.

- 96 -

He switches channels to CCTV1, where there is some news of a panda at the local zoo.

Mr. Black changes channels again to BBC, where there is news of gay marital and family rights.

He switches again to NBC, where there is a documentary on the prosecution of elephant hunters being shown.

Finally, he switches to CNN, where there is news of a Russian airplane crash that has killed over 100 people.

Mr. Black flips though a couple of more channels.

Feeling tried, Mr. Black finally falls asleep with the TV still on...

- 97 -

2:00 AM

Mr. Black sleeps...

Meanwhile, the movie *2012*, about the end of the world, is on the television...

- 99 -

3:00 AM

A buzzing sound wakes Mr. Black up—it's a mosquito. Mr. Black tries killing it by clapping his hands, and then by spraying it. Upset at getting woken up, he gets up from bed and walks to the closet and changes into his pajamas.

Mr. Black turns off the television and light, then returns to sleep.

- 100 -

The buzzing sounds returns...

Mr. Black turns on the light and looks around for the fly but doesn't see it.

So he switches off the light again and closes his eyes, but he still hears the sound...

Then he quickly turns on the light again, and searches for the bug once again...

Again he cannot see the fly and turns off the light, but the buzzing noise persists...

He turns on the light again and spots the mosquito flying around the light. He gets up from bed and angrily pursues it with bug repellant. He chases the fly back and forth in the room becoming more and more angry to the point of desperation. Mr. Black then goes into the kitchen and mistakenly picks up a chopping knife thinking it's a fly squatter.

- 101 -

He pursues the mosquito, chopping up and down with the knife, but it continues to evade the angry Mr. Black. Eventually it lands on the ceiling light.

Frustrated, Mr. Black stacks a stool and chair onto a table in order to reach the mosquito. He gets on top and claps, but the fly zips off. Mr. Black then stands on his tiptoes and tries again and again, only for the mosquito to get away...

Then he turns off the lights.

Finally, he claps and kills the fly between his hands.

- 103 -

4:00 AM

Mr. Black is sound asleep.

- 105 -

5:00AM

Mr. Black dreams that he is walking towards his desk and begins to work. He looks up to see a lot of documents and his boss. His boss starts twirling around and around like a balloon... He kicks the balloon and it rises all the way up to the sky. Then he sees it coming down and suddenly, pins fly towards the balloon and pop it.

- 106 -

The balloon spins in circles as it deflates, but then starts to rise, now growing bigger and bigger until it turns into a hot air balloon. Mr. Black is running in the clouds with the hot air balloon. Unexpectedly the color of the balloon changes into a rainbow as it moves higher and higher towards the sun. Mr. Black continues to dream that amongst the clouds there are bricks of gold, a lot of mansions, and a big chandelier. Then he is in a field of flowers with a red sports car when he sees a sexy woman. He dreams that he is having hot sex with the woman in many different positions... but then she become pregnant. Mr. Black starts dreaming that he is Superman zooming through the air, up into the clouds, past thunder and lightning, and more white clouds.

- 107 -

Then he dives down, descending lower and lower until he sees an umbrella and reaches for it. The wind pulls him along and now he's heading upside down when he spots the city below. He is now in his office building falling downwards fast and then he's in a house that he shares with a woman, but still he's falling fast until he wakes up!

Mr. Black screams! He wakes up puzzled by the dream. What was the thing with the woman in his house? He paces back and forth for long time then sits on the bed and notices its six o'clock.

- 109 -

Mr. Black can't fall back asleep so he turns on his game station and shuffles through his games until he decides on playing *Tetris*.

He rearranges the Tetris blocks little by little, shifting and spinning them...

- 110 -

...Until he ultimately loses. The falling blocks remind him of the dream he just had of falling from the sky so he turns the game off and decides to play *Super Mario* instead.

He starts playing, but slowly his mind drifts to thinking about taking the train in the morning. He continues playing until the princess character enters, which reminds him to call Miss Violet. The game goes on and his mind continues to wander. This time he thinks about the car crash victim he saw laying on the street the night before. He keeps playing till he eventually rescues the princess and wins the game!

- 111 -

Feeling like a hero for winning the last game Mr. Black wonders what super hero best suits him. Amongst them all he decides on the Hulk!

He starts playing but quickly loses 50 points fighting against Superman. He then gains 75 points against Spiderman, but loses 50 points in the next round. Transformer enters and Hulk first wins 75 points until Transformer transforms into a big truck and knocks him down and for a 50 point loss. Finally he gains 100 points defeating the evil, red Hulk! Victory!

- 112 -

At this point Mr. Black's cell phone starts vibrating, and then his alarm clock goes off! It's seven o'clock! He looks at the phone and it's his boss calling, Yikes!

Mr. Black clicks the hang up button.

He picks up his briefcase and leaves...

Outside on the street he walks further and further into the distance until he is just a small dot. Another day begins in the cycle of life.

(End)

ACKNOWLEDGMENTS:

Xu Bing Studio
Wu Lifan
Dong Tianye
Grace Zhuang
Rachel Shen
Linda Wu
Dollion Zhang
Zhao Yong
Maya Kramer
Vivi Yan
Jin Jiangbo
Eddy Li
Sun Peishao
Cindy Yang
Eura Yu

SPECIAL THANKS TO:

Yan Danjie
Zhang Xuesong
Zheng Hao
Wang Hua
Jin Yangping